JOHN CHARLES

MAINSTREAM *SPORT*

JOHN CHARLES

GENTLE GIANT

MARIO RISOLI

MAINSTREAM
PUBLISHING

EDINBURGH AND LONDON

First published in Great Britain in 2003 by
MAINSTREAM PUBLISHING (EDINBURGH) LTD
7 Albany Street
Edinburgh EH1 3UG

ISBN 1 84018 802 2

This edition, 2003

A catalogue record for this book is available from the British Library

Typeset in Baskerville MT and Stone Print

Printed in Great Britain by
Cox & Wyman Ltd

ACKNOWLEDGEMENTS

I wish to thank everyone who shared memories of John Charles with me. I am especially grateful to, in alphabetical order, Umberto Agnelli, Venanzio Cinus, Siriano Collini, Gareth Davies, George Edwards, Peter Harrison, David Hartshorne, Bobby Henning, Xavier Jacobelli, Don Murray, Charles Pickard, Richard Shepherd, Ceri Stennett and David Watkins. Staff at the main libraries in Cardiff, Hereford, Leeds and Merthyr Tydfil also provided invaluable help. Thanks also to my father, Saverio, for his tireless research skills, and my wife, Catherine, for her support and encouragement.

CONTENTS

CHAPTER ONE – FAREWELL SWANSEA

Twenty-seventh December 1931. Edward and Lillian Charles – already parents to a young daughter, Maureen – were celebrating the birth of a first son at their home in Alice Street, in Swansea's humble Cwmbwrla district. They called him William John Charles. Born at No. 9 in a row of 36 council-owned terraced houses, he was to become one of the world's greatest footballers.

It was no surprise to see Edward – known as Ned – coaxing his first son to kick a ball. Once a useful half-back himself, Ned played for Swansea Town reserves, but his playing days came to an end at Cwmbwrla Park when he broke a leg while turning out for a local team called Cwm Mission.

In May 1935, Lillian gave birth to a second son, Melvyn, and he too was encouraged to play football. Mel would become a fine player in his own right and in April 1955 the Charles brothers would play alongside each other for Wales for the first time, in a Home International Championship match against Northern Ireland at Belfast's Windsor Park.

The Charleses were a typical working-class family. Ned was a steel erector at the steelworks in Margam, just outside Swansea, and Lillian was a housewife who devoted herself to caring for the children. 'It was basically two families living in one house,' recalls Mel Charles of his upbringing in Alice Street. 'Mum, Dad, Maureen, John and myself lived in the middle room and my aunt lived in the back room. We didn't have a television, only a radio. We didn't know what television was.'

Money was tight in the Charles's household. 'I used to wear all of John's clothes,' says Mel. 'They went down right through the family. We used to get a new outfit every Whitsun. We ate mostly baked beans with toast. That was what we were brought up on, although we would have chicken every Christmas.'

John and Mel were seven and four respectively when Winston Churchill announced Britain was at war with Nazi Germany. The Second World War brought destruction to many towns and cities across Britain but it was particularly unkind to Swansea, which was heavily bombed by the *Luftwaffe*, the arrival of which was always preceded by a horrifying orange-yellow flare that would puncture the night-time darkness.

Germany's attacks on Swansea began in the early hours of 27 June 1940, and culminated in the devastating 'three-night blitz' in February 1941. Houses disintegrated, water mains were shattered, roads were blocked by charred rubble and the town centre was reduced to a mass of mangled iron. The *Luftwaffe* launched 44 raids on the South Wales town, killing 387 people, injuring 851 and damaging nearly 28,000 properties.

At the height of the bombings Ned and Lillian's two boys were evacuated to Llandeilo, a picturesque market town in Carmarthenshire, west of Swansea. 'I stayed with my sister and John stayed with someone else,' remembers Mel. 'But John was sent back home because he and another boy called Danny Sullivan were killing chickens. They were buggers, those two. I think they were killing the chickens and then trying to sell them.'

John and Mel were close, with Mel following his older brother in everything he did. 'John did a paper round, I did a paper round. John boxed, I boxed,' explains Mel. 'When John joined the cadets, I joined the cadets.' The cadets was an extra-curricular activity based at Manselton Senior School, open to all young boys, not just Manselton pupils. 'We only joined the cadets so we could have a uniform,' smiles Mel. 'We had an Army kit – brown shirt, long trousers and boots. It was all free. At the time most kids were wearing shorts but we would have a pair of longs. We used to think we were grown up.'

Like all brothers they had their squabbles. 'We used to fight like hell. I remember one time just before Guy Fawkes' Night,' continues Mel. 'We decided to do "Penny for the Guy" so we could raise the money to buy fireworks. I was ten and John said to me, "You stay off school and take the Guy around." So I missed school for a week doing "Penny for the Guy". We got the money to buy the fireworks, which were a mixture of bangers and sparklers. Anyway, John kept all the bangers, which were the things to have, and gave me all the sparklers. Didn't we have a bloody fight! Dad had to separate us. We also had a fight over rabbits. John had a black one and I had a white one. John's rabbit died and he wanted my white one.'

Occasionally, they would team up to scrump apples from a nearby orchard. Mel would be the lookout on top of the wall while John stole the apples and hid them under the mattress of their bed. One night, the antics ended in a beating from their strict father. The man who owned the orchard, a Mr Pope, knocked on the door of No. 9 Alice Street. Ned answered and was told his two sons had been seen pinching apples. Ned refused to believe the accusation and said, 'They couldn't have taken your apples, they're in bed.' After Mr Pope left, Ned confronted his sons who were pretending to be asleep. 'He started shaking the bed and all these apples started dropping onto the floor,' laughs Mel. 'He hit the hell out of us with his belt, and it was some belt. We didn't take any more apples after that. They were beautiful sweet apples as well.'

John was educated at Cwmdu Junior School before moving to Manselton Senior School at the age of 11. David Farmer, a classroom contemporary at Cwmdu, remembers John's early sporting ability. 'He was not only good at football, he was good at cricket.' Farmer recalls a school cricket match at Cwmrhydyceirw, in the Swansea Valley. 'He was a very pacey bowler and in this match he was bowling at a spot on the length. He was bowling so fast it became dangerous and John had to be taken off.'

John was only interested in sport and had no inclination for the academic side of school. Farmer says on one occasion, after misbehaving during lessons, John was summoned to the front of the class and caned by the teacher who told him between each whack, 'Wake up, Charles! Wake up! You will never make a living playing football!'

In an era without amusement arcades and home entertainment, boys growing up in Swansea during the 1930s and 1940s spent their leisure time playing football, cricket and other sports. The Charles boys were especially fortunate since Cwmbwrla Park, a hundred yards from Alice Street, was virtually on their doorstep.

'In those days boys played football, rugby, cricket or they boxed. There was nothing else for us to do. We didn't have television or video games,' says Glyn Davies, who was at Manselton with Charles and who played alongside him for Swansea Schoolboys. Davies, who went on to play for Derby County, grew up on the other side of Cwmbwrla Park, in Pentregethin Road.

'Everybody used to end up in the park. We'd throw some coats down and play football. A two-a-side game would become three-a-side, then four-a-side and it would grow and grow,' says Davies. 'We used to have competitions, boys living in one street would play boys living in another. They were marvellous days. The only things we had to worry about were the air raids.'

John and Mel were among the vast numbers playing football at Cwmbwrla. 'During the holidays we played football all day in the park and we'd be there every day,' says Mel. 'We used to have half a pitch each and you could end up playing 20-a-side. Sometimes there were so many kids playing in the park that you couldn't get on. That's all we did, play football. We'd leave our house at eight in the morning and we wouldn't go back home until nine at night.'

Mel's recollections are backed up by an interview his father gave in 1958 to the now-defunct *Empire News*. 'John and Melvyn have been soccer crazy ever since I can remember,' said Ned. 'At home their mother seldom saw them. They spent every moment of their spare time in the fields and parks around Swansea kicking a ball about.'

Even though Ned introduced them to the sport he played as an amateur, Mel insists his father did not push his boys into pursuing football as a career. 'We didn't know what we were going to do. We had no idea we were going to end up as professional footballers,' explains Mel, who would sign for Arsenal in 1959 – two years after his brother's big-money move from Leeds United to Italian giants Juventus. 'My father never said, "I want you to be footballers." It sort of happened naturally. He let us do our own thing. I'm not having a go at him but Dad didn't take much interest in us.'

Cwmbwrla Park hosted some decent footballers during the 1940s and John, along with his friends, would watch and listen. 'There was a lot of knowledge being thrown about free of charge,' explains Davies. 'We learned the little tricks of the game at Cwmbwrla – how to pass the ball, how to receive it, how to play it first time, how to keep it moving on a muddy surface. There were a lot of good players about. Some went into the Welsh League and could have gone even further but didn't, either because of bad luck or circumstances.'

In those days of food rations and coupons for clothes, a pair of football boots was a luxury that most families could not afford. Ned, however, hit on a clever solution that allowed his sons to play football wearing their everyday boots. 'Dad was something of a cobbler and he put these leather strips on our boots,' says Mel. 'The strips acted as pegs. If we didn't have them we'd be slipping all over the place. When we finished playing football, Dad would take off the strips and we could wear them to school.'

The young John had a knack of wearing shoes without laces and on one occasion, while playing a kickabout game in Alice Street, it cost his father a pane of glass. He took a shot at a heap of coats that were serving as a goal only for his shoe to fly off and shatter the front window of a neighbour's house. Ned was never happy with his sons playing football in the street, often warning them that if they did not stop a policeman would be along 'to lock them up'. This hollow threat fell on deaf ears.

John's childhood reads like something out of *Boy's Own*. With his gang of friends he would walk to Bracelet Bay, in the scenic resort of Mumbles, where they would dive into the sea from rocks. They would also go swimming in the lake at Afon-Llan, taking some bread so they could light a fire and make toast. Mooching through some of the town's many bombed buildings was another favourite – but frowned upon – pastime.

Then there was boxing. While in the cadets John tried his hand at 'the noble art' and it soon became apparent Ned's eldest son had the attributes to forge a career in the ring. 'John was a very good boxer. He could have been a professional footballer or a professional boxer,' says Mel. John would continue to box when he was in the Army doing his national service and there was even talk of him fighting Swansea-born heavyweight Dick Richardson.

Glyn Davies, who boxed against the young Charles, recalls, 'We used to go around the different clubs on a Friday night to box. John was a good boxer. He was a nice size and he had quick hands. He could have fought for the Amateur Boxing Association (ABA) title. We had a boxing club at Manselton and one of our teachers, Herbie Morris, loved the sport. They would match boys up based on age and size. We all got a pasting now and again, even John.'

When John was ten, Dai Curvis, the Swansea 'southpaw' boxer who lived near the Charles family and who was carving out a name for himself in professional boxing, approached Ned about taking John under his wing. Ned was keen, not so John or his mother. According to Ned, his wife was 'horrified' at Curvis's offer. Although John would later be crowned Army heavyweight champion, Ned later admitted his son was not cut out for the brutality of boxing. 'John's disposition was all wrong for boxing,' he said. 'In the ring you've got to have the killer instinct, you must be mean to all opponents, hurt them as much as you can. And as John confessed when I raised the point with him, "I don't like to hurt people."' Curvis's two sons, Brian and Cliff, took up boxing and, trained by their father, they both became British welterweight champions.

In a country where rugby is the national sport, Manselton Senior School had a reputation for putting the emphasis on football. It had won the Martin Shield – Swansea's schoolboy championship – in 1935, sharing it with Danygraig Senior School, and did so again two years later, this time sharing it with Townhill Senior School who dominated the schoolboy scene during the late 1930s.

Soon after moving to Manselton, Charles, aged 11, made the school team playing as a left-half. 'John was a natural sportsman,' recalls Davies. 'He was good at every ball game. He played cricket, he was a good tennis player. He was also good at table tennis.' In his first season with the school team, Charles was a schoolboy championship winner. 'We walked away with the title that year,' continues Davies. 'We hammered most sides and I don't think we lost a game. We were a bit bigger than the other teams, and physically stronger.'

A year later, Charles won a place in the Swansea Schoolboys side where he continued to play left-half. He was one of four Manselton boys to get picked. Davies, Enoch Williams and Brian Sykes – whose father was Swansea Town scout Joe Sykes – were the other three.

The schoolboy side played at St Helens, the home of Swansea Rugby Club, and the youngsters were watched by good-sized crowds. One match, against Aston Schoolboys, attracted 20,000.

Terry Medwin, who would go on to play for Swansea, Tottenham and Wales, recalls playing alongside Charles in that schoolboy side of the mid-1940s. An inside-forward in the team, he says, 'Even at that young age John was a bit special. It wasn't because of his height or bulk. He wasn't that big then. There were seven or eight lads in that team who were taller than John. You could just tell that something was on the way. He had a lot of things going for him. Perhaps the biggest thing was his inner strength.'

Charles would become renowned for his awesome physical stature. In his prime he stood 6 ft 1 in. tall and weighed 13 st. 10 lb., most of it muscle. But in his early years, no one would have guessed the slight Charles would blossom into the 'Gentle Giant'. Indeed, when he was a 14 year old on the Swansea Town groundstaff, Roy Paul, the club's star player – who later skippered Manchester City to FA Cup glory in 1956 – referred to Charles as 'a slip of a boy'. Adds Medwin, 'All the lads in the schoolboy team stopped growing at 16 or 17 but John carried on and became a man-mountain.'

Bobby Henning was centre-forward for the Swansea Schoolboys and as the goal-getting striker he should have dominated the write-ups in the local paper, the *South Wales Evening Post*. Yet Charles, playing in the unglamorous half-back position, began to steal his thunder. 'I remember meeting John for the first time at the trials for the schoolboy team and he was the boy to look up to. Even then he always stood out and he was attracting all the attention,' says Henning. 'He always got a mention in the local paper, no matter how the game went.'

It was rare for Charles not to be acknowledged in a schoolboy match report. In a 10–0 mauling of Briton Ferry Schoolboys during the 1944–45 season, the *South Wales Evening Post* said the Swansea defence 'was well served by John Charles'. Henning bagged a hat-trick in a 4–0 win over Aston Schoolboys in December 1945 but 'Charles, at left-half, played an intelligent game'. In a 5–1 victory against Cardiff Schoolboys in January 1946 'the Swansea half-backs [Glyn Davies and Charles] were so complete that their forwards enjoyed a field day'. And in a 3–0 win over Bristol Schoolboys, Davies and Charles 'kept plying their forwards with perfect passes and at the same time held the Bristol attack in a vice-like grip'.

Medwin, who grew up close to Swansea Prison, where his father worked as a prison officer, recalls, 'Because I grew up in a different part of the town the only time I mixed with John was when we were with the schoolboy team. But one time I remember going with him to his house in Cwmbwrla. We planned to play football there in the afternoon and I was a sort of guest. He said to me, "Come on, Terry, let's go and have something to eat." I thought to myself, "Oh, that's nice of you, John." So we went into his house and he got a fresh loaf out, cut four slices of bread, buttered them and added strawberry jam. You were really living if you ate this in the 1940s. Then he cut three slabs of cake. It looked delicious. And do you know what? John ate the lot. I didn't have any of it. John scoffed all the bread and all the cake.'

The English Schools' Trophy, the schoolboy version of the FA Cup, was the silverware every side wanted to win. Swansea had a good record in the competition. Runners-up in 1934 and 1935, they lost to Manchester Schoolboys on both occasions. They won the trophy for the first time in 1939, beating Chesterfield Schoolboys. With the likes of Charles, Medwin, Henning and Davies in the team, the class of 1945–46 fancied their chances of bringing the trophy back to South Wales for a second time. 'You could see John was going to be a very good player. He was a natural, so quick and strong,' explains Davies, who was right-half in the schoolboy side. 'John was a bit more aggressive in those days. As he got older he quietened down. You knew which way he was going to go and that was up. There were only two things that could have stopped him – a bad injury and bad luck. Fortunately he avoided both.'

Swansea Schoolboys began their campaign against Bristol Schoolboys and easily dispatched the West Country side 3–0. Then came Reading Schoolboys, containing a young Johnny Brooks who would play for Tottenham and England. They were beaten 2–1, setting up a quarter-final clash against Leicester Schoolboys to be played at St Helens. In front of 20,000 people Swansea failed to book a place in the last four, drawing 1–1. Still, the *South Wales Evening Post* singled out the two Manselton pupils, Charles and Davies, for praise. The Swansea half-back line, it declared, is 'considered one of the best ever fielded by Swansea'.

The Welsh team travelled to the East Midlands for the replay. Medwin recalls the trip. 'John liked some fun. There was a bit of devilment in there. Whenever we went away with the schoolboy side, our parents used to give us a shilling and we'd end up playing cards for halfpennies or pennies. Anyway, we were playing cards in the room in Leicester and John started giggling. I asked him what he was laughing about. He said, "Nothing." But he carried on. He was taking all my pennies off me and do you know why? I was sitting in front of a wardrobe that had a mirror on it. Of course John could see what cards I had in the mirror.'

The replay was staged at Filbert Street, the home of Leicester City, with the hosts' Lord Mayor and his wife among the 14,465-strong crowd. It ended in disappointment for Charles and his teammates as the home side ran out 2–0 winners. 'We were very disappointed with that result,' says Medwin. 'I thought we were good enough to win the trophy that year. The Leicester match was the only game we lost that season. They were too strong for us.'

Charles could take comfort from the glowing report in the *Leicester Mercury* which described him as 'an outstanding player'.

During the train journey back to Swansea, Bobby Henning witnessed the joker streak in Charles. 'The boys were sitting in different carriages. I was in a different one to Charlo. He came to our carriage door and said, "Do you want some ginger beer in there?" He handed over this bottle with something gold-coloured in it. The bottle was warm and it wasn't ginger beer inside. Someone had urinated in it. I don't know if it was Charlo.'

For Swansea, there was some consolation when they won the Welsh Shield, thrashing Aberdare 9–0 on aggregate. In the first leg at St Helens, they won 3–0 with Charles, according to the *South Wales Evening Post*, 'always endeavouring to initiate attacks'. In the return game at Aberaman Park, Charles scored in a 6–0 win. This was Swansea's first victory in the competition for eight years, although they had not competed during wartime.

Charles's outstanding performances for the schoolboy side did not go unnoticed. He had caught the eye of Yorkshireman Joe Sykes, who played centre-half for Swansea Town during the 1920s and 1930s and who was now scouting and coaching for the Second Division club. Sykes – who was known as 'the doyen of carpet passes' in his playing days – moved to Swansea from Sheffield Wednesday in 1924 and stayed there until his death in 1975. He was highly respected, bringing young players like Medwin, Ivor Allchurch and Cliff Jones to the Vetch Field. 'Joe could spot talent,' remarks Henning. 'He was the best. Everyone looked up to Joe.'

Sykes called at 9 Alice Street and invited John for a trial at the Vetch. It came as no surprise when Haydn Green, then Swansea Town manager, offered the 14 year old a place on the groundstaff for fifteen shillings a week. Charles had the option of working as an electrician's apprentice but by now was set on becoming a professional footballer and he accepted Green's offer. Charles was the first of three groundstaff boys to join The Swans in the summer of 1946. Harry Griffiths soon followed, then Henning.

The groundstaff boys were assigned the laborious jobs around the Vetch – sweeping the stands, cleaning boots, weeding and forking the pitch, tidying the dressing-rooms, painting the railings, scrubbing the baths and other menial chores. At the time it was regarded as a rite of passage for those who dreamed of making a living as a professional footballer.

'We would arrive at the ground at about nine in the morning and we'd finish at about three in the afternoon,' recalls Henning. 'Weeding and re-seeding the pitch at the end of each season was the worst job. That was a real back-breaker. I remember they gave John and me the job of sweeping the North Bank after a big game. We didn't pick anything up, we just spread all the rubbish about. It looked worse than before and the groundsman played hell with us.'

That was not the only time Charles and Henning crossed the groundsman, Jim Fairweather. One afternoon he caught the pair playing football on the Vetch pitch, which was strictly out of bounds until matchdays. 'Jim always took two hours off for lunch. He used to go to The Glamorgan pub on Mumbles Road,' says Henning. 'When he had gone, we decided to have a kickabout in the goalmouth. It was about one in the afternoon and there wasn't anyone about. This one day he came back early and he played hell with us. He told us, "I'm taking you to see the manager tomorrow." And he did.'

By now Billy McCandless had replaced Green in the Vetch hot-seat. The Swans were relegated to Division Three in 1947 and after a poor start to the following season Green resigned. 'We went into McCandless's office but Jim didn't come in with us, he stayed outside,' continues Henning. 'McCandless was quite nice to us. He didn't talk about playing on the pitch at all. "How much am I paying you lads then?" he asked us. We told him. "Have a rise next week," he said. So we came out with a rise. From fifteen shillings a week we went to twenty-five. When Jim saw us he asked, "Well, what did he say?" We told him he'd given us a rise and started laughing our heads off.'

Henning also remembers the morning when the groundstaff boys were asked to cement in the bases of the newly installed steel columns that would support the Centre Stand. The youngsters decided to leave their permanent mark, writing their names in the wet cement – R. Henning, T. Jones, H. Griffiths and so on. 'We came back from lunch and noticed how John had spelt his surname. He'd written Chales instead of Charles,' laughs Henning. 'He tried to rub it out. He nearly dug a hole trying to get rid of it but the cement had dried.' Charles's error has long since been covered up.

While he was on the groundstaff the former Manselton pupil suddenly shot up in size. As Henning remembers, 'When we were playing for Swansea Schoolboys, John was 4 inches shorter than me, but when he was about 15 he started to sprout. We had this tea cabin at the Vetch and I'll always remember John standing at the door one day. He looked like he'd just got out of bed. His trousers were halfway up his legs. When he started on the groundstaff a year earlier they fitted him. All of a sudden he just grew out of them.'

With no money to replace his wardrobe Charles would wear his father's trousers. One night, the bashful teenager was invited next door, to a party thrown by Betty Harris, his neighbour's daughter. With the party in full swing, there was a knock at the door. Betty answered. It was Ned. 'John are you in there?' he cried. 'I want my trousers because I'm going out!' A chorus of giggles followed.

When the groundstaff boys had finished working at the Vetch, they would play table tennis in the ground's now-demolished Double Decker Stand, or have a game of snooker in the town centre. En route, the gang would tease the many spivs who sold knock-off goods from the backs of lorries. If it was raining, Charles and his friends would play cricket underneath the exit of the Centre Stand.

They would also take the Mumbles tram to Victoria Park for a game of bowls and Henning recalls one such occasion when he accompanied Charles and Harry Griffiths. 'We were on the tram and the conductor yelled to the driver to close the doors. Just as he was about to do it Harry jumped out before a woman and a child who ended up getting caught in the doors. John had a right go at Harry and they ended up fighting on the road, one was kicking and the other was thumping.'

Charles had not lost his appetite for stealing apples, as fellow apprentices Henning, Griffiths and Terry Jones discovered one afternoon as they returned home from the Vetch. 'We stopped at this shop and I bought an apple. As the lady went into another room to get my change, three apples suddenly dropped to the floor,' says Henning. 'Charlo had his coat over his arm and he was trying to put the apples into a patch pocket but he missed the hole. We got out of the shop as quickly as we could and belted up the road. We never went back into that shop.'

At the Vetch, Charles played for Swansea Town's 'A team' in the local league and occasionally he made the Welsh League side but, with the first team playing well and challenging for promotion in 1948–49, a senior debut seemed a long way off. McCandless was not going to tinker with a winning team and, with the Swansea public clamouring for a return to Division Two, blooding youngsters was low on his agenda. But Charles was not unhappy. He was in the presence of his big hero, Roy Paul and, while performing his groundstaff duties, he would listen to the first-team players and watch them in training, learning all the time. He was keen to pick up hints on how to succeed in professional football and would follow the first-team players everywhere, so much so that Paul nicknamed him 'the Shadow'. Charles started to hang out at the Italian café on Nelson Street, near the Vetch, where the first-team players sometimes ate after training. Paul recalled one afternoon when he and his astonished teammates watched Charles devour two steak pies, a plate piled high with potatoes and vegetables and two helpings of apple tart, all washed down with tea. 'I'm a growing lad,' said Charles when he noticed his colleagues were watching him in amazement. Paul never forgot that remark and every time he and Charles met up to play for Wales during the 1950s, he would say to him, 'Still a growing lad, John?'

Leaving his hometown club never entered Charles's thoughts. To feed his hunger for competitive football he would turn out for the Gendros junior side, a local Swansea team.

'I was playing for Newport County when John was on the groundstaff at Swansea,' says Harold Williams, a winger who would join up with Charles at Leeds United. 'Joe Sykes, who was a close friend of mine, would talk to me about him. He'd say, "Harold, this fella is going to be a great player. What a fantastic player he's going to be." I thought to myself, "I don't know about that" because John was a bit slow then. But I've never forgotten Joe saying those things and he was proved right. The funny thing about it was that Frank Barson, who was also a coach at the Vetch, never mentioned John to me.'

Sykes also enthused about the teenager to Paul, Swansea's captain. 'This lad is going to be great. He's got the lot – strength, heading ability, ball control, timing and body balance.' After such a glowing appraisal, Paul was keen to watch the youngster in action. He was not impressed, however, believing Charles looked 'too nice a lad to come into the hurly-burly of league football'. According to Paul, a former coal miner from the Rhondda, he was 'too dainty' and 'afraid to go in resolutely and use his strength'. His scathing verdict was, 'Plays like an amateur'. When Leeds eventually snatched him away in 1948, Paul did not notice the youngster had gone. Paul later admitted he was ashamed of his first assessment of the player who, arguably, became the finest all-round footballer the world has ever seen.

For all Sykes's talk, Charles was nowhere near the first team. 'The trouble at Swansea when we were on the groundstaff was that they had 40 bloody professionals on the books,' explains Henning. 'There were three players for every position and we apprentices just weren't going to get a game. We stood a better chance of playing by going to another club. The older players were on contracts so the manager would play them.'

This was Charles's situation at the Vetch when Jack Pickard first saw him on a hot August afternoon in 1948, playing in a kickabout game at Cwmbwrla Park. Pickard was Leeds United's part-time scout in South Wales. Born and bred in Leeds, the divorcee had moved to Swansea before the First World War to take photographs of the Mumbles and the Gower, which he sold to the public. He remarried and settled in the town before being made manager of the Willerby & Co. men's outfitters shop on the High Street.

Pickard had never enjoyed a career in the game. He played centre-half for Armley Church School in Leeds and had trials with the now-defunct Leeds City. He served in the First World War and lost the sight in his left eye in 1916 while on duty in Brownstown, Northern Ireland, ending any chance of him becoming a professional footballer once the war ended.

Billy Hampson, who was appointed Leeds manager in 1935, gave Pickard the job of unearthing young talent in the South Wales area and sending it up to West Yorkshire. As a scout he preferred a low-key approach and the parks of wet and windswept mining villages were his favourite hunting grounds. Not all Pickard's recommendations were taken on. He had told the Yorkshire club to sign Roy Paul and Trevor Ford but his advice fell on deaf ears. Both players went on to become big stars in the First Division, Paul with Manchester City and Ford with Aston Villa and Sunderland.

When Pickard spotted Charles, he was working for a new manager, Major Frank Buckley, the Boer War veteran and one of the most famous names in English football. In 1939, Buckley took Wolverhampton Wanderers to the FA Cup final where they were surprisingly beaten by Second Division Portsmouth. Twice he came close to bringing the First Division championship to Molineux. In 1938 his side was pipped to the post by Arsenal. The following year, they were beaten by Everton.

Pickard's first glimpse of Charles was serendipitous. After locking up at Willerby's, he and his wife, Blodwen, made their way to Cwmbwrla Park to watch a Swansea League fixture between St Joseph's and the Nickel Works. As they strolled through the park, Pickard noticed a group of boys playing with a light rubber ball behind the goalposts.

'Among the bigger lads was one who dominated the scene,'

recalled Pickard, who died in 1983. 'He seemed to be everywhere the ball went and always able to do something out of the ordinary with it. Even to me, after watching so many footballers in my time, it seemed uncanny, for the ball seemed to be glued to his feet. I asked my wife to carry on to see the game and said I would join her in a few minutes. I couldn't take my eyes off this boy. She suggested I was wasting my time and that I would miss the game I had gone to see.'

Pickard stayed and asked a bystander who the 'gaunt-looking boy who's bossing this lot with the ball' was. 'He's young Charlo,' came the reply. 'He's here nearly every day. I believe he's on Swansea Town's groundstaff.' Pickard stayed a few more minutes before joining his wife to watch the Swansea League game, believing Charles – who 'was like a general preparing for battle' – was out of his reach.

Pickard returned to his home in William Street, opposite the Vetch, and told his son, Charles, of his discovery. Charles Pickard recalls, 'I remember Dad telling me quietly, "I've just seen this boy playing in Cwmbwrla Park. He's beyond. He's got everything." He went to watch John in the park a couple of times.'

The scout was captivated by what he had seen. He later told a newspaper that he felt 'as excited as a fight manager who knows he has found a world heavyweight champion'. He added, 'I couldn't sleep at night. I lay awake systematically going over his footballing strong points. I tried hard to find a fault in his make-up. The only possible snag I could think of was that he was rather weaker on the left side than the right but even that shortcoming seemed to be more than compensated for by all his other qualities. It also occurred to me that he was rather gaunt. I couldn't be sure that he was naturally inclined that way or if he was just in the process of growing quickly.'

Pickard was more critical of the teenager in his handwritten memoirs. Charles 'gave the impression of being lazy, with no ball control, aimlessly booted the ball . . . he was very slow and cumbersome on the turn and lethargic in his movements'. But the good points outweighed the bad. He had the 'priceless' gift of two good feet, was cool and confident, and also 'looked likely to grow and be of a powerful build'.

Pickard assumed Charles was Swansea Town's property and there was no way he could send him up to Leeds for Major Buckley to take a look at him. One day, however, Ned Charles came to see Pickard at Willerby's. Ned was frustrated by his son's lack of progress at Swansea and was considering getting him a job at his steelworks. At the Vetch, John was doing menial jobs, all for twenty-five shillings a week. Ned felt his son might as well become a labourer in the steelworks. At least he would get more money. Ned told Pickard that with the amount his son was bringing home he was 'unable to put enough food in the lad's belly, let alone being able to buy clothes to put on his back'.

Explains Charles Pickard, 'Ned told my dad that all John was doing at the Vetch was cleaning the stands and picking up rubbish after the matches. He knew Dad had sent players up to Leeds and he asked if he could send John up. Dad said to Ned, "Has John signed anything?" Ned said he hadn't. "Are you sure, Ned?" He said he was sure. "John isn't a Swansea Town player – he just works at the ground."' Charles was registered at the Vetch as an amateur, on a Welsh League form. This meant any Football League club could poach him since, in the eyes of the Football Association (FA), he was not a Swansea Town player.

Pickard could send the 16 year old he described as a 'young magician' to Leeds for a trial.

He rang Buckley and told him, 'I'm not exaggerating when I say that I have a boy down here in Swansea who has it in him to become a great player. If you miss him you'll miss the finest proposition in the British Isles. If you feed him on steaks and help him to regain some of the strength he's lost through growing, he'll become the greatest footballer in Britain.'

Pickard visited Ned and Lily in Alice Street one Thursday evening to discuss the possibility of their son going to Elland Road for a trial. John was out playing cricket and Mel was dispatched to bring him home. Decades later, John Charles recalled that visit. 'When Mr Pickard came round to see my parents and mentioned Leeds, my mother said, "John can't go up to Leeds – he hasn't got his passport." That's how some people thought in Swansea. My mother had never been out of the town.'

Ned was keen for his son to make the 250-mile trip to Yorkshire.

So too was John who knew his chances of playing for The Swans were remote. But Lily was not thrilled at the idea of John moving north. As Ned later explained, 'My wife was the big stumbling block. Naturally, like any other mother, she had no desire to see her son leave home and Leeds is a long way from Swansea. She said she'd much rather he didn't go but to avoid a major domestic upset Lily eventually gave John her blessing.'

Before he left the house, Pickard told John, 'You have it in you to become one of the greatest footballers in Britain. You can play for Wales before you are 20. You have all the ability to make your family proud of you. You can do all these things if you remember this advice – when you report to Leeds listen to all the coaches and say nowt.'

Charles was not the only Swansea groundstaff boy to be having a trial at Leeds. Joining him were his close friends, Henning and Griffiths. 'The day after Pickard offered him a trial John told us what had happened and suggested we go and see Pickard at the shop because he might be interested in us going up as well,' says Henning. 'So all three of us went into Willerby's and we asked Pickard if we could go to Leeds with John. He said he would arrange for us to go for a trial as well.'

Both clutching a pair of football boots and a small suitcase, Charles and Henning met Pickard at Swansea's Victoria Station on 18 September 1948. Griffiths, in London playing for Swansea's Combination side, would join up with his two colleagues in Leeds later that day. Pickard saw the pair safely onto the 6.30 a.m. train to Crewe, where they would change for Leeds City Station, and waved them off. Charles's remarkable football journey had started.

CHAPTER TWO – BUCKLEY'S BOY

After a draining eight-hour train journey, Charles and Henning made their own way to Elland Road. From there, they were taken to a boarding house on Beeston Hill, about three-quarters of a mile from the ground. This would be their home for the next few weeks.

'It was only a terraced house but apart from us there were four navvies staying there plus the husband and wife who ran the place,' remembers Henning. Later that afternoon they met Harry Griffiths at Leeds City Station. His arrival made the conditions even more cramped. 'The three of us were put into one room. Looking back, I don't know how we all fitted in,' adds the former Swansea Town forward.

The trialists trained with the Leeds United squad every morning and played a number of games for the 'A team'. Recalls Henning, 'We played a team from a mining village in one game and another time we played at Huddersfield.' Major Buckley, now approaching his 66th birthday, would decide if any of them were to be offered contracts with the Second Division club. When he took on young players the Major used a four-point formula – they must be strong, they must love the game, they must be able to play with both feet, and they must have guts. Those not fitting the bill were politely shown the door.

In his first trial match, Charles was picked for the unfamiliar role of right-back. Charles, who had always played at left-half, was stunned when he learned of the news. This was Buckley's way. He wanted to see how players performed in different positions and in Charles's case, he wanted to see if he had a right foot. By the time Buckley left Elland

Road in 1953, Charles had played in five different positions. 'A genuine footballer,' the Major declared, 'should be able to perform successfully in any position on the field.' Another of his favourite sayings was, 'I don't care how good a player is, if he can only kick with one foot he's only half a footballer.' It would have been interesting to hear the Major's thoughts on the great Hungarian, Ferenc Puskas, who was all left foot.

Watching Charles that day at Elland Road were Buckley's right-hand men. They were trainer Bob Roxburgh, the former Newcastle United and Blackburn Rovers right-back, former England captain and Leeds manager Willis Edwards, who was in charge of the reserves, and former England wing-half Ken Willingham, who was helping with coaching duties at Elland Road.

Charles got off to the worst possible start. In the opening minutes of the game the ball came to him and he lunged forward to volley it clear but missed completely. Because of that lapse, his game could have disintegrated altogether, but Charles quickly settled down and impressed the trio of coaches who were convinced his early blunder was simply a case of stage fright. Buckley also took a look at Charles during his trial period. He kept his views private but inside he shared Jack Pickard's excitement. 'By Jove,' thought Buckley when he first saw the Welsh boy play. 'A natural two-footer who does the simple things easily and the difficult things even more easily.'

After two weeks, decision day arrived for Charles, Henning and Griffiths. They were summoned to Major Buckley's office and one by one they learned their fate. 'I remember we were called to the Major's office on a Wednesday evening,' says Henning. 'We went in one at a time. I was first and he said, "I don't need you at the moment. I'll send for you if I do." Then Harry went in and he said the same thing to him. John went in last and when he came out he said, "I've got to come back up Friday." That was it. They wanted John. We all went back to Swansea together that night but John returned to Leeds on the Friday. Harry and I did quite well but obviously not well enough. Anyway, I was so homesick I was glad to come home, so was Harry. John didn't have that problem though.'

Charles Pickard, who worked as a bus driver in Swansea, was in his native Leeds when the Major made his decision. His father had asked him to pay the Leeds manager a visit to ask him what he thought of the three players he had sent up. 'I'll always remember what Buckley said to me. "I'm keeping this boy called John Charles. If ever I've seen a winner he's the one." I asked him about Bobby and Harry. He said, "Those two are more content to go into the billiard room and play snooker."' Charles Pickard played with Griffiths in a local team, The Ysgolians, and did not agree with the Major's assessment. 'I said to him, "I tell you Mr Buckley, Harry Griffiths will play for Wales." And he did,' smiles Pickard. Griffiths would win his one and only Welsh cap in April 1953, in a 3–2 win over Northern Ireland in Belfast.

The two 'rejects' were eventually both taken on by Swansea Town. Henning played ten times from 1955–57 but Griffiths would have a far better career, making 422 appearances for The Swans from 1949–64 and briefly managing the club in the mid-1970s. He became assistant to John Toshack when he was made manager but died tragically at the age of 47 when he collapsed in the Vetch treatment room from a heart attack before a league game in April 1978.

As for Charles, Buckley took to him the very first time they met, when the diffident teenager was ushered into his office for an interview. Buckley ran the football club like an Army battalion and detested bad manners. Players who smoked or stood with their hands in their pockets in his presence were thrown out of his office. But Charles did all the right things. Like a soldier waiting for inspection, straight-backed with arms at his sides, he stood in front of Buckley, who was sitting at his desk, and he waited until he was spoken to. Recalling his first impression of Charles, the late Buckley said, 'I was confronted by an Adonis of a youth. I liked his bearing and his respectful approach. Somehow, he looked like a footballer. He looked like a fine, upstanding young man but he was far too shy and modest to say much about himself.'

Buckley offered Charles a place on the groundstaff, found him digs and, noticing Charles was growing out of his suit, ordered him to report to a tailor for a new one to be paid for by Buckley. Had Leeds turned Charles away, Jack Pickard had a contingency plan for the teenager. Believing he would 'give a good account of himself in the boxing ring', Pickard would have contacted either Johnny Best, one of the country's leading fight promoters, or the British heavyweight champion, Bruce Woodcock, suggesting they should take on and train this 'powerful, tough, young man'. They were telephone calls he never had to make.

At Elland Road, Charles was financially better off since Leeds were paying him three pounds and ten shillings a week. He was doing the same jobs as he was doing at the Vetch, such as sweeping the stands and doing odd jobs, but the big difference was that Charles knew he had a far better chance of playing first-team football with his new club. Buckley had a reputation for throwing young players into league action. At his former club, Wolves, he had made Stan Cullis captain when the centre-half was only 19 and also gave wingers Jimmy Mullen and Alan Steen their senior debuts at the tender age of 16.

Charles also had the comfort of knowing Buckley rated him highly. On one particular day, when the Leeds manager was talking to a local journalist, Phil Brown of the *Yorkshire Evening News*, he spotted Charles and another groundstaff boy, Grenville Hair, sweeping the Elland Road stands. He summoned them over. 'Come here you two!' Then he introduced them to Brown, saying, 'This is Grenville Hair. With a bit of luck he'll play full-back for England.' Then he turned to Charles. 'He'll play centre-half for Wales and won't need any luck. He'll be the best centre-half since Cullis.'

Back in Swansea there was uproar when McCandless and the Swansea Town directors discovered what Leeds had done. Across from the Vetch, Charles Pickard was standing outside the bus depot where he worked when McCandless and Sykes approached him. 'McCandless told me there was murder at the Vetch because my father had sent John to Leeds,' he recalls. 'There was uproar in the town. But Dad did nothing wrong. He did everything right. It was Swansea's fault.' After McCandless had berated him for his father's actions, Pickard junior told the Swansea manager he was about to lose Griffiths as well as Charles, since his father was sending him to Norwich City for a trial. Later that night McCandless signed Griffiths. Pickard senior was furious when he found out his son had 'opened his mouth' and refused to speak to him for two months.

Swansea protested to the FA, claiming Leeds had acted illegally in signing Charles, but after an investigation the FA found in favour of the Yorkshire club. Pickard, who always insisted he had acted within the rules, was vindicated. Buckley himself would never have signed the player if it breached FA regulations. He was a disciplinarian, a military man, who wanted things done correctly and 'at the double'. He wore plus-fours, bawled at players who did not say 'Good morning' and ordered his wife and daughter to refer to him as Major. Before Charles signed for Leeds, Buckley personally checked all the details of the transfer to ensure it was valid. After the Charles case, the FA tightened the rules on player registration. In future, Pickard would not be allowed to approach players as he had done with Charles.

Charles had moved to Leeds without fulfilling his two childhood ambitions. The first was to play for his hometown club. The second was to play a schoolboy international for Wales. He was on course to win his first cap when the war broke out, disrupting the schoolboy international programme. In 1947, David Beynon, manager of the Swansea Schoolboys side, tried hard to arrange a match against England so Charles could win his cap but the schoolteacher was unsuccessful.

In prising him away from the Vetch, Leeds quite possibly took advantage of Swansea's preoccupation with winning promotion back to Division Two. Relegated in 1946–47, McCandless was building a side that would eventually storm to the Division Three (South) championship in 1949. When Charles, Henning and Griffiths were in Leeds, The Swans went top of the table and, from 18 September to 16 October, McCandless's side recorded seven straight wins, scoring twenty goals. 'Pickard stole a jewel and you can't blame him for that,' says Glyn Davies. 'You've got to blame Swansea. They should have tied John down. Maybe they didn't appreciate what they had. But you've also got to remember the war had just finished and things were changing. People were coming back from the war and there was a lot of upheaval. McCandless had a good side which was attracting big crowds at the time and he was concerned with winning promotion, which he did.'

Terry Medwin, who joined The Swans two years after Charles's departure, is not so sympathetic. 'The club certainly slipped up with John. It wasn't a well-organised club. They weren't aware of the player he was going to become and I don't think they knew how to keep hold of him.'

Joe Sykes was devastated at losing Charles. According to Henning, the man who perhaps really discovered him was the most hurt. 'Joe thought the world of John and he felt let down. He never talked to us about what happened,' says the former striker. 'John going broke his heart because he really rated him.'

Sykes never held any grudges against Charles and said he 'always thought he would win international honours'. Added Sykes, who died in 1974, 'Unhappily we lost a player who could have helped us to get promotion to the First Division in the very year (1956) Leeds went up. Swansea Town regarded John Charles as one of their discoveries and when he was whisked away to Leeds, I must confess it was one of the biggest disappointments of my life.'

His remarks, which appeared in the *South Wales Evening Post* in January 1959, when Charles was sweeping all before him at Italian club Juventus, incensed Jack Pickard. His anger and contempt at Sykes's comments are made clear in the private notes he penned daily at his Swansea home. As far as he was concerned, Charles had been forced to leave his home town in order to make a name for himself. Similarly, ten years later, Welsh international centre-half Ray Daniel was to leave Swansea for Arsenal.

> You will note the people who lamentably failed to recognise the soccer talent in John Charles while he was a despised and unappreciated boy working on the Vetch Field ground for a miserable pittance . . . and yet when the Major had made a star of John Charles for Leeds United, the same people who had despised and openly scoffed and sneered at him and his family, fell over themselves and absolutely crawled and fawned on John in their efforts to climb on the bandwagon of his success, and attached themselves to him in one way or another to claim they helped him or knew he had football in him. Those hypocrites stand out vividly to me as most despicable and treacherous rats.

Buckley's man in South Wales became a vilified figure after the Charles affair. He was seen as the Englishman who stole a promising Welsh player for an English club. 'My name was smeared. I was slandered and persecuted,' he said. 'There even came a time when I was subjected to threats. How I suffered for my honest transaction but if anybody down here thought I'd show the white feather they were wrong.' When he went to the local parks to watch football games, people would give him an unwelcoming stare before passing on the word, 'Leeds scout 'ere.' Even Charles Pickard was given stick. 'Some of it was good-natured, some of it wasn't. People would come up to me and say, "Your old man stole John Charles." Don't forget, in those days Swansea were getting crowds of 20,000–25,000.'

Undeterred, the ex-soldier continued to scour the playing fields in his patch, not least the diamond mine that was Cwmbwrla Park, and over the next few years Pickard would send further talent to Elland Road. Among his finds were Charles's younger brother Mel, goalkeeper Gary Sprake, midfielder Terry Yorath and striker Carl Harris.

'Dad never got the credit he deserved in Swansea but they thought the world of him in Yorkshire,' continues Charles Pickard. 'John was my dad's best find. He would have been any scout's best find. Dad was very proud of John. Anything that was in the newspapers about him he would cut out and keep.'

Charles never publicly criticised his hometown club for the way they treated him. In fact, he said The Swans 'had done everything for me' and that working for Buckley was simply an opportunity he could not miss. After all, the Major was one of the biggest names in English football. His wheeling and dealing in the transfer market at Wolves netted the West Midlands club nearly £111,000 – an astronomical sum in the late 1930s. What would have appealed to Charles was Buckley's reputation as a maker of football stars. Cullis and Mullen, who both went on to play for England, were two such 'Buckley Babes'.

Buckley soon got to work on his raw prodigy. He felt Charles was not strong enough on his left foot and he was also unhappy with his leaping ability. When he first arrived at Elland Road he could jump no higher than a foot. For a fortnight Charles was given special heading lessons and most afternoons he was summoned back to the ground to practise shooting with his left foot. Charles was furious but he was later grateful for these extra training sessions.

He played regularly for the Leeds 'A team' at right-back and the steelworker's son had played a dozen games in his new position when Buckley decided to switch him a second time. For a Yorkshire League encounter against Barnsley, Charles was told to play centre-half. The Major believed this might be the ideal role for the player who was now 6 ft tall and weighed 13 st.

Charles described the Barnsley match as 'the turning point in my career' because after that game he decided centre-half was his favourite position. 'I enjoyed playing at centre-half more than wing-half. Centre-half, I felt, was my natural position.' He then graduated to the Central League side – Leeds' second team – for a game against Preston North End at Deepdale and in January 1949, just days after his 17th birthday, he turned professional, receiving a £10 signing-on fee while his weekly wage rose to £8 a week.

During his early days in West Yorkshire Charles became close friends with Leeds outside-left Peter Harrison who was given the same digs as the Welshman. 'After I signed for Leeds the Major took me into the snooker room and introduced me to everybody,' recalls Harrison. 'Then he said to Charlo, who was playing snooker, "John, take Peter to your digs." When I first saw Charlo I thought, "What a rough-looking bugger." He looked as rough as a badger's backside. I didn't want to go into digs with him. He was scruffy and looked hard but he turned out to be a nice kid.'

At the time Charles was living in Morley Terrace, Beeston. The rent, thirty shillings a week, was paid by the club. 'The landlady was called Daisy and we called our digs "the Ranch House" because there were so many people living there,' adds Harrison. 'Apart from Daisy there were these two old men and one of them had his son with him. Then there was a Liverpudlian, an Irishman, John and me. There were eight of us altogether. Three of us shared one bed – me, John and the Irishman. Because he wasn't as big as us we used to kick the Irishman out of the bed during the night so Charlo and I would have the bed between us.'

Charles and Harrison soon became inseparable. 'I don't know why we became such good pals because we were completely different,' explains Harrison. 'John was quiet and shy whereas I was outgoing and would talk to anybody.' Wherever one went the other followed. Charles would spend weekends at Harrison's family home in Grantham. Each was best man at the other's wedding and they talked about opening a fish and chip business together. 'We used to go to the pictures a lot and there were always long queues when a big film was on,' says Harrison. 'We'd go to the front of the queue and say, "John Charles and Peter Harrison. Leeds United. Two tickets." And they let us straight in whereas everyone else had to wait two hours. It was a bit cheeky I suppose.'

Another favourite haunt was the snooker club in Burtons Arcade, in the city centre. 'Whenever we argued it was nearly always over snooker,' says Harrison, who later played for Bournemouth, Reading and Southport. 'It used to cost us sixpence a game or five games for half a crown and the loser paid. If Charlo was losing he would start arguing. Say I was 27 points ahead. He'd start saying, "How did you get those 27 points?" Then he'd accuse me of cheating. He never wanted to pay up because he was so tight.'

Occasionally the pair would break the club curfew on going out at night before a Saturday game. Buckley told his players they must be in bed by 10.30 p.m. from Wednesday night onwards but Charles and Harrison thought nothing of defying the Major's orders. To avoid being recognised Harrison would wear a trilby and paint on a moustache while Charles would don a flat cap. They would catch the tram into the city centre, take in a film at either the Odeon or the Tower cinema and stop off for a drink on the way home. 'Instead of walking like young footballers we used to adopt an old man's walk, just to make sure no one recognised us,' smiles Harrison.

The two players were hardly model tenants. They were thrown out of their digs in Morley Terrace because the landlady grew tired of their antics. 'We used to wrestle and bugger about in the house,' remembers Harrison. 'One night, because we were messing about, Daisy's cat, Smokey, escaped and we had to go out and find it,' remembers Harrison. 'Me and John were wandering the streets going, "Smokeeeey. Smokeeeeey." We found it eventually. John was always acting the goat with Daisy. At the table he'd say, "This egg isn't cooked properly" and, "These tomatoes aren't right". She used to go mad. "You either eat it or go without!" That was John. He didn't realise what he was doing but I was older than him and should have known better. In the end Daisy told us to get out.'

They found new lodgings in Wesley Road, in a house owned by

an elderly woman who lived there with her daughter and son-in-law. That, too, ended in eviction. 'One day we had the house to ourselves and we started buggering about. I threw a cup of water at Charlo and it ended up hitting the wallpaper,' recalls Harrison. 'It was this embossed pink wallpaper and when the water dried it left a dark stain. Charlo says to me, "What are we going to do, Pete?" We decided to wipe water on the rest of the wallpaper thinking it would hide what we'd done so we got a damp cloth. You should have seen the sight of it at the end – it looked even worse, much worse! We were in the other room when the landlady came back. All of a sudden we heard this scream. "What's that?!" We left not long after that.'

Archer Road, in Beeston, was their next port of call, a terraced house owned by an elderly couple called Mr and Mrs Weston. Says Harrison, 'They were lovely people and they really looked after us.' The house did not have its own toilet, which meant sharing a lavatory at the end of the street with four or five other families. Residents took turns to clean it. David McAdam, then a left-half at Leeds, lodged with the Westons before Charles. 'You had something to wee in at night,' he recalls, 'but if you wanted to do the other thing, you had to unlock the door and go down to the end of the street.'

When Buckley's men faced Scottish top-flight side Queen of the South at Elland Road in a friendly on 19 April 1949, they were floundering in the bottom half of Division Two. They had also been embarrassingly knocked out of the FA Cup by Third Division Newport County and had won just one league game in the last ten.

This meaningless Easter Tuesday match against The Doonhamers from Dumfries would change Charles's life forever. Tom Holley, Leeds' first-choice centre-half, had suffered an ankle injury in a 1–0 defeat at West Bromwich Albion on 6 April. His replacement, Roland Depear, failed to impress when he stepped in for Holley earlier in the season after the stalwart broke bones in his hand. Buckley decided to give 17-year-old Charles, who had served his apprenticeship in the Yorkshire League and Central League sides, his chance. The man he had to mark was The Doonhamers' Scottish international centre-forward, Billy Houliston.

Ten days earlier, Houliston had ripped apart an England defence that included Neil Franklin and Billy Wright in Scotland's famous 3–1 win at Wembley – their first post-war victory against the 'Auld Enemy'. Houliston did not find the net that day but he unlocked England's rearguard for James Mason, Billy Steel and Lawrie Reilly to score their goals. Houliston was the big attraction and the reason this friendly against the Scottish club attracted a respectable 18,000 crowd.

Recalls Harrison, 'When Charlo was told he was going to play in the first team he wasn't at all excited. Not like me. When I found out I was making my debut I wanted everyone to know. But that was John – he was so level-headed for a young man. He never got excited about anything. Whenever he got a Welsh cap he would just shove it in the bloody drawer! If it was me I would have got a glass cabinet to put them in.'

As Charles tied his bootlaces in the dressing-room, Buckley sat beside him and gave words of advice and encouragement. Shyly, almost apologetically, Charles took to the field wearing the number 5 shirt. Behind him in goal was Harold Searson. At right-back was Jimmy Dunn and at left-back Jimmy Milburn. At right-half was Jim McCabe and left-half was Tommy Burden. Before the kick-off Houliston looked at the match programme and enquired about this John Charles who would be marking him. When told he was a 17 year old making his first-team debut he was delighted. 'Having had such a strenuous game at Wembley, I thought it would be an easy match for me for a change.'

Charles had a blinder on his senior debut. In the very first minute he tackled Houliston, won the ball and then fed it to his forwards. That set the tone for the rest of the match as Charles tamed the man who had tormented England. 'This young chap had all the tricks of the trade,' said the surprised Scot. 'To be honest, he played me out of the game. I knew then that he would turn out to be the best in Britain.' The match ended in a 2–1 win for Leeds and when the final whistle sounded, Houliston shook his marker's hand and told him he had a great future in the game. 'I watched that game and Charlo didn't give Billy Houliston a kick,' says Peter Harrison. 'He was only 17 yet he stopped a top international player touching the ball. It was as if he had been playing at that level for years.'

Watching from the stand, McAdam witnessed Charles's baptism in the first team. 'Even at that age,' he remembers, 'Charles was an accomplished player. Houliston came with a big reputation but John didn't let him into the game. That was the beginning of the end for Tom Holley.'

Not long after coming off the pitch Houliston heaped praise on Charles, hailing him as 'the best centre-half I've ever played against'. After the game the young defender returned to his digs in Archer Road. He had cancelled out the man who ran the great Billy Wright ragged ten days previously, yet Charles, to Harrison's astonishment, did not talk about his debut. 'That was Charlo all over. He never got excited about anything,' says his former housemate. 'It was just a game of football to him. He took it all for granted.'

Charles received rave reviews in the local press the following day. Richard Ulyatt, a football reporter on the *Yorkshire Post*, wrote:

> Lacking the bite of a league fixture, the pace was not as fast as usual for many of the players. Charles was not one of these for his opponent, William Houliston, whose refreshing vigour is welcomed by everyone except goalkeepers and centre half-backs. Young Charles came through the ordeal no worse than the England players at Wembley a week ago and from his cool assurance, his tactical skill and sturdy build, it seemed evident that United's manager, Major Buckley, has found a player of great promise.

Holley, who, like McAdam, watched the Queen of the South game from the stand, knew he would never play for Leeds again. Says Harold Williams, 'I'll never forget what Tom said after the Queen of the South game. He said, "When I saw John play for the first time I thought it's time to get my boots and get out." Tom never saw the first team again after the Queen of the South game. Tom wasn't in John's class. He knew after that game that his position had gone to someone else.' After 12 years at Elland Road, Holley retired at the end of the season and moved into journalism, becoming a highly respected football writer for the *Yorkshire Evening Post* and

Sunday People. As for Charles, he would remain in the Leeds first team until his departure to Juventus in 1957. Only injury and national service commitments stopped him playing.

Holley, who died in 1992, never forgot the 90 minutes that signalled the end of his career at Leeds. 'As I had been training in the evenings I had seen nothing of John,' he recalled. 'Trainer Bob Roxburgh had told me time after time that this boy, even when he was 16, was a winner. Within 20 minutes of the start of the game against Queen of the South I knew that my football days weren't simply numbered, I knew they were finished. I knew that John Charles, though only 17, was already a man destined to hold that centre-half position with distinction for a long time to come.'

Four days after the Queen of the South friendly, Charles made his league debut against Blackburn Rovers at Ewood Park. Once again Charles proved to be an irremovable barrier, snuffing out Willie Fenton as Leeds ground out a 0–0 result. That display earned him his first headline – 'CHARLES'S FINE FORM' enthused the *Yorkshire Post.* Charles kept a second successive clean sheet in the home clash against Cardiff City. He 'gave a completely satisfactory home debut', wrote Ulyatt. But then he tasted defeat in the final fixture of the season with Leeds going down 2–0 against Queens Park Rangers at Loftus Road.

While the players were in London for the Rangers match, Bruce Woodcock, the heavyweight boxer from Yorkshire, was fighting the American Lee Savold at the Harringay Arena. Showing a generous streak, Buckley arranged for the team to stay an extra night in London so they could watch the fight. The team were booked in at their usual King's Cross hotel in the capital but, due to a shortage of rooms, two players had to find other accommodation. Buckley put Charles and Len Browning in a taxi and asked the driver to take them to a hotel. They were driven to the opulent Mayfair on Park Lane, a salutary experience for the boy from Alice Street. 'At the time it was the best hotel in London,' says Browning. 'John and I walked in there with only a toothbrush in our pockets. You can imagine what we felt like. We weren't given one room, we were given a suite of rooms. It was unbelievable. We never stopped for breakfast the following morning because we were too scared to go into the restaurant and eat. Everyone was in their finery and the ladies were all wearing long dresses. We felt completely out of place.'

It was during this period that Charles fell in love with a Leeds girl, Margaret White – known as Peggy – who worked as a clerk for the Midland Bank at their city-centre branch in Vicar Lane. She and Charles first met on a Saturday night at the Astoria dance hall, which was often frequented by the Leeds players. 'The girls were on one side of the hall and the blokes on the other, having a drink,' explains Harrison. 'We'd decide which ones we liked and then ask them to dance.' Charles, at the dance hall with Harrison, was captivated by Peggy's dark looks. 'I remember John saying, "I fancy her." She was an attractive girl. She looked Spanish or Italian,' adds Harrison.

The first Mrs Charles recalls her initial encounter with the strapping Welshman who had just broken into the Leeds first team. 'He came over and asked me to dance,' says Peggy. 'I didn't know who he was. The girl I was with told me he was a Leeds United player. Then after dancing he asked if he could take me home. It was two trams to my house and there were no taxis in those days. My dad was a big Leeds fan and he recognised John when he came into the house. He was quite overcome. John was very quietly spoken and didn't have much to say. The next day he took me to a cricket match but I never thought the relationship would become a long-term thing.'

Not long after their first date, Charles took his girlfriend to Swansea to meet his family, a telltale sign that their relationship was serious. They stayed in Alice Street for a week. 'They had an outside toilet which had newspaper on the walls. There was no bathroom – everyone washed in the sink. I didn't come from a well-off family but this was a real eye-opener,' remembers Peggy. 'The house was small but it was full of people. John's two younger brothers, Mel and Malcolm, were there, and his sister, Maureen, who had just had twins. Somehow we all managed but I couldn't wait to get out.'

The following season, Charles, at centre-half, was ever-present for Leeds and on 12 November 1949, he scored the first of his 157 goals for the club, against Plymouth Argyle at a windswept Home Park. With the score standing at 1–1, and with just four minutes remaining on the clock, the visitors were awarded a penalty. 'Without any hesitation John strolled up, put the ball on the spot and banged the ball into the net, no problem,' recalls former Leeds inside-left Frank Dudley. 'Even when he was only 17 or 18 John was the best player in our team.' The goalkeeper he beat on that dreary winter's day in Devon was Wales international goalkeeper Bill Shortt. Charles was only months away from becoming his international teammate.

Dudley, who joined Leeds in June 1947 and witnessed Charles's meteoric rise from groundstaff boy to the first team in eight months, recalls the away journeys on the team bus. 'I always took an apple to eat after the game. When I was eating it John would come up to me and with that deep Welsh voice of his he'd ask, "Can I have the core, boy?" I used to give him the core when I had finished and I used to think about that after John was sold to Juventus for what was then a huge fee.'

Charles quickly emerged as a key man in the Leeds team with Buckley publicly stating Charles was better than Cullis at the same age. His excellent form was rewarded with a Welsh cap, against Northern Ireland at Wrexham in March 1950. 'John was a tremendous centre-half,' says Len Browning, who Charles would eventually replace at centre-forward. 'He was never out of position and he could command the field. He made everything look so easy.' Former milkman Harold Williams, who had joined Leeds from Newport County before the 1949–50 season, adds, 'John was something special. He was phenomenal in the air, had two great feet and he could move like a ballerina. He would never try and do anything stupid. He just did the simple things, and he did them well. Buckley said he was the best player he had ever seen and he said that early on. Stan Cullis was one of his favourites but he said John was better.'

By the middle of February there was talk of promotion after Leeds won six league games on the bounce, the undoubted highlight a 3–0 win over Tottenham Hotspur which was watched by an Elland Road crowd of 50,476. Tottenham won the Division Two title by nine points that season.

On 25 February 1950 came a trip to Ninian Park where they faced Cardiff City. On an overcast afternoon, The Bluebirds won

1–0 with Welsh international George Edwards fooling Charles to head the winner. Edwards admits that on the evidence of this game he did not think Charles would become an international superstar. 'I saw our outside-right, Mike Tiddy, coming down the right wing,' remembers Edwards. 'I was on the left wing. I could see he was going to cross so I cut across the goalmouth, raced past John and headed home. John didn't know what I was doing and I remember he was left flat-footed. Looking back, you wouldn't have said a legend was in the making there.'

Leeds finished fifth that season, five points behind runners-up Sheffield Wednesday who dashed their promotion hopes at Hillsborough on 25 March. Leeds were holding the home side 2–2 but with 23 minutes left the defence caved in – according to one report Leeds 'crumpled up like a boxer under a heavy blow to the solar plexus' – and Walter Rickett, Hugh McJarrow and Gerry Henry ensured a 5–2 win for The Owls. In the *Yorkshire Post* Ulyatt suggested Leeds' Welsh centre-half, coming to the end of his first full season and still only 18, looked tired. 'Charles, grand youngster though he is, is still only a youngster. He looked to me as if he is beginning to feel the strain of his first season in league football and was never happy against the thrusting McJarrow.'

In that season's FA Cup Leeds really made an impression. After beating Carlisle United, Bolton Wanderers and Cardiff City, Leeds booked their place in the sixth round of the competition for the first time in the club's history and they were drawn to face Arsenal at Highbury. The Gunners were littered with star players – Dennis Compton, Laurie Scott, Joe Mercer, Walley Barnes, Alex Forbes, Jimmy Logie and Don Roper.

The pundits gave Leeds no chance but the pessimism failed to prevent a mass exodus to North London with 150 coaches making the trip from West Yorkshire to Highbury. In front of 62,273 people the underdogs produced an heroic display with Charles dominating Roper in a fascinating duel. 'Even though John was only 18, he was probably the best thing in that Leeds side,' admits Dudley. Many of Charles's former teammates rate this as his finest match for Leeds at centre-half. It was certainly the game that put Charles on English football's map.

For 52 minutes Leeds held firm but then Forbes charged down

the left wing. He passed to Roper who centred to Reg Lewis. In vain, Charles stretched out his left leg to try and block the pass before Lewis toe-poked the ball past Searson. The visitors came close to forcing a replay – George Swindin brilliantly saved a Dudley header with his knees while Ray Iggleden hit the crossbar. Arsenal went on to lift the cup, beating Liverpool at Wembley. After this epic quarter-final, Compton walked over to the disconsolate Charles as he was leaving the pitch. 'He said to him, "Well done, son" and John was quite thrilled about that,' remembers Dudley. 'John was quite outstanding that day and he felt very proud after what Denis had said to him.'

Charles had firmly established himself as a first-team player in 1949–50. 'I imagine,' says Harrison, 'that his was the first name on the team sheet.' Buckley was delighted with his progress and began comparing him to Billy Wright, the England captain he had groomed at Molineux. 'John Charles is the greatest I've ever had,' enthused the Major. 'I have never seen anyone like him in 50 years of the game.' Bob Forrest, an inside-forward who joined Leeds in 1953, recalls Buckley's appearance on *This Is Your Life* when Wright was its subject. 'The Major was asked who he considered to be the best player he had worked with. Everyone expected him to say Billy Wright but he said John Charles!'

Buckley, well educated, well spoken and with a distinct military bearing, was not one for favourites in the dressing-room but he made an exception with Charles, 'Every Friday we used to have a team chat with Major Buckley,' says Dudley. 'Sometimes John would nod off but the Major would just say, "Don't wake him up. He doesn't need to listen to what I've got to say." But we ordinary mortals had to listen.' Adds John Reynolds, another of Leeds' Welsh contingent, 'If anyone was late for training the Major would chop their bollocks off but if John was late he'd never say boo to him.'

None of Charles's ex-colleagues recall Buckley rebuking his Welsh international. Forrest says, 'When we played practice matches, the Major used to shout things at the players over the public address system using a microphone.' (Buckley was forced to stop using the system after the club was inundated with complaints from residents on the Heath estate opposite the ground who objected to his colourful language.) 'If you played a bad pass he would shout, "The fuckin' ball won't go through the man!" But if John made a bad pass it was always, "Hard luck, John." We used to take the mick out of Charlo about that.'

Charles also experienced Buckley's unique – some would say eccentric – approach to management during this season. The Leeds manager was rarely without the company of his terrier, Bryn, named after inside-forward Bryn Jones whom Buckley – when he was at Wolves in 1946 – sold to Arsenal for a world record £14,000. His methods were unconventional. A big believer in sharpening the mind, Buckley made his players sniff essence of beef or essence of lamb before games. 'It made us want to spew,' recalls Harrison. On freezing days his players would be massaged with whisky, Buckley claiming it would help their bodies deal with the cold. One such occasion was before an FA Cup match against Manchester United in January 1951. 'The Major said to Bob [Roxburgh], "Get the whisky out." Bob got these eight bottles of whisky out. We were wondering what was going on,' says Harrison. 'We ended up being massaged with it. The United players must have smelt it on us and thought we were pissed up because we ended up losing 4–0.'

In training sessions, Buckley would play music over the Elland Road public address system and order his players to pair up and dance along the touchline. 'He said dancing was very good for our balance,' explains Browning. 'Quite often John, who was the biggest in the team, paired up with Harold who was the smallest. You can imagine what they looked like.'

Buckley's most controversial idea was the monkey gland injections and capsules given to his players during the 1950–51 season. The Major told his bemused dressing-room that monkey gland extract sharpened the mind and would make them think two or three seconds faster than their opponents. Players were given a weekly jab and ordered to take three white capsules of gland extract daily. In reality it was a psychological trick – the 'stimulant' was an inoculation against the common cold.

'The Major said Winston Churchill had monkey gland injections during the war to keep his mind alert and active,' says Browning. Buckley first introduced the injections in the summer of 1937, when he was manager at Wolves. It created quite a stir and the subject was even raised in the House of Commons, prompting a statement from Walter Elliot, the Minister of Health, who said that he did not think a special investigation was needed. 'The Major was a great believer in anything that could make us better,' says Harrison, 'We had the injection in our backside. If you said you wouldn't have it then you were told you wouldn't be considered for the first team. We had a course of injections for three or four months.' Did the injections work? 'Well, I remember playing West Ham on Christmas Day. The Major said to us, "As from today the monkey glands should take effect." We were 3–0 down at half-time. We lost 3–1 in the end.'

Promotion once again eluded Leeds in 1950–51, with Buckley's boys finishing fifth for the second time in succession. There were no FA Cup heroics this time as Leeds were thrashed 4–0 by Manchester United at Old Trafford in the fourth round. 'I'll never forget Charlo being pulled down by a United player in that game,' recalls Harrison. 'He stayed down, then after a while he got up and everyone inside the ground started clapping. Afterwards he said to me, "There was nothing wrong with me, Pete, but I knew I'd get a good clap if I got up after staying down for a bit."'

This nondescript campaign turned out to be a milestone in Charles's career since it saw him switched from centre-half to centre-forward. Buckley made his move on 23 March 1951, when his team visited Manchester City at Maine Road. It was one of seven positional changes Buckley made following a 2–0 defeat at Hull the previous day. Charles was replacing Len Browning who was ill, although Harold Williams says the Leeds coaching team thought Charles was 'wasted at centre-half' and was moved up front to spice up a forward line that had failed to score in three of the last four games. 'Are you quite sure I'm good enough?' Charles asked Buckley when he was told to put on the number 9 shirt. 'Quite sure,' replied his manager. 'You are tall, good in the air, a natural ball player, and having played centre-half you should know the tricks of centre-forward play.'

When Buckley told the *Yorkshire Evening News* the Welshman would play at centre-forward, the newspaper said the Leeds manager had 'sprung a soccer sensation' and called it 'a dramatic bid to achieve greater striking power in his attack'. The Major's changes failed to work as Leeds were crushed 4–1, their heaviest league defeat of the season. On a personal note Charles had a decent 90 minutes. 'I scored our goal,' says Harrison, 'but it was Charlo who made it for me. Even though it was his first game as a striker that day, Charlo looked the part. Everything came so easily to him. He could even have played goalkeeper for Wales.' Jimmy Dunn, the full-back who served Leeds for 11 years, said, 'Moving John Charles up front was the best thing the club ever did.'

There were mixed reports in the press regarding Charles's display at Maine Road. The *Yorkshire Post* was unconvinced about his change of role. 'John Charles tried very hard and well, like the all-round and wholehearted footballer that he is, but he was comparatively innocuous in front of goal. His distribution on approach was, on the other hand, excellent.' The *Yorkshire Evening News* was kinder. Under a headline that read 'CHARLES SHINES AS LEADER' it said, 'Only Charles had any snap in his finishing proving himself a good leader.'

Charles was back at number 9 for the next game two days later, a home clash against Hull whose centre-half was the classy Neil Franklin, capped 27 times by England. He was not convinced by his manager's judgement. 'You saw me, I didn't get a kick,' said Charles, referring to the previous game at Maine Road when Buckley told him he was staying in attack.

In a blizzard and on a muddy, snow-covered pitch, Buckley's faith was rewarded. Charles drove home two spectacular goals in his side's 3–0 win. Ulyatt sensed he had a big future in the number 9 jersey. In his match report he wrote, 'Charles got his goals by moving about the field; here was no orthodox down-the-middle centre-forward but a man with a football brain, able to sense the right position to take up.'

Despite his success against the Boothferry Park outfit, Charles was still not sure if he was centre-forward material and as the 1950–51 season drew to a close he could not envisage a long-term future as a striker. 'I never saw Charlo have a bad game. It was harder for him to play badly than well,' says Harrison. 'One Friday night when we came back to our digs late – it was about eleven o'clock and everyone had gone to bed – I said to Charlo, "Do you want a drink of hot milk?" And Charlo said, "I'll tell you what's good for you – hot milk with Mackeson in it."' Mackeson, a milk stout sweeter than Guinness, had a reputation as a nourishing drink and was a favourite with women. 'So I put some in the milk and we drank it,' adds Harrison. 'We were as sick as dogs that night but Charlo still played well the next day.'

The former winger also remembers the FA Cup match against Middlesbrough on a foggy Saturday afternoon in January 1951. Charles's father made the trip from Swansea to watch his son play in this third-round tie. 'Charlo and I went to meet Ned at the railway station. His train hadn't arrived so we went back home. We went back and forth, back and forth – the station was a good quarter-of-an-hour tram ride from our digs and we must have gone back there five times before Ned's train finally came in. I think it arrived at one o'clock in the afternoon – and we were playing in a cup match in two hours' time! We didn't get to the ground until 2.10 p.m. and all that going back and forth really took it out of me. I felt knackered during the game but John had a blinder and we won 1–0. What happened earlier in the day hadn't affected him at all. He was a big, strong lad.'

Charles was restored to centre-half for the 0–0 draw at Notts County but a week later he was back at centre-forward against Grimsby Town at Elland Road, scoring the only goal of the game. It would be another 12 months before the Major pencilled him in at number 9 again.

CHAPTER THREE –
PRINCE OF ELLAND ROAD

For two years, from 1950–52, Charles was something of a stranger at Elland Road. Now that he had turned 18 he was called up to do his national service. Placed with the 12th Royal Lancers, he was stationed first at Barnard Castle, North Yorkshire, and then Carlisle. The Army could have refused Charles leave to play for Leeds but in the words of Frank Dudley, 'He had a very understanding commanding officer who used to let him off every weekend.'

He could not make every game, however, as Army commitments took Charles to Belgium and Austria. Buckley, like many managers in the game, feared national service would halt Charles's progress but was proved wrong. In fact, Charles insisted his spell in the Army improved his game. He became renowned for his prowess in the air (Dudley recalls him scoring one header after leaping nine feet off the ground), a skill Charles attributed to learning how to play basketball at Barnard Castle. He knew nothing of this American sport – he described it as 'a cissy's game' – and when some of his colleagues asked him if he wanted to take part, he agreed only because it meant avoiding some 'unpopular duties'. Basketball improved his jumping ability and kept him in shape. Away from the daily rigours of training, Charles was in danger of putting on weight but he discovered playing 20 minutes of basketball burned up as much energy as 50 minutes of playing football.

While in the Army he took up another sport, his schoolboy

pastime of boxing. While working out in the Barnard Castle gymnasium, Charles's sergeant-major asked him if he fancied fighting. Charles agreed and won his first 11 amateur heavyweight bouts, all by a knockout. His trainers were convinced he was a potential champion. When Charles's father bumped into his commanding officer at a football match at Elland Road, he was told, 'Your son is a better boxer than a footballer.'

The Amateur Boxing Association stepped in and barred Charles from boxing since he was a professional footballer and professionals in other sports were not allowed to enter the amateur ring. 'The law is quite clear,' said Lieutenant G.T.A. Peters, secretary of the Northern Command Sports Board. 'Anyone who makes money from any sport cannot box under ABA rules.' The Leeds player was forced to hang up his gloves. 'It is a big disappointment,' he said after learning of the ABA decision. 'I like boxing but I shall have to concentrate more on football now.'

When he finished his national service he received a letter from the boxing manager, Jack Solomons, enquiring if he wanted to take up boxing professionally. Charles toyed with the idea and went to his close friend, Peter Harrison, for advice. 'He asked me, "What would you do, Pete?" I told him to forget it,' says Harrison. 'I'd boxed in the Army and I saw lads get some good hidings. I witnessed one lad get such a bad beating I packed it in myself because I thought that fella could have been me. I said to John, "Stick to football" and he did.'

Trooper W.J. Charles dazzled in Army football. He was an automatic choice at centre-half but occasionally played at right-back and in 1952 he captained his side to victory in the Army Cup. Charles left a lasting impression on his superiors, shown by a letter sent to the *Yorkshire Evening News* by Lieutenant-Colonel G.J. Mitchell. The Army Football Association's secretary was enchanted by three displays in particular. The first was in Belfast when he produced 'an exhibition of centre-half play not equalled in the Army since'. The second came in Brussels against the Belgian Army in 1951, when Charles not only 'won the game off his own bat' but 'had the partisan Belgian crowd on their toes shouting in amazement at this young giant every time he kicked the ball'. The third was also against the Belgians, this time in Dulwich a year later, when he quelled 'the rather cocky' Belgian international centre-forward, Rik Coppens. Coppens went on to star for his country in the 1954 World Cup.

'We of the Army Football Association will never forget John Charles, for to us he was the acme of fairness and the ideal sporting player who always gave his best, no matter whether it was in a platoon or representative Army football,' wrote Mitchell. 'There was great sorrow in his camp when he finally terminated his national service, though we did not try to get him to extend it!'

While wearing His Majesty's uniform Charles developed cartilage trouble. Before he resumed his professional career at Elland Road he underwent an operation to remove one of the two cartilages from each knee. It could have wrecked – or certainly hindered – his career but Charles made a recovery that staggered his doctors. 'I joined Leeds in 1952,' says full-back John Reynolds, born in Briton Ferry, near Swansea, and who was another Pickard discovery. 'I first met John when another Welsh lad, George Williams, was showing me to my digs. He saw John on the way and introduced us. He was on crutches at the time because he'd just had his cartilages out. He was very young to have that sort of operation but in the end it never affected him.'

Charles missed a large chunk of the 1951–52 season because he was sidelined following surgery. He returned to action, somewhat ironically, against Swansea Town on 1 December 1951. He was back at centre-half, replacing utility man Roy Kirk, and the match ended 1–1. 'Because we were from the same part of the world, John and I used to travel back home together,' continues Reynolds, whose promising career ended after he damaged cruciate ligaments in a Youth Cup match against West Bromwich Albion. 'It was an overnight journey. We'd catch the 10.45 p.m. train at Leeds and we'd get to Swansea Victoria at eight the following morning. If we were sleeping in one of the old carriages and there were three of us, we'd toss to decide who slept where. The loser would end up sleeping in the overhead rack.'

Charles stayed in defence until the match at Nottingham Forest on 11 April 1952. Leeds' promotion challenge was wavering after a 2–1 defeat at Luton, and Buckley, for the second time, experimented with Charles at centre-forward. He failed to find the net but Buckley persevered with him up front in the next two games, against Bury and Forest again. Charles fired blanks although the team did collect three points out of a possible four.

A month earlier Leeds received the first of many offers for their coveted defender. It came from First Division club Sunderland who offered £15,000 plus the creative inside-forward Ivor Broadis, a player who interested Buckley. But the Major had no desire to part with Charles – 'I cannot tell you what he is worth, he is priceless' – and told his counterpart at Roker Park, Bill Murray, there would be no deal. 'People argue about what was John's best position, centre-half or centre-forward,' says Browning. 'In my opinion he was best at centre-half. He was as good a centre-half as I've ever seen. When I was transferred to Sheffield United and we came up against Leeds I always wanted John to play centre-forward because there he was more reliant on his teammates. If you could cut the supply to him, you had a good chance of stopping him. But at centre-half he could command the field.' Harry Gregg, the Northern Ireland goalkeeper who played for Doncaster Rovers and Manchester United, came up against Charles on many occasions. He also believes centre-half was his best position. 'Trying to get around Charles,' he says, 'was like trying to get around a double-decker bus.'

There were some forwards who caused Charles problems. One was Southampton's diminutive Charlie Wayman. The man from Bishop Auckland was feared for his twisting, turning and darting runs. 'Charlo hated playing against him,' reveals Peter Harrison. 'I was 5 ft 6 in. tall and Charlie was no bigger than me, but he was nippy and he had two good feet. Charlo found it hard playing against him. I've never seen a player have a really good game against Charlo except Charlie Wayman.' Browning agrees. 'John liked playing against the normal centre-forwards and he would outjump them in the air. But Wayman was little and he used to play deep and run at John. He gave him more trouble than most.' Charles admitted Wayman – 'fast, clever, always at you' – was one of only two players who gave him problems. The other was Northern Ireland international Wilbur Cush, who joined Leeds after Charles was sold to Juventus.

Leeds' faltering form at the end of the 1951–52 season meant they missed out on promotion for a third time, finishing sixth, four points behind Cardiff City who took the runners-up spot. Buckley was under pressure. He had been brought in to lead Leeds into the top flight but four years on the club still languished in Division Two. To freshen up the side for the next campaign he made two notable signings, winger George Meek from Hamilton Academical and, in October, inside-forward Albert Nightingale from Blackburn Rovers.

Charles might also have been playing alongside his younger brother at Elland Road in 1952–53. While John was in the Army, Jack Pickard had sent Mel to Yorkshire and Buckley took him on as a groundstaff boy. After nine months, Mel, who, unlike his older brother, suffered severe bouts of homesickness, returned to Swansea for a short holiday and never returned. On the day he was due to return to Leeds, Mel's neighbours in Alice Street threw a farewell party for him. Just as he was about to leave for the railway station he decided to stay home. 'When I was living in Leeds I used to listen to Welsh Rarebit on the wireless. They would sing 'We'll Keep A Welcome' and tears used to run down my face,' recalls Mel who enjoyed seven successful years at Swansea Town before joining Arsenal in 1959. 'But John never had problems with homesickness. If he moved somewhere, he just seemed to accept it. I was much more of a home-bird. I never wanted to leave Swansea. Maybe John might have helped me settle in Leeds, but he was in the Army when I joined so I didn't see much of him. I only saw him at weekends.'

There were differences between the two brothers. On the pitch they showed completely different temperaments. 'If someone kicked John he wouldn't retaliate. He would just get up and carry on. He really was a gentle giant,' explains Mel. 'But I was different. If someone kicked me I'd always get them back. I'd wait my time but I'd get them.'

In public Charles was extremely shy. Whenever he went out with Peggy he would cover up the Leeds badge on his blazer to avoid people approaching him and talking about football. If he was invited to a function, such as those organised by the Leeds supporters, he never went alone because he would feel uncomfortable. He always coaxed some of his teammates to go along with him. 'John wasn't very outgoing,' says Len Browning. 'He was quiet, never said a word.' Yet inside the dressing-room the players saw a different side to him. Charles was one of Elland Road's comedians, forever playing practical jokes. Sometimes he would soak his teammates with a hosepipe or while one of them was having a bath he would hide their clothing. On one occasion he urinated over the back of Harold Williams while the winger was washing in the hot bath. There was three feet of snow outside and both players were naked but Williams chased Charles around the Elland Road car park.

Charles was not afraid to fool around with the club's directors and one who sampled Charles's humour was Harold Marjason. 'We were playing in London and staying at our usual hotel in King's Cross,' remembers goalkeeper Roy Wood. 'We went for a walk on the Saturday morning and in front of us were three directors; one of them was Marjason. They had just walked past someone with an Alsatian and John noticed Marjason veer away from the dog, obviously a bit scared of it. So John says to me, "Watch this." He went right up behind Marjason and started barking and growling. Marjason jumped six feet into the air. He wasn't a young man and could easily have had a heart attack. Any other player would have been put on the transfer list after that but not John.'

Charles had his own running gag with Wood. During training he and Dunn would exchange passes until they were two or three yards away from Wood's goal, then Dunn would lift the ball up into the air for Charles to volley straight at the goalkeeper. 'He wasn't bothered about scoring,' says Wood. 'All he wanted to do was hit me with the ball.'

Charles started the 1952–53 season at centre-half but Leeds began poorly and after five defeats, five draws and just two wins Buckley moved Charles to centre-forward for a third time after watching him score both goals in a 2–1 win over Halifax in a West Riding Cup fixture in early October. That match convinced Buckley that Charles should stay up front. The versatile Jim McCabe took Charles's place in defence.

Since Browning's transfer to Sheffield United he had tried three players at centre-forward – Frank Fidler, Barry Smith and John Hastie – but none of them proved effective. Charles, he felt, was the answer and in the next ten league games 'Big John' fired in fifteen goals, including two hat-tricks, against Hull and Brentford, both at Elland Road. From scoring the fourth goal in the 4–1 win over Barnsley on 18 October until bagging his hat-trick in the 3–2 win over Brentford on 29 November, Charles scored all of his team's ten goals. In the *Yorkshire Evening News*, Ronald Crowther described his display against Hull, when he claimed his very first hat-trick, as 'one of the finest displays of devastating marksmanship that I have ever seen from an Elland Road leader in post-war times'. The visitors fielded their fourth-choice centre-half, James Duthie, because Neil Franklin, Tom Berry and Frank Harrison were all unavailable, but this should not have detracted from Charles's performance. His first goal was the result of a brilliant, flowing move, which began with his goalkeeper, Jack Scott. He threw the ball to Harold Williams who beat two men on the wing before passing to Albert Nightingale who fed Charles and 'in a flash the ball was in the net'. His second was a 'lightning-like' left-foot shot that gave Hull's goalkeeper, William Bly, no chance and the third came from the penalty spot. When it came to spot-kicks, Charles was a master. 'Whenever we had a penalty the fans would rush to the end of the ground where Charlo was going to take it,' remembers Peter Harrison. 'He used to absolutely blast the ball. It was a miracle he never broke the net.'

Against Brentford four weeks later, Charles scored what he has always considered the finest goal of his glorious career. It came in the last minute and on an icy, treacherous pitch. Charles picked up the ball inside his own half, beat two players, ran towards the visitors' goal, teased goalkeeper Alf Jefferies off his line, and slotted the ball home. 'I hesitate to use the phrase a one-man win but this was the nearest I have seen to it for a long time,' wrote a mesmerised Richard Ulyatt. Former England striker Tommy Lawton, who was enjoying an Indian summer at Brentford, became Charles's latest admirer after that game, hailing him as the greatest player of his era. Buckley went even further – 'Charles is the best in the world.'

A week earlier, after he scored twice in the 2–2 draw at Everton, the Goodison Park faithful were convinced they had just seen the next Dixie Dean. Recalls George Meek, 'At the time Wolves, Arsenal and Manchester United were the best teams in the country and John would have walked into any of those sides. He was more than 6 ft 1 in. of solid muscle. Running into him wouldn't have been like running into a brick wall – it would have been like running into a brick wall that was moving towards you. At the time there were forwards like Nat Lofthouse and Trevor Ford who would barge goalkeepers into the net but that wasn't John's way. I always thought if I was his size I would have trampled over everybody on a football pitch, but John didn't want to do that.'

In between games and after training, Charles, with a ball under his arm, would retreat behind the West Stand on his own. There, and sometimes in night-time darkness, he would practise his shooting, all the time improving his accuracy and power. After one game, Ron Crowther, the sports editor of the *Yorkshire Evening News*, and his deputy Jack Gillings, were driving past Elland Road when they heard what sounded like gunfire outside the ground. They stopped their car to investigate and saw the immense figure of Charles repeatedly kicking the ball against the base of the stand's wall.

Charles remained at centre-forward for the rest of the season, firing a third hat-trick in a 4–0 drubbing of Rotherham at Elland Road. He scored two breathtaking goals in that clash. His first saw him run half the length of the pitch before rounding Rotherham goalkeeper John Quairney and finishing coolly. His third saw him ride tackles from Jack Selkirk, Horace Williams and Quairney before finding the net. Eric Stanger in the *Yorkshire Post* described it as 'a goal that bore the stamp of greatness'.

Another match that stood out for 'Big John' was the 5–1 win over Swansea Town at Elland Road, in December 1952. Charles netted twice in the demolition of his hometown club and Billy McCandless, who was still Swansea's manager, was no doubt contemplating what might have been.

But Charles was not comfortable at centre-forward and after scoring his 18th goal in 15 games, in a 2–1 FA Cup defeat at Brentford, he nervously knocked on the door of Buckley's office and asked to be moved back to centre-half. Buckley was staggered. 'You've scored all those goals and you want to go back to being just a stopper?' he asked. Charles nodded, but the Major thought he was wasted in defence and told him he was staying where he was.

Playing up front was proving far more lucrative for Charles since he was receiving 'under the counter' payments – then illegal – from club chairman, Sam Bolton. For every goal the Welshman scored he received a cash bonus from Bolton, a lifelong Leeds supporter who was managing director of a motor haulage company, Thomas Spence Ltd. 'Every time Charlo scored Sam Bolton would come up to our digs and give him one pound,' says Harrison. 'That was a decent amount because, don't forget, we were on twelve pounds a week in those days. You could have a good night out for one pound. You could play snooker, go to the pictures, have a couple of drinks and still come home with change. Charlo used to say he would give me fifty pence for every goal I created for him. I created a lot of goals for him but I think only once did he give me anything.'

Bolton, nicknamed 'the Black Adder' by the Leeds players because he drove a black Ford V8 Pilot car, tried to further reward Charles. Recalls Roy Wood, 'In one match – I can't remember against which team – John had scored a hat-trick and on the Monday after the game Sam Bolton went up to him and said, "John, congratulations on your hat-trick. Go to my garage because there's three gallons of petrol waiting for you – one for each goal." And John said to him, "But Mr Bolton, I haven't got a car." None of us players had a car in those days.'

Despite Charles's goals – in 28 league outings he scored a remarkable 26 goals – Leeds were never in the promotion hunt that season and for the final match, a meaningless clash against Doncaster Rovers at Elland Road, Buckley handed a 17-year-old centre-half called Jack Charlton his senior debut. 'Everyone played on a Saturday – the third team, the second team and the first team,' says Charlton. 'We used to go into the dressing-room where the team sheet was pinned up to see if we were playing. I looked at the bottom of the list because I was in the junior side at the time but my name wasn't there. So I looked at the second team and my name wasn't in that. I looked at the first team and there I was. It wasn't half a shock. John Charles was there looking at the sheet with Eric Kerfoot and I'll always remember John pointing to my name and saying, "Who the fuck is that?" I just stood there and said, "That's me."'

When the players were changing in the dressing-room, Charlton, pale and thin – and later nicknamed 'the Giraffe' – never took his top off at the same time as the muscular Charles who was blessed with broad shoulders and narrows hips. 'John could have been the world heavyweight champion if he wanted to,' says the former Republic of Ireland manager. 'He was a big, strong, solid boy. I was very thin. When he had his shirt off, I kept mine on otherwise the other players would have thrown sand in my face.'

In January 1953, Charles and Peggy were married at St Mary's Church in Beeston. They tied the knot two months after the Welshman was best man at Peter Harrison's wedding in the same church. 'We had a weekend relationship while John was doing his national service,' says Peggy. 'We sort of drifted into marriage.' The newlyweds moved into a club house in Cross Heath Grove, on the Heath estate where Leeds owned several houses. 'Peter Harrison had got married so I think John thought we should too,' adds Peggy. 'I'm positive it happened that way because everything Peter did, John did. I didn't think twice. I thought marrying John was the right thing.'

In August 1954 the Charleses had the first of their four sons, Terry. Soon Charles joined the handful of Leeds players who would push their babies in prams around Elland Road every Friday morning while the wives went shopping. 'It started with just two of us, me and Jimmy Dunn,' says Bob Forrest. 'Then a few of the other players joined. After a while there were about half a dozen of us pushing prams about. The lorry drivers used to toot at us as they were driving past Elland Road.'

Following Leeds' disappointing tenth-place finish in 1952–53, Buckley decided to move on and took over as manager of Walsall in Division Three (South). After two years at Fellows Park he retired from the game at the age of 71. He lived in Walsall until his death in December 1964.

The Leeds board hired Horatio 'Raich' Carter to replace him. Ironically, Carter, a former England international inside-forward, had replaced Buckley at Hull in 1948 after the Major joined Leeds. As player-manager he won promotion to Division Two with The Tigers in 1949, resigned two years later after falling out with the board, but returned to management in Ireland, with Cork Athletic, where he won the FA of Ireland Cup in 1953.

The players, including Charles, never warmed to the egocentric Carter, who loved talking about his achievements during his – admittedly distinguished – career. 'Raich was such a bloody big-head. Everything he talked about, it was always about himself,' complains Archie Gibson.

Charles rarely says a bad word about anyone in public, but he makes an exception for Carter who 'loved himself'. Said Charles, 'Carter was very opinionated. He had this view – "I do it this way so you do it this way." He wouldn't let you argue. He would take the credit for what you'd done.' Some of Charles's former teammates, such as George Meek and Harold Williams, are convinced Carter was jealous of his Welsh international. 'Raich was a famous person and I don't think he liked the fact John was stealing the limelight,' explains Meek. But Carter, well aware Charles was the player who could fire Leeds into Division One, kept him on his side.

Bolton and his fellow directors made it clear to Carter that he was expected to win promotion to the First Division, a feat Buckley, with all his idiosyncrasies, had failed to do. He quickly decided to build the team around the awesome goalscoring power of Charles, who was retained at centre-forward for the following term.

Charles opened his 1953–54 account in stunning fashion, hitting four in the 6–0 drubbing of Notts County in front of a modest 18,432 crowd at Elland Road on a wet August afternoon. Three days later he hit a hat-trick – the second of five that season – in the 4–2 win over Rotherham, again at home. The emphatic opening-day win meant a 6,000 increase on Saturday's gate but, as the *Yorkshire Post* put it, for the first half an hour they 'must have wondered if they were at the right ground: even Charles could not get going'. The visitors raced into a two-goal lead but Charles and Albert Nightingale levelled before the interval and 'Big John' finished The Millers off after the break.

Then came the first defeat of the season, a 4–3 reverse at Swansea. John's younger brother, Mel, was playing centre-forward for The Swans and stole the headlines from his more illustrious sibling, breaking the deadlock after just 30 seconds. The older Charles had his revenge the following week when the Welsh side travelled up to Elland Road for the return fixture. Leeds won 3–2 with Charles scoring twice. Terry Medwin, his old teammate in the schoolboy side, was playing for The Swans and remembers Charles's first goal. 'A ball came over and it beat our defence and it also went well over our goalkeeper, Johnny King,' he says. 'It fell to John but he didn't head it in, he chested it over the line.' His second, which took the breath away, was vividly described in the *Yorkshire Post*. 'From halfway he ran side by side with Swansea's centre-half [Tom Kiley] watching the ball in the air rather like a cricketer judging a catch on the boundary. As it dropped Charles controlled it, pushed it forward past his guardian opponent, round another foe, drew the goalkeeper out and slipped the ball into the goal.'

Charles was in unstoppable form, scoring 19 goals in the first 14 matches. He bagged three more hat-tricks that term, against Bury, Rotherham and Lincoln City. 'I've seen John score goals with his head you wouldn't believe,' says Harold Williams. 'His accuracy and power were phenomenal. I once asked him, and I asked in jest, "Who is better heading the ball, you or Tommy Lawton?" He turned to me and said, "Have a bet on me." As a centre-forward, John took some looking after. He was so big, so strong and so good in the air.' George Meek, who, like Williams, set up many goals for Charles, says, 'John wasn't playing against bad players, he was playing against some very good defenders but it didn't matter how good the centre-half was, he still scored.'

One goal stands out in Peter Harrison's memory. 'I can't remember who we were playing but it was at Elland Road,' he says. 'A goalkick came to John who was about 30 or 40 yards from the opposition's goal. He took the goalkick on his chest, controlled it with his knee, turned and hit it. The ball flew into the back of the net. I thought to myself, "Bloody hell, what a goal."'

Charles's staggering tally of 42 league goals that season remains a club record but it was not enough to win promotion. In fact, Leeds failed to improve on the previous season, finishing tenth. Understandably, Carter and the Leeds directors feared losing their prize asset. The whole country knew of Charles's exploits and it was only a matter of time before the First Division clubs made formal bids for the marksman. Burnley and Sheffield Wednesday were reportedly interested, so too were Glasgow Rangers in Scotland. Leeds' determination to hold onto Charles was about to be tested.

The 1954–55 season started poorly for Carter. It began with a 2–0 opening day win over Hull. Then it all went horribly wrong, Leeds losing the next five league matches, against Rotherham (twice), Lincoln, Bury and Stoke. Carter's men conceded sixteen goals in those five games. The centre-half position was a problem. Loyal club man that he was, Jack Marsden was no John Charles. Jack

Charlton was tried in the home match against Lincoln but, having just come out of the Army, he was ill-equipped for the rigours of Division Two football and Leeds lost 3–2. In the dressing-room after the match, Charlton saw another side to the so-called 'Gentle Giant'. 'I'd just come out of the Army and I wasn't feeling in the mood to get pushed around,' says Charlton, a World Cup winner with England in 1966. 'In this game John came back to defend a corner-kick and he started telling me where to go. I said to him, "You fuck off! We've been handling this all game, we don't need you here!" And he just looked at me. Anyway, when we got back into the dressing-room he got hold of me by the shirt and said, "Don't ever talk to me like that again!" I said I was sorry and told him we should forget what had happened. I never spoke to him like that again.'

The press was critical of the team, accusing the players of relying too heavily on Charles who, because of his achievements the previous season, was now a marked man. On the Lincoln defeat, Eric Stanger in the *Yorkshire Post* wrote, 'United's ideas were mostly limited to booting the ball down the middle to Charles, irrespective of whether he was closely marked or not.' On 6 September, after a 5–3 defeat at Bury, Leeds captain Tommy Burden was put on the transfer list. Carter handed the captaincy to Charles, a decision that surprised Richard Ulyatt who thought the introverted Welshman was 'not really the sort one would have pointed to as the forceful leader of men'. But this was a shrewd move by the manager. Charles may have been the silent type, but he was well liked, inspired loyalty and, more importantly, he had the respect of his teammates. This was shown when one of the players, Keith Ripley, lost his baby son, Peter, through acute pneumonia. 'It was the day of the funeral and Peter was laid out upstairs in our house in Normanton, but my wife and I were so upset we wouldn't go and look at him,' says Ripley. 'John came to the house with flowers from all the lads. When he found out we wouldn't go upstairs he said to me, "Look, you've got to see the little boy." Because it was John I went upstairs and I'm so glad he said that. I wouldn't have done it for anybody else. He was a great pal. That was something I won't forget and I still get emotional now when I think about that day.'

With his defence in crisis, Carter also moved Charles back to centre-half, his favourite position, with Bob Forrest switching from inside-forward to centre-forward. 'If we needed John we played him up front,' recalls Forrest, one of Buckley's last signings. 'If we were leaking goals we would put him at centre-half. He was the best centre-half I've ever seen. He could head a ball clear as far as the halfway line and he wasn't one to just boot the ball upfield – he always placed it to one of his teammates.'

His first game as skipper, at home to Stoke, was an unhappy one as Leeds lost 1–0. It was a rare Charles mistake that allowed John King to score his side's winner in the 35th minute. The dismal run finally came to an end three days later when Swansea, with the help of Albert Nightingale's hat-trick, were beaten 5–2 at Elland Road. Charles, still at centre-half, was back to his brilliant best in the 1–0 return game at Stoke. Forrest gave Carter's men the lead and Stoke piled on the pressure as they looked for an equaliser. For most of the second half every outfield Stoke player was camped in the Leeds half but, as Ulyatt wrote, 'John Charles was here, there and everywhere, blocking this loophole and stopping that one . . . he was head and shoulders – metaphorically if not quite literally – above all the other players on the field.'

A 1–1 home draw against Nottingham Forest and a 2–1 win at Ipswich – Charles missed the latter match with a groin injury – followed and seven points out of a possible eight should have lifted the gloom from Elland Road. But, on Monday, 27 September 1954, Charles dropped a bombshell when he handed in a transfer request. Asked the reason for doing so, he replied, 'I want to play in the First Division. I have no quarrel with United but it is my ambition to get into the highest class of soccer.'

He had finally grown impatient. With his 23rd birthday approaching, he had no desire to spend the best days of his career in Division Two. Money was not an issue. This was the era of the maximum wage and, whichever club he played for, Charles would earn no more than fifteen pounds a week. Nor could he receive bigger bonuses than two pounds for a win and one pound for a draw.

'I am dumbfounded,' said Carter when asked his reaction to Charles's request. Sam Bolton was equally stunned. 'I am staggered. Charles has not said anything about wanting to leave us for the First

Division.' Percy Woodward, a Leeds director, remarked, 'Charles and I were at the reserve match on Saturday and he said nothing about it then.' The player was also silent on the matter when he went to Elland Road on Sunday morning for treatment for his groin injury. As Woodward wryly put it, 'He must have done some hard and concentrated thinking between Sunday midday and 10 a.m. on Monday when he handed in his request.'

Bolton announced that he and his fellow directors would meet in the Elland Road boardroom on Wednesday night before the floodlit friendly against Hibernian to discuss Charles's request. Arsenal and Cardiff City both declared an immediate interest in buying Leeds' golden boy and there were also telephone calls from Chelsea, Sunderland, Sheffield Wednesday and Blackpool. Charles said he would prefer to join Cardiff because 'they've got a lot of Welshmen on their books'.

Cardiff were desperate to beat the Londoners to his signature. How they needed Charles. The Bluebirds' defence was leaking like a sieve, letting in twelve goals in two games, both against Preston North End. 'If Leeds United agree to let Charles go then Cardiff City will leave no stone unturned in order to get his services,' proclaimed Cardiff chairman Sir Herbert Merrett, who told Bolton he was prepared to write out a £40,000 cheque for the player. That would have shattered the record transfer fee of £34,500 paid to Notts County by Sheffield Wednesday for Jackie Sewell in March 1951, although Newcastle United chairman Stan Seymour said Charles would be cheap at £40,000. 'All I can say is that anything Arsenal can do Cardiff City can do. For a long time now I have been a keen admirer of John Charles and I am convinced he could do us a power of good,' added Merrett. 'In view of that, we are prepared to go to the limit because I have made it known that Cardiff City would always go after Welshmen of note.'

Cardiff, looking for a star to bolster their team, had tried to sign Charles before, in 1952. On that occasion Leeds were prepared to sell and Charles was only too happy to return to his native Wales. Albert Lindon, Cardiff's chief scout, packed his bags for a 'top secret trip' to Elland Road where he was to have a 'quiet chat' with Buckley. The Major told Lindon he was 'ready and willing' to part with Charles but the asking price would be a record £35,000.

Cardiff balked at the asking price and Lindon returned to Ninian Park without his man. Just two years later they were prepared to hand over £5,000 more.

In public, Buckley said Charles was not for sale but privately he declared he would part with him at the right price. When a number of clubs were chasing after the defender, team skipper Tommy Burden asked the Major, 'You're not going to sell him, are you?' Buckley was unambiguous with his answer. 'You watch me. I like money in the bank to cover my salary. He'll go if I get the right money.'

Come the evening of Wednesday, 29 September, the Leeds directors scurried behind closed doors at Elland Road to decide whether or not to sell Charles. Waiting outside the boardroom was Cardiff City's assistant secretary Trevor Morris who had made the long trek from South Wales so he would be first in the queue to sign the Welsh international. Morris had been told he could go up to £50,000.

In the *Yorkshire Post* that day, Eric Stanger described the decision the club had to make as 'the most difficult in the club's 35-year history', but, in a courageous opinion piece, Stanger admitted he would not blame Leeds for selling Charles since £40,000 would help the club's cash-flow and allow Carter to strengthen other areas of the team. 'Events have proved that, by himself, John Charles cannot bring about a Leeds United revival either on the field or through the turnstiles.' He continued, 'Too much reliance, it has struck me, has been placed on Charles in the past by his club and by his colleagues. I dislike intensely the idea of him being lost to Yorkshire football but his transfer might – and I emphasise that – prove in the long run to be a blessing in disguise. All the same, I'm glad I don't have to make the decision.' The *Yorkshire Evening News* conducted a poll asking its readers whether Charles should be sold or not. The result was close, 51 per cent believing he should stay and 49 per cent saying Leeds should take the £40,000.

The meeting lasted two hours and forty-five minutes, with the Leeds directors unanimously agreeing not to sell Charles. The player, who was at the ground preparing for the Hibernian game, was summoned to the boardroom and told the news. His reaction was philosophical. 'I'm still anxious to play in the First Division but what can I do?' he told reporters. 'I was called into the meeting and told the club would not let me go. I was not really surprised.' Not surprised because only a week earlier Bolton, as if he anticipated Charles's request, had gone on record saying the Welshman would not be sold. 'Our aim is to get into the First Division and we can't do that by selling our star player.'

For Morris, it was a wasted journey. 'Naturally I am very disappointed after travelling so far,' said the trilby-wearing Morris. 'But I believe in personal contact and had the verdict been yes I should have been on the spot to get in first with my club's offer.'

Over the loudspeakers, before the Hibernian game kicked off, Bolton announced to the anxious Leeds supporters that Charles was staying. Elland Road was engulfed by a tremendous roar. Not only was Charles their best player, he was also a folk hero in this corner of Yorkshire. This was the champion who sent letters of encouragement to handicapped children and visited hospital patients. One such patient was his former teammate, Len Browning, who was in Selby's Gateforth Sanitorium after contracting tuberculosis. The illness forced him to retire from the game. 'I was in hospital for 20 months and John came to see me frequently,' recalls Browning. 'As soon as I came out, the first place I went to was Turin. John had joined Juventus and he invited me and the wife over. We stayed in his apartment and he took me to watch Juventus train.'

Bolton had not heard the last of Cardiff. In November 1955, Merrett pushed to sign Charles once more. In a telegram sent to the Leeds chairman, Merrett made a cash offer of £40,000. Leeds declined to reply and a furious Bolton, worried that Cardiff's bid would unsettle the player, told Wales's national newspaper, the *Western Mail*, 'The Leeds United board have no intention of transferring Charles and such a thing as a new offer of £40,000 by Cardiff has never been discussed by us and we do not intend doing so.'

He may have been disappointed by having his transfer request turned down but Charles decided to knuckle down and help his team win that elusive promotion. Apart from the trip to Bristol Rovers and the FA Cup matches against Torquay United, when he wore the number 9 shirt, Charles was used in defence for the remainder of the season. In a nail-biting race, Leeds finished fourth, one point behind champions Birmingham City and second-placed Luton Town who went up. It could have been so different had they not started the season so badly.

His wait for top-flight football finally came to an end in 1955–56 when Leeds finished runners-up to Sheffield Wednesday. The season began with a defeat at Barnsley. Charles, at centre-half, was tormented all afternoon by their impetuous winger, Arthur Kaye, and it was Kaye who hit the winner in a 2–1 victory. With a chorus of slow handclapping ringing in their ears, Carter's players overcame Bury at Elland Road, Jock Henderson the unlikely hero with an 80th-minute winner.

After a 4–1 home win over Rotherham, Arsenal were linked with the Welshman but Bolton was unperturbed. Charles's decision to buy a house in Leeds was viewed as a sign he was committed to the club.

Charles scarcely had an off day but one of his worst games for the club came on 15 October, in the 4–0 drubbing at Sheffield Wednesday, a result that questioned Leeds' promotion credentials. More than 27,000 watched Albert Quixall torment the best centre-half in Britain. 'It must be a long time since the Welsh international was so often chased, caught and dispossessed as he was by Quixall,' wrote Ian Guild in the *Yorkshire Post*.

A brief spell at right-half followed but he was back at centre-forward for the trip to Bristol Rovers on 29 October. The service from wingers Meek and Overfield was non-existent, Charles was marked out of the game – 'the penalty of his fame' – and Leeds lost 4–1. In February, for the visit of Second Division leaders – and eventual champions – Sheffield Wednesday, Carter asked Charles to fill the inside-right berth so he could be more involved in the build-up play, with Bob Forrest filling the centre-forward position. On a snow-covered pitch, both players scored in the 2–1 win and the Charles–Forrest partnership was such a great success that Carter kept it for the rest of the season. Charles may have been followed around the pitch by Ralph O'Donnell, a centre-half converted to left-half, but Richard Ulyatt described this performance against Wednesday as 'the best game Charles has ever played for Leeds United . . . Charles was the complete footballer in defence and attack'.

Carter's side were there or thereabouts for most of the campaign but it was their strong finish that clinched promotion, Leeds winning nine of their last ten games. Charles was again formidable in front of goal during the season, scoring 29 times. Recalls Jack Overfield, 'We had two good wingers at the time – George Meek was one and I was the other! Our gameplan was to keep crossing the ball for John, me from the left and George from the right. That way we were bound to get goals because you couldn't miss John with a cross – he was like a lighthouse.'

Not all his goals were headers. He scored with a 30-yard shot in a 4–3 defeat at Plymouth Argyle and swerved past the entire Liverpool defence in a 4–2 home win over The Reds. In a 6–1 mauling of Fulham at Elland Road on Good Friday 1956, a match that saw Charles score the ninth hat-trick of his career, goalkeeper Ian Black experienced the awesome power of Charles's shooting. In the sixth minute Black got a decent hand to his 25-yard shot, but it was struck with such venom that it still flew into the net off both posts. His third – and Leeds' sixth – came from a 20-yard free-kick, the ball flying past Black 'like a shell from a gun'. Adds Meek, 'Whenever we needed a goal, John would score it. He took a lot of pressure off the other forwards. As long as he was on the pitch we could get a goal out of nothing. Of course there were games when he didn't score but I don't think any defender who played against John could say they totally stopped him.'

Leeds celebrated promotion at Hull City's Boothferry Park on the final day of the season, but arguably the decisive result came a week earlier when Bristol Rovers were beaten at Elland Road in a promotion showdown in front of 49,274 people. Rovers were in second spot, two points ahead of third-placed Leeds. Anything but a victory for Carter's men and it would surely be Division Two football for another season. Rovers took a third-minute lead when David Ward headed George Petherbridge's cross past Roy Wood. Charles, wearing a steel brace to protect the two front teeth loosened following a collision of heads during a 'very hectic' friendly against Uruguayan side Rampla Juniors, equalised 14 minutes later. 'That was the best goal I've ever seen him score,' explains former wing-half Keith Ripley. 'John was running across the Rovers penalty box, George Meek crossed but the ball was going past John. But John, who was a good 12 yards out, went up for the ball, turned and thumped it into the far corner. A trapeze artist would have been pleased with the movement he showed. It was a fantastic goal and I can still see it clearly today, after all these years.' In the 27th minute Charles set up the winner, whipping the ball across the face of the Rovers goal for Overfield. He also saw a 25-yard shot hit the post. It was hit with such force that the ball rebounded straight back to him.

Leeds now needed three points from their last two games, at Rotherham and Hull, to be sure of promotion. At Millmoor, with half the 19,871 crowd cheering for Leeds, Rotherham were put to the sword 2–0, Nightingale scoring both. After the game, and sniffing grounds such as Old Trafford, Molineux and Highbury, Sam Bolton paid tribute to Charles. 'John has always been prepared to play where we wanted him, at half-back, inside-forward and centre-forward. More than that, he has always realised that his great reputation could not have been achieved without the cooperation of every player in the team.'

Bolton was responding to suggestions Leeds were a one-man team. The press dubbed them 'John Charles United' – a tag that angered Charles (he described it as 'unfair and untrue') and upset his teammates. 'People said John was half the team but I didn't agree with that,' says Overfield. 'We played to him but if he was missing through injury we could cope without him because we had a lot of good players in the side. It doesn't matter how good a centre-forward is, he won't score goals if he doesn't get the service.' Roy Wood agrees. 'It wasn't a one-man team at all. There were ten other players beside John and, to be fair, John always said that himself. John had his stinkers, like every player. He always got the write-ups in the newspapers but some reporters weren't even at the matches. I knew one who used to go to the pub and get his information from people who had just been to the game.'

Leeds needed only a draw at Carter's former club Hull on 28 April to join Sheffield Wednesday in the First Division. They were firm favourites since Hull had already been relegated and Charles, to the delight of the 15,000 travelling supporters, blasted Leeds ahead after five minutes but Hull fought back and Tom Martin levelled before half-time. Leeds, clearly nervous, were clinging on for the draw but in the 62nd Charles gave them breathing space when he made it 2–1 from the penalty spot after Meek was fouled. He showed his class with that spot-kick. It was a high-pressure moment but Charles thumped the ball into Bernard Fisher's right-hand corner after sending the Hull goalkeeper the wrong way with a cheeky dummy. It was Charles who instigated the two attacks that led to Harold Brook scoring twice to seal a 4–1 win – 'a flattering scoreline', admitted the *Yorkshire Post*. Afterwards, in the visitors' dressing-room at Boothferry Park, the players celebrated with Moët & Chandon champagne, drunk out of white teacups.

On their return to Leeds, and before they joined Lord Mayor Sir James Croysdale for a toast, around 2,000 people greeted the players outside the Civic Hall shouting, 'Two, four, six, eight – who do we appreciate!' Bolton, Carter and the Lord Mayor made speeches but the crowd wanted to hear the captain. To cries of 'We want John!' he was handed the microphone although his message was brief and hardly Churchillian. 'With the support you have given us, we have done very well. Promotion is a great thing.'

Jack Pickard, the man who sent Charles – 'the player more responsible than anybody else for gaining promotion' – to Elland Road seven years earlier, was a notable absentee at the promotion party. He was not invited, a gaffe which upset the scout. 'Neither the club nor John Charles had the elementary decency to remember to invite me to the celebrations and functions, or to enquire why I wasn't present, and I never did receive any letter of regret at my non-appearance, or apology re any oversight in respect of me not receiving an invitation,' he wrote in his memoirs.

After an absence of nine years, Leeds were back in Division One and Charles was finally able to grace English football's biggest stage.

CHAPTER FOUR – THE £65,000 MAN

By the time the 1956–57 season kicked off on 18 August, Charles was the biggest draw in the domestic game, second only to Stanley Matthews, the Blackpool and England winger. When Everton arrived at Elland Road on a wet, vile afternoon for the curtain raiser, the Leeds public pinned their hopes of a victory on their illustrious Welsh international.

Leeds won handsomely 5–1 and, typically, Charles did get his name on the scoresheet but he was upstaged by 34-year-old Harold Brook who scored a hat-trick inside half an hour. Five days later Leeds beat Charlton Athletic 2–1 at The Valley, Charles getting both goals. The visitors found themselves enjoying a numerical advantage after a minute when Charlton centre-half Derek Ufton dislocated his shoulder as he fell awkwardly trying to tackle Charles. While Ufton rolled about in agony, the Leeds striker was free to shoot at the Charlton goal but Charles, living up to his 'Gentleman John' tag, kicked the ball into touch. The 100 per cent record fell the following Saturday when Tottenham Hotspur dished out a football lesson at White Hart Lane, Raich Carter watching his side take a 5–1 beating. Welcome to Division One.

But Leeds came back with a 4–0 win over Charlton. In that game Charles, in the words of the *Yorkshire Post*, scored a goal 'no other forward in the world could have got' when he squeezed a chip between goalkeeper Edward Marsh and the upright, an opening 'about large enough for a tennis ball'. The team jumped into second spot after winning four of their next six games – including impressive victories over Wolves and Manchester City – with Charles, at inside-right, proving he could score in the First Division as freely as he did in the Second, notching ten in the first eleven games.

When Aston Villa visited West Yorkshire on 22 September, Leeds were just one point behind the leaders, Manchester United's 'Busby Babes'. Leeds continued their superb start with a 1–0 win which was achieved inside a half-destroyed Elland Road. Four days earlier the uninsured West Stand had burned down because of an electrical fault in the roof. The fire destroyed the dressing-rooms, club offices, boardroom and press box. Lost in the blaze were the kit, boots and physiotherapy equipment. Injured players were treated at the home of former trainer Arthur Campey while the players and match officials changed in the dressing-rooms belonging to the Whitehall Printers sports ground where a coach waited to take them to Elland Road. The same coach was the venue for the half-time team talk.

Carter, keen to maintain momentum, insisted the match should not be cancelled and Charles leading his teammates through the West Stand's twisted, smouldering remains to take on Villa on a sultry afternoon was a surreal sight. 'The atmosphere was very odd,' recalled Charles. 'Running out was funny. You went into the car park and then nothing.' The Welshman scored the only goal of the afternoon. Billy Baxter did a decent marking job on Charles but was unable to prevent him chesting down Bob Forrest's 20th-minute cross and beating goalkeeper Nigel Sims with a clinical strike which the Elland Road faithful were accustomed to seeing.

With his players wearing new boots, and with no time in which to break them in, Carter feared the worst for his players' feet but afterwards a delighted Bob Roxburgh smiled, 'Not a solitary blister.'

The excellent run of results was maintained at Kenilworth Road when Charles's two headers earned his team a 2–2 draw against Luton Town. 'A player's eyes close automatically the moment he heads a ball, but John's didn't,' says Jack Charlton. 'I've got a photograph of John jumping above me and heading the ball. The ball is on his forehead and his eyes are wide open. Incredible.'

It was back down to earth against Cardiff City at Ninian Park. The Bluebirds had collected only two points from their last five matches but they walloped Leeds 4–1. Charles's presence put an extra 10,000 on the gate but Cardiff striker Gerry Hitchens, who would later join Charles in Italian football, stole the show, scoring twice. Derrick Sullivan, Charles's Welsh international teammate, marked the Leeds star out of the game.

The 1–1 home draw against Birmingham City in mid-October showed the heavy marking Charles was receiving could benefit his teammates. 'I was told that whenever we had a corner I was to stay near John in case the ball dropped loose,' explains Keith Ripley, who scored the goal against Birmingham. 'There were always three or four players around John which was good for the other players. I scored with a tap-in but really the credit for the goal should have gone to John because he had four players around him.'

Charles scored two hat-tricks that season, both against Sheffield Wednesday. Several of his teammates recall the second game, a 3–2 win at Hillsborough at the end of March 1957. 'We were shocking that day but John scored three goals,' says George Meek. 'That's the sort of thing he could do.'

Owls defender Jimmy McEvoy was assigned the task of stopping Charles. 'I wasn't playing in that game so I watched it from the stand and McEvoy never gave John a kick,' recalls Ripley. 'But John got three headers and we won 3–2. I was glad we won but I felt sorry for McEvoy who was magnificent that day. John could destroy good defenders.' Overfield adds, 'John was the worst player on the pitch. He really did have a poor game but they gave him three chances and he scored from all three.'

In the first game against Wednesday, Charles was at his devastating best. He was closely marked by Don Gibson, who, in the words of one newspaper, stuck to him 'closer than a brother'. Three times he shook off Gibson and each time he scored. His third, a 25-yard shot, was hit with such ferocity that the ball was nestling in the back of the net before the diving Owls goalkeeper, Alan Hinchcliffe, hit the grass.

The November trip across the Pennines to Old Trafford to face Manchester United's 'Busby Babes' turned out to be a classic encounter. In front of 52,131 people Leeds lost 3–2 – Charles's late penalty ensured a tense finale – but Eric Stanger described it as 'the best Leeds display since the war'. United were constantly linked with buying Charles. Their centre-forward Tommy Taylor, one of eight United players who tragically died in the Munich air crash in 1958, was in the Army with Charles and the pair became good friends. Then there was fellow Welshman Jimmy Murphy, United's assistant manager who had just taken charge of the Welsh national side. Murphy thought the world of 'Big John'. 'Whenever I look at him I see the Messiah,' he once said. 'Jimmy tried to sign John,' reveals Mel Charles. 'I'm so glad he didn't because if he had we would probably have lost him in Munich.'

When Leeds played champions-elect United at Elland Road that season, a game the Manchester side won 2–1, Charles scored with a magnificent free-kick from just outside the penalty area. Murphy later said it was the most powerful shot he had ever seen. As the Leeds players mobbed Charles, United manager Matt Busby turned to his number two. 'I think someone in the wall must have moved, Jimmy.' To which Murphy replied, 'Whoever it was, he was a damn good judge. Anyone who got in the way of that shot would have ended up in the net with the ball.'

Carter's side was involved in another classic game in April 1957, against Arsenal at Highbury. Charles inspired a dramatic comeback against the Londoners who were 3–0 ahead with the Clock End showing only 26 minutes remaining. Enter Charles. He headed Overfield's corner past Welsh teammate Jack Kelsey. Leeds were transformed and Forrest made it 3–2 three minutes later before Charles headed an 86th-minute equaliser, converting Meek's pass. 'Leeds without John,' Kelsey would later say, 'is like London without the Tower.'

After this game Charles was approached by a plump, smartly dressed Italian by the name of Luigi 'Gigi' Peronace. Peronace, from the Calabria region in southern Italy, spoke fluent English. He was scouting for the Italian club Juventus, of Turin, and told Charles the club was interested in signing him. Juventus belonged to the hugely wealthy Agnelli family who also owned the Fiat car empire (Gianni Agnelli had been the club's president until 1954 but he was now busy with Fiat's affairs and the responsibility of running Juventus was handed to his younger brother Umberto). Charles, however, thought little of Peronace's approach since Leeds had never been willing to let him go in the past.

Peronace had been monitoring Charles's progress since 1955 when he was working for another Italian club, Lazio. Staff at Elland Road had often noticed an Italian man strutting around the ground and on one occasion he watched Charles train through the window of Raich Carter's office. He asked Carter if Charles was for sale. The answer was no. Harold Williams, who ran the Railway Inn public house in Beeston after he retired from playing, says, 'Peronace used to come into my pub and he'd ask me various things about the club and John. It was obvious that he was after one thing and that was Charles.' Peronace was also a visitor at the Charleses' home in Morley. 'He used to suddenly appear at the house,' recalls Peggy Charles, 'and he'd talk about Italy, saying, "You will love Italy and they will love you."'

According to Umberto Colombo, the Juventus right-half who became good friends with Charles after he moved to Turin, it was Jesse Carver, and not Peronace, who first alerted Juventus to Charles. Carver had coached *I Bianconeri* (the Black and Whites, Juventus's nickname) from 1949–51 and won the Serie A championship, *Lo Scudetto*, in 1950. 'The whole John Charles thing came about not because of Gigi Peronace but because of Jesse Carver,' says Colombo. 'Peronace worked for Carver and Carver told him to speak to the Agnellis about Charles. Juventus signing the player had as much to do with Carver, even though he had gone by that time, as with Peronace.'

The Calabrian, who was responsible for Eddie Firmani's £35,000 transfer from Charlton to Sampdoria in 1955 and who would also take Jimmy Greaves, Denis Law and Gerry Hitchens to Italy, decided to formally recommend the Leeds player to Juventus president Umberto Agnelli after watching Charles against West Ham at Upton Park on 14 January 1956. Charles scored a brilliant goal in a 1–1 draw. Peronace returned to Turin and told Agnelli he had seen 'the greatest centre-forward in the world'. Agnelli had his doubts when Peronace told him the player was nearly 14 st. and nearly 6 ft 2 in. tall. 'If he's that big he can't be very quick,' he countered.

Recalling how his club's interest in Charles came about, Agnelli says, 'Peronace told me there was this great player in England and that we should go over and see him. I sent someone over to watch Charles and this person said he was outstanding. I was not sceptical because Peronace knew football very well. The only thing that scared us was buying a player in England at that time. It was normal for Italian clubs to buy players in South America but not England. It was inconceivable for an Italian club to go to the homeland of football and buy a player. People were scared of that. Juventus wanting to buy John Charles was seen as something of a scandal. The English press was very condescending about it.'

It would take Peronace 14 months to convince Agnelli to watch the Leeds star in action. Juventus were having a terrible season and one of Italy's richest and most glamorous clubs was in real danger of being relegated in 1957. Agnelli knew he needed to rebuild the team for the following season and that a quality centre-forward was the priority. Agnelli chose to watch Charles play for Wales in a Home International Championship match against Northern Ireland, at Windsor Park in Belfast. The match finished 0–0. It was a dull affair, hindered by strong winds, but Agnelli was impressed with Charles who was captaining his country for the first time. 'That day he didn't play so well,' remembers Agnelli, 'but you saw he had great potential. He had all the attributes of being a great player so we started talking to the people at Leeds and that is how the deal came about.'

Sam Bolton and his directors, after years of resisting tempting offers, were ready to sell Charles. The club was £40,000 in debt and a new stand needed to be built.

Leeds, though, would not transfer Charles to another British club. If he was going then he was going abroad. The front-page headline of the *Yorkshire Evening Post* on 16 April 1957 read, 'JOHN CHARLES FOR SALE – EXPORT ONLY: £65,000 TURIN BID.' Agnelli, admitting Charles was on his shopping list, told the British media, 'We need Charles badly and we are determined to get him. I saw him play for Wales against Ireland last week and I said to myself, "What a player – if in a good team." He did not play well but the greatness was there. In flashes he showed what he could do on form in a good side. Some of those who were with him were not good.' If he signed for Juventus, said Agnelli, Charles would receive a £10,000 signing-on fee – then a staggering amount – an apartment and a car. It would be a dream move for the Charleses who now had a second son, Melvyn, and were expecting a third child.

Agnelli began talks with Bolton. '*Charles fenomeno inglese sarà da oggi bianconero?*' (Will the English phenomenon Charles become a Juventus player today?) asked the Turin-based sports daily *Tuttosport* on 17 April, clearly ignorant of where Charles had been born. Agnelli said he was 'acting fast' because 'I fear competition'. And competition he apparently had, in the shape of Spain's finest, Real Madrid, and two other Italian clubs, Lazio and Internazionale of Milan. Lazio's English manager, the Liverpudlian, Jesse Carver, who wanted to bring Charles to Turin when he was coaching Juventus, had been at Elland Road the previous Saturday for talks with Carter about the possible transfer of his Welsh international. Newspapers claimed Lazio had tabled a £50,000 bid.

It was, however, the Spanish club that Agnelli saw as his biggest threat. 'I am frightened of Real Madrid,' he confessed. He knew that if it came down to a straight fight between Real and Juventus, the lure of playing for the reigning European Cup holders, and for a team that boasted wonderful players such as Alfredo Di Stefano, Vincent Kopa and Francisco Gento, would be impossible for Charles to resist. Additionally, if the press was to be believed, Real Madrid's package of £70,000 to Leeds and a further £30,000 to Charles eclipsed anything the Italians had to offer.

Leeds succumbed to Juventus's £65,000 offer but the transfer was a drawn-out affair. Over the telephone, Agnelli made his first offer for Charles. It was £45,000, to which Bolton responded, 'That amount would not buy his bootlaces.' Agnelli said he was prepared to offer cash and loan Leeds their Swedish international forward Kurt Hamrin for a year. Furthermore, Juventus would play two friendly matches at Elland Road with Leeds taking the gate receipts. Bolton asked Agnelli to fly over to discuss the deal further. 'Charles, although he has wanted a transfer during his time here, to Arsenal and to Cardiff City, could have done no better with them financially than he has done with United,' explained the Leeds chairman. 'We were not hurting him financially by keeping him. But if he can receive a sum from a foreign club of £10,000 upwards – even £30,000 has been mentioned – then it is obviously unfair to stand in his way.' To his credit, Bolton also said 'attention had to be paid' to the club's overdraft.

The proposed sale of Charles to Juventus was a massive back-page story. A foreign club was trying to sign a British player, which was almost unheard of in 1957 (Firmani, it must be stressed, was a South African of Italian origin), and the rumoured sum was nearly double the British transfer record. It prompted the BBC to devote a large chunk of its *Sportsview* television programme to discussing British footballers' salaries and comparing them to what Charles might earn playing in Serie A. The Leeds player was a guest on the show, along with Fulham's England international Johnny Haynes, although Charles's appearance proved an anti-climax since he knew so little about his proposed transfer to Juventus. Those tuning in would have heard him say he did not want to leave Britain but going to Italy might mean pocketing a £10,000 signing-on fee. If he stayed in Britain his earnings, because of the maximum wage, would be no more than £1,780 a year.

Charles was offered £10,000 by a Leeds businessman to stay at Elland Road. From 17 April, his semi-detached home was besieged by the press. As two-year-old Terry and 15-month-old Melvyn played in the back garden, the waiting hacks asked 25-year-old Peggy if she wanted to go to Italy. 'If the answer has anything to do with me, it will most definitely be yes. The offer for John is wonderful. There have been so many rumours in the past that I hardly dare build this one up.' Her husband, knowing the move could set them up financially for the rest of their lives, was equally enthusiastic. 'I was only too relieved when Mr Bolton told me the club would let me go to a foreign side. I will today go to any club that is willing to pay me the "thick money" that is being reported. I understand that in addition I shall get a new car and a flat with coal and lighting laid on. I should regret it all my life, as a married man with two children and a third due at any time, if I turned it down. I could never hope to earn that sort of money here, however long I played here. I'm 26 next Christmas, you know.'

Agnelli arrived in London at 5 p.m. on 17 April after catching the 2.30 p.m. flight from Milan's Malpensa Airport. Wearing a light sports jacket and grey flannel trousers he fielded a barrage of questions from football reporters as he was escorted from arrivals to his waiting car by Gaetano Bolla, the general manager of Fiat (UK).

'How much will you pay Leeds?'

'It depends.'

'Will you go to £70,000?'

'£70,000 is quite a lot of money.'

'Is there a limit to how much you will pay?'

'There is a limit. Even John Charles has got a limit.'

'Have you seen Charles play?'

'Yes, once. In a match in Belfast.'

Agnelli stayed overnight at the swish Claridges Hotel before being driven up to Leeds with his entourage, Peronace and Bolla. To shake off the press, the Italians were to meet Bolton, Carter and Percy Woodward at a secret location on the outskirts of the city, at the factory belonging to John Waddington Limited, the board game manufacturers, in Hunslet. They were due to join up with Charles at the Queens Hotel in the centre of Leeds later that evening.

By now Juventus's only rivals for Charles's signature were Inter. Nothing more was heard of Lazio, and Real Madrid's proposed £100,000 offer never materialised. Antonio Calderón, Real's club manager, said the European champions were never in the running. The rules laid down by Spanish football's governing body, the Real Federacion Española de Futbol, stated that each club could own no more than two foreign players and Real had already reached their quota with Di Stefano, an Argentinian, and Kopa, a Frenchman.

But Inter were still on the scene and the Milanese side was in the country to play Birmingham City in the Fairs Cup. From the team's base in Leamington Spa, Alberto Valentini, Inter's secretary-general, sent a telegram to Bolton saying his club was keen to buy Charles but then their interest suddenly evaporated and the path was cleared for Juventus. 'I must say the Inter president (Angelo Moratti) behaved very well. He didn't want to start an auction for Charles,' explains Agnelli. 'We were first to the player and, because we were the first, he let us buy him. He wasn't going to start a battle. That was fortunate because if that had happened the player would have cost more than £65,000. It would have been good for Leeds if there was a battle between us and Inter!' *Tuttosport* had its own explanation for Inter's abrupt withdrawal, claiming Agnelli had promised to sell them Italian international inside-forward

Giampiero Boniperti, although this never happened and Boniperti finished his career at his beloved Juventus.

At the Queens Hotel, Charles was represented by Teddy Sommerfield and the BBC football commentator Kenneth Wolstenholme. Sommerfield looked after Charles's interests outside of the game, such as after-dinner speaking, and had become good friends with the Leeds and Wales star. Used to dealing with television celebrities such as Eamonn Andrews, he was not au fait with football matters, so he asked Wolstenholme, one of his clients, to assist him. The previous day, after learning Juventus were on their way to Yorkshire for transfer talks with the First Division club, he sent Charles a telegram. 'Am leaving London first thing in the morning with Kenneth Wolstenholme. Do nothing until we arrive. Teddy Sommerfield.' Charles wanted to meet the pair at Leeds City Station but was prevented from doing so by hovering newspapermen and so the three met inside the hotel.

Wolstenholme, speaking shortly before his death in March 2002, recalled the events that day. 'The story came out that John might be going to Juventus and Teddy, who was my manager, rang me on Maundy Thursday and told me to get the train to King's Cross because we were going to Leeds,' he said. 'Teddy, quite rightly, told John that he would help him because the whole business could be very complicated. I knew how Teddy worked, he was a great negotiator. I had had an argument with the BBC about money. I was going to accept what they were offering but he said not to. I thought it was the end of my career but Teddy got his way.'

Sommerfield and Wolstenholme were smuggled in through the back entrance of the Queens Hotel to avoid the press who were camped in the lobby. They were taken to room 222 on the second floor where Charles was waiting. There, Sommerfield went through the Juventus contract with a toothcomb. 'Teddy was from Warrington but he was of Jewish extraction. He was chunky and swarthy,' said Wolstenholme. 'The people of Leeds mistook him for one of the Italians. When we got off the train, one of the railway staff said, "Don't help him, he's come to take our John away." And at the hotel one of the porters grabbed me and said, "Don't let that wop take our John away from us." When we met John he was under the protection of the hotel staff to stop the press getting hold of him. If they did he would never have been able to get away.'

The Leeds and Juventus officials arrived at the hotel at 8.30 p.m., five hours after Charles and his two representatives. They discussed their side of the deal further down the corridor, in room 233, and at 10.10 p.m. the telephone rang in room 222 – Agnelli wanted to meet Charles. That was the sign the two clubs had agreed a fee. 'What the Juventus people didn't know was that Teddy spoke and understood Italian but he never let on when they were around. I remember him asking for a copy of the standard contract for a player in Italy. They said, "*Si, si, si*, we'll get one translated for you." Teddy said, "Just give me one now and I'll have it translated." The talks went on until well into the night. John didn't know anything about Juventus or where they played. They gave him a well-drawn up contract. They were decent people to do business with. John was happy with the move. He could see a great future, a lot of money and a lovely house.'

Good Friday was only ten minutes old when a tired-looking Agnelli made his way down to the hotel lobby and told the media Charles had 'agreed in principle' to join Juventus. He refused to reveal how much he was paying both Leeds and the player. 'What we have paid is a question that concerns myself, my club, Leeds United and John Charles only.' Despite Agnelli's guarded approach the terms of the deal soon came to light. Leeds received £65,000 – a British record and only £10,000 less than the world record fee paid by AC Milan to Penarol for Uruguayan international forward Juan Schiaffino – plus Juventus would visit Elland Road during the 1957–58 season for a friendly. 'When we saw the Leeds United directors at the Queens Hotel they were saying to John, "We don't want you to go" and "We don't want to lose you." But when they got that £65,000 cheque from Juventus we didn't see them again,' laughed Wolstenholme. 'They took it and couldn't wait to put it in the bank. They didn't even stay to toast the deal. Juventus offered Leeds what was a hell of a lot of money in those days and Leeds were all for picking up that money.'

Charles was offered a two-year contract and a £10,000 signing-on fee, payable in monthly instalments over those two years. If he had joined a British club he would have received a signing-on fee of

£10. The club would also provide him with an apartment and a Fiat car. His weekly salary at Juventus of 28,000 lire (£16) was actually less than he was earning in English football but the rich pickings came in the form of bonuses – 49,000 lire (£28) for a home win and 70,000 lire (£40) for an away win. More generous three-figure bonuses came his way when Juventus won the big games, against Milan, Inter and city rivals Torino. Charles could expect to receive windfalls of £100 or £200. After one victory over Milan, Charles claimed to have been given £800 because Umberto Agnelli had won a sizeable bet with the Milan president. 'The money we paid for Charles was a lot for the Juventus balance sheet,' admits Agnelli 45 years later. 'The people of Leeds wanted that amount to justify the sale of this player. The deal was about money, nothing else. The amount of £65,000 was a lot of money at the time but we got it back by selling Kurt Hamrin to Padova.'

Only two factors threatened the Charles transfer. The player might fail a stringent medical in Turin and Juventus could be relegated. If the Turin side dropped into Serie B then the deal was void since *stranieri* (foreign players) were not allowed in Italy's second division. In those days two clubs were relegated from Serie A each season and Agnelli returned to Italy knowing Juventus were anchored in the bottom five, just four points ahead of bottom club Palermo and in real danger of being one of the two clubs that would fall through the trapdoor.

But Charles still had three games to play for Leeds. At Sunderland on 19 April, Carter's men lost 2–0 and the draining transfer saga appeared to have taken a toll on Charles whose presence attracted a 56,551 gate. Playing at centre-forward he missed two easy chances that could have earned the Yorkshiremen a point. In the 20th minute, with the score at 0–0, he chested down Harold Brook's long ball, burst through the Sunderland defence but fired wide from ten yards. Then, with 20 minutes to go, George Aitken miskicked and the ball fell to Charles who uncharacteristically pulled his shot wide.

Charles scored twice in the 6–2 defeat at Birmingham the following day before his emotional farewell against Sunderland in front of 29,328 people at Elland Road on Easter Monday. He signed off in spectacular fashion. Despite the close attentions of

Sunderland centre-half Ray Daniel, a fellow Welsh international and native of Swansea, he scored twice in a 3–1 win taking his tally for the season to 38. Leeds finished their first season in the First Division in a respectable eighth place. In the *Yorkshire Post* Geoffrey Winter wrote, 'The black eyes of Gigi Peronace, the Juventus scout who was there to take delivery of John Charles when the match was over, glistened with excitement and satisfaction whenever the great man got possession of the ball. "That's my boy" they seemed to say.'

The day after the Sunderland game Charles caught the overnight train to London. From there he would fly to Italy for his medical. 'John didn't really want to leave Leeds, not as I saw it,' says Keith Ripley. 'Personally, I didn't think he'd go. We were all good pals. In the summer we'd play cricket against the supporters clubs and we'd have tea in each other's houses. To me he seemed a very happy man. We were all disappointed he left because we all thought he was the best player in the world.' Adds Jimmy Dunn, 'For someone of his class he was being paid peanuts in England. I don't think he was happy with the money.' John Reynolds has his own theory on why the club parted with their star attraction. 'They sold John to pay for the West Stand. If the stand hadn't burnt down I don't think John would have left. Having to rebuild the stand put pressure on the directors to sell him.'

The flight to Milan, only an hour and a half drive from Turin, was fully booked, so Charles boarded a flight to Rome's Ciampino Airport. From there he took a domestic flight to Turin's Caselle Airport where he was met by Agnelli and the usual horde of *tifosi* (supporters), journalists and photographers. 'We could not wait to see this giant of a man that we had all heard so much about,' says Bruno Boldi, a full-back and a bit-part player at the club. 'I was quite surprised that we bought a player in England.' Around 2,000 Juventus supporters greeted him at the airport, many of them shouting, '*Ecco il nostro salvatore!*' – Here comes our saviour! He was hugged and kissed. A black and white Juventus shirt was pinned on his towering frame.

'I read in the news that we had bought the best footballer in England,' says Umberto Colombo. 'Everybody was saying, "Who is this man?" because up until now we had never heard of him. He did

not play in England's national team so how could he be the best
player in England? There was great confusion, so I went out and
bought all these newspapers and magazines to find out about this
man who was supposed to be the best player in England. I used to
follow the England national team and I had never seen John Charles
playing for them. I picked up a magazine which had an article
about John Charles called "King of Soccer". I thought to myself,
"How can he be the King of Soccer if he doesn't even make the
national team!" I carried on reading this article and that's how I
found out he was Welsh and not English. I was quite ashamed of
myself. I thought I followed English football yet I didn't know about
John Charles.'

Charles was booked into the luxurious Hotel Principe di
Piemonte and the following day he met his new teammates at the
Stadio Combi where Juventus trained. Giampiero Boniperti, the
club's long-serving captain and one of Italy's star players, was asked
by photographers to pose with his new teammate for a newspaper
picture. 'They took a photograph of me presenting John with his
shirt and I was so taken by his size,' recalled Boniperti. 'He then
came back to my house and through an interpreter I kept asking
him to stand up. "*Alzati,* John! *Alzati*!" I kept measuring myself up
against him and saying, "Now we are going to win everything!"'

Colombo, the only Juventus player who had a grasp of English,
was assigned the task of helping Charles to find accommodation. 'I
was the first Juventus player to meet him,' adds Colombo. 'I
remember seeing John for the first time as if it was yesterday. He
had a magnificent physique, so upright and straight and he was
wearing a collar and tie and a blue blazer with the Leeds badge on
it. Because I spoke a little bit of English they asked me to take him
around Turin to find an apartment for him and his family. John
wanted a ground-floor flat with a bit of garden space so his children
could play there.' They eventually found the right apartment on Via
Susa, in the Borgo San Paolo area. 'Finding the right place wasn't
too difficult because there were a lot of apartments available,'
continues Colombo, 'but they didn't stay in Borgo San Paolo long.
After a year they moved to a lovely villa in the hills where they had
more space, more fresh air and where there was less traffic.'

Then came Charles's all-important medical at the Molinette

Hospital. His prospective employers were aware of the knee operations he had undergone in the Army but Charles passed with flying colours and the doctor who undertook the medical, Professor Amilcare Borsotti, enthused, 'I have never seen a better human machine in a lifetime in medicine.'

The Welsh international took part in a discreet training session at the Stadio Combi. 'When we saw John play for the first time we were all impressed by his stature, his presence, his physical power and his athleticism,' recalls Boldi. 'Everybody – the directors, the players, everybody – pinned their hopes of winning on him.' *Tuttosport* journalist Mino Mulinacci was also excited by this *straniero*. He wrote, 'All in all he gave the impression that he is a first-class player. He confirmed the qualities that made him so famous in Britain. He looked well built, strong against his opponents and gifted with clear tactical vision, able to run away from his marker and play the ball first time. He's quick off the mark and at full speed he runs with a beautiful style. He used his left and right feet to control the ball. In the air, naturally, he is excellent and his timing is perfect.' Bruno Roghi, of the Milan-based pink sports daily *La Gazzetta dello Sport*, penned a memorable and colourful description of the new Juventus player. 'He has the features of Marlon Brando, the body of a light-heavyweight boxer, the legs of a classic dancer, the breathing of a tiger and the bite of a cobra.'

Giorgio Stivanello, a winger who supplied many goals for Charles during his five years in Turin, recalls his first encounter with the Welshman. 'We were at our training ground when this man appeared with the directors and the coach. The coach [Teobaldo Depetrini] said to me, "Stiva, stay a bit longer because I want you to put some crosses over for this man." So I took my position and John took his position,' says the Venetian. 'I saw that John was standing well outside the penalty area. I thought, "What's going on here? You can't head the ball outside the box, you must be in the penalty area. What's he up to?" Anyway, I crossed the ball as the coach asked and this man gets up and – bang! He headed the ball with such power it could have been a shot. I kept crossing and he kept heading with the same power. I've never forgotten that day.'

In his very first *partitella* (practice match) Charles was marked by left-back Bruno Garzena who broke into the Juventus side in

1952. 'I was a natural full-back but for this match I was the centre-half and John was the centre-forward. I soon found out what sort of player had arrived at Juventus!' says Garzena. 'I was a strong, muscular player but I looked at this massive man who weighed 90 kilos and thought, "How do I tackle him?" He would come at me like a big beast and he would jump over me. I didn't know where to start.'

Charles was due to return home on 28 April but he decided to stay an extra day to watch Juventus's 1–0 win over Napoli at the Stadio Comunale in Turin. His wife, back in Leeds, had just given birth to a third son, Peter. 'John sent me a telegram,' says Peggy in an unimpressed tone. 'It said, "Congratulations on birth of baby son."' On hearing of the baby's arrival, Boniperti took Charles to his home and cracked open a bottle of champagne. On Monday, 29 April, Charles left Italy for Cardiff to prepare for Wales's opening World Cup qualifier against Czechoslovakia at Ninian Park.

Juventus, thanks to a decent finish to the season which saw them win four of their last six games, steered clear of relegation. All obstacles to the Charles deal were cleared and, for two years at least, 'Big John' would wear their black and white shirt. 'I was really looking forward to going to Italy,' adds Peggy. 'I had never been abroad before in my life.'

Leeds struggled after selling Charles, as many had feared and predicted. The board promised Carter that some of the Juventus money would be ploughed back into the team but he was given only £24,000 to spend. He bought Airdrie centre-forward Hughie Baird (£12,000), Glenavon half-back/inside-forward Wilbur Cush (£7,000) and Shamrock Rovers inside-forward Noel Peyton (£5,000). Filling Charles's shoes was an impossible task but in fairness·Baird scored 20 goals in 39 appearances in his first and only season at Elland Road before returning to Scottish football with Aberdeen because he was unable to settle south of the border. Leeds, though, were not the same without 'Big John'. They finished 17th in 1958 and 15th the following year before succumbing to the drop in 1960. By then Carter was long gone. He departed the club in 1958, after the board failed to renew his five-year contract. Carter was bitter and accused Bolton and his directors of expecting too much, especially as less than half of the Charles money was used to bring in new players. 'OK, we got £65,000 for John, which was a hell of a fee, but it was a big loss for Leeds United,' says Jack Charlton. 'The team didn't play with much confidence after he went. It's hard when a player who is half your team – and John was half our team – goes. The moment he left things started to fall apart. We didn't have that something extra to stay in the First Division. Maybe we were too dependent on John but when a guy scores more than 30 goals a season, you've got to find someone to replace him and we didn't manage to replace him.'

Chapter Five – *Il Gigante Buono*

Turin is a rich, industrial city that lies in the shadow of the Alps. The capital of the Piedmont region in the north-west of Italy, it is the fourth largest city in the country after Rome, Milan and Naples. Home to the Fiat automobile empire, it is one of Italy's most important economic centres. The city may lack the spectacular Renaissance charm of Florence, the breathtaking beauty of Venice and the unrivalled history of Rome, but Turin is 'the Gateway to Italy', an elegantly planned Baroque city renowned for its arcades and squares. It was a world away from wet and grey Leeds.

Charles was the first of three major signings made by Juventus in 1957. Just days after he completed his £65,000 move, Agnelli swooped for the brilliant Argentinian inside-left, Omar Enrique Sivori, paying River Plate a world-record £91,000. Then he paid Padova £58,000 for Bruno Nicolé, a record for an Italian player. Nicolé, a striker who had not long turned 17, was one of the revelations of the 1956–57 season but Charles's phenomenal success at centre-forward with Juventus forced him to play most of his games on the wing.

Agnelli's decision to secure Charles before Sivori was cunningly deliberate. The transfer fees in Britain were far lower than in South America and Agnelli feared that if Leeds saw Juventus paying such an amount for Sivori they would have demanded the same figure for Charles.

Sivori was the complete opposite to the Welshman, in size and temperament. Whereas Charles was placid and never prone to retaliate, Sivori, who played football with his socks rolled down to his ankles, was fiery, volatile and possessed a spiteful streak that would continually land him in trouble with the football authorities. 'Sivori was an impetuous man, a real rascal,' explains Giorgio Stivanello. 'He broke one or two legs during his career and served no end of bans. John was totally different. In the dressing-room you wouldn't know he was around.' Whereas Charles was modest, Sivori was egotistical. During matches he would run past opponents and tell them, 'You know you are playing against the best player in the world?' This displeased Umberto Agnelli who felt Sivori was not behaving in a manner expected of Juventus players. It also led Charles to dub his teammate 'the greatest linguist in the world' because 'he could say, "I'm the greatest footballer" in every known language'.

Along with Antonio Angelillo and Humberto Maschio, Sivori was one of *el Trio de la Muerte* (The Deadly Trio) that helped Argentina to win the *Copa America* in spectacular fashion that year. His partnership with Charles was awesome. A classic big man–little man pairing, in their five years together they scored a staggering 195 goals between them and Juventus won three Serie A championships and the *Coppa Italia* twice. Charles brought power, pace and aerial supremacy to the Juve attack and Sivori dribbling ability, unpredictability and ingenuity.

'I first met John a couple of days after he arrived in Turin,' remembers Sivori. 'We were staying in the same hotel, waiting for the club to sort our apartments out. Although we came from two different cultures – he was from Britain and I was a Latin American, and although we couldn't exchange one word to one another, and I mean one word – I had this immediate instinct that we would do very well together. Those early days, when we ate our meals staring at each other's face and not saying a word to one another, brought us together as if we had the longest conversations.'

Agnelli hoped his new signings would herald the dawn of a new era at the Stadio Comunale. The 1956–57 *campionato* was a disaster for *La Vecchia Signora* (the Grand Old Lady) as Juventus are affectionately known in Italy. A ninth-place finish – just four points clear of Triestina, the second of the two relegated clubs – was seen as a complete humiliation for the club that had won *Lo Scudetto* on nine occasions. Bruno Garzena blames the dismal showing that season on a lack of leadership. 'Although the Agnellis owned the club there was a vacuum at the top,' he explains. 'Gianni Agnelli was looking after other aspects of the family business and his brother, Umberto, was seen as too young to run the club. It was a bad time for Juventus. There was a fear of relegation, a massive fear. For the first and only time in its history, the club was fighting relegation. Imagine a club like Juventus, with all the players it had, in that position. This fear of relegation was like woodworm, gnawing away at us. In those days there were 18 teams in Serie A and 12 of them were fighting to avoid going into Serie B. The other six fought for the championship and Juventus was always one of those six. Relegation was inconceivable.'

The Italian press, renowned for its sardonic approach, had some fun with a struggling team that was coached by a man called Sandro Puppo. The newspapers would often refer to the Juventus players as *pupazzi* (puppets), a play on the coach's surname. Puppo was dismissed during the 1956–57 season and temporarily replaced by former Juventus player Teobaldo Depetrini, the club's youth-team coach. Puppo tried to build a team of emerging young players (Castano, Garzena, Emoli, Stacchini, Colombo, Mattrel) around an Argentinian inside-forward, Juan Vairo, and a Brazilian striker, Leonardo Colella, but neither South American was a success and the plan failed. 'We weren't that bad a team in 1956–57. It wasn't as if we were losing matches 6–0. We drew a lot of games and if we lost it was usually by one goal,' says Flavio Emoli, who played right-half for Juventus. 'We were a good group of young players and you had to give Puppo credit for that. He might not have been a great coach but he looked after the Juventus nursery. Most of the players came from the youth team. But the Agnelli family did not want a repeat of the 1956–57 season. They wanted a big team and that's why they went out and bought John Charles and Omar Sivori. There was a real optimism at the club once they bought those two players. We all sensed we were about to win things.'

Apart from the introduction of Charles, Sivori, and to a lesser extent Nicolé, there was another significant change for 1957–58.

The team had a new *allenatore* (coach) in the shape of 46-year-old Ljubisa Brocic, a much-travelled Yugoslav who previously coached Red Star Belgrade, Egypt, Albania and Yugoslavia. The refining touches followed. Goalkeeper Carlo Mattrel was recalled from Ancona where he was on loan, replacing Giovanni Viola. Another loan player returning to the Comunale was centre-half Rino Ferrario, who had spent the previous season at Triestina. Umberto Colombo's conversion from inside-left to left-half completed the jigsaw.

Brocic took his first look at Charles in a friendly match in Sweden, against AIK Stockholm at the end of June. To help him settle, Charles was put in the same room as Colombo, who by now had become the Welshman's interpreter. 'I was always with John in Sweden. If they needed a player to share a room with John they always asked me,' explains Colombo. 'It was a way for me to improve my English and for John to learn Italian. We had some fun and games talking to each other! He knew hardly any Italian and I couldn't understand his English because he spoke with a Welsh accent. He didn't speak Oxford English and that's the only English I could understand. I had to keep saying to John when he was talking to me, "John, please speak slow!" But he learned Italian quickly and in the end his Italian was better than my English.'

In the Rasunda Stadium on the outskirts of Stockholm, Charles scored twice in a breathtaking 10–1 victory over AIK. Kurt Hamrin, playing in his native country, netted a hat-trick with Sivori (two), Boniperti, Antonio Montico and Stivanello completing the rout. After the match Sivori hailed Charles as 'the best centre-forward in the world'. Alec Stock, the Leyton Orient manager who was about to take charge of Roma, watched Juventus hand out a football lesson to the Swedes. 'He [Charles] is the first or second best player in the world,' commented Stock. 'He is the best we've ever had in Great Britain. He has an outstanding personality, a physique of steel and a wonderful temperament.' The press was equally generous in its praise of the new signing. '*LA JUVE IRRESISTIBILE: CHARLES IL MIGLIORE IN CAMPO*' (Irresistible Juve: Charles The Best Player On The Pitch) was the *Tuttosport* headline. Turin's sporting daily described Charles as 'a colossus'. The eighth Juventus goal, converted by the Welshman, was the pick of the ten. As he prepared to shoot at goal he was challenged by two AIK defenders who fell 'as if hit by a digger' when they made contact with Charles's immense frame. 'He not only demonstrated he is a champion but he was the leading light of the team,' said the newspaper's match report. 'He pulled the team along. He coordinated the play. He built up the action and imposed the way his team manoeuvred. The whole team was infected by his enthusiasm and style of playing.'

The front page of the Stockholm daily *Tidningen* read 'JOHN CHARLES KO'S AIK', while *Dagens Nyeter* said, 'John Charles will pull big crowds in the Italian championship next year. He is one of the greatest that ever touched the grass at the Rasunda Stadium. We have not seen anything similar since the time of Puskas and Kocsis.' The *Svenska Dagbladet* proclaimed, 'Charles is worth every single penny that Juventus has paid for him.'

Juventus played a couple more friendlies in Sweden before returning to Turin. Against CK Gimonos, Charles scored four in a 7–1 win which resulted in *Idrottsbladet* comparing him with Gunnar Nordahl, Hasse Jeppson and Silvio Piola – three brilliant forwards – and saying he was worth more than those three put together. The final friendly was in Boden, 75 miles below the Arctic Circle, and Charles failed to make the scoresheet in a 3–1 win.

After these displays, no one could blame Agnelli for rubbing his hands with glee. The £65,000 paid to Leeds looked like a good piece of business. 'I remember the tour of Sweden very well, particularly that game against AIK,' says Garzena. 'They were a lovely attacking team. Eight of their players went on to play for Sweden in the 1958 World Cup final. They had just drawn 2–2 with the Manchester United "Busby Babes" and beaten the Soviet Union. They attacked with seven players, two up front and five behind them. For 80 minutes AIK played in our half. We defended and every time we got the ball we scored. We went to Sweden just to play AIK but after this game the Swedes begged Agnelli to play more friendlies. The whole of Sweden wanted to see us.'

The Juventus management flew home convinced they had signed a *fuoriclasse* (world-class player) in Charles. Depetrini, who reverted back to youth-team coach following Brocic's arrival, said, 'I had seen Charles in training and I knew I was dealing with a player of great class but in Sweden he surpassed all expectations. He is a world-class player. I think he's better than Nordahl at his best. Charles is more complete because he is better in the air, he plays with tactical intelligence and he makes the others play. He scores by getting rid of not just one defender but two or three. I believe he will do the same in our championship. He will do just as well even though our defenders won't be so kind.' Depetrini's claim that he was better than Nordahl was quite a compliment. Nordahl, known in Italy as *Il Pompiere* (the Fireman, his profession in his native Sweden), was in the autumn of his career with Roma when Charles signed for Juventus but in his heyday at Milan he scored an astonishing 210 goals in 257 matches and was *capocannoniere* (top scorer) on five occasions.

On returning to Italy Charles experienced *ritiro* (retreat), which was the Italian pre-season ritual in which teams were taken to an isolated location for training in almost monastic conditions. All clubs chose a mountain hideaway – in Juventus's case it was at Cuneo, 35 miles south of Turin – where they stayed for three weeks, away from their wives, families and the outside world. Players mixed training with relaxation and there was a strict night-time curfew of 10 p.m. The British players who joined Italian clubs hated *ritiro*. Even Charles, who embraced the Italian way, admitted he was 'bored to tears' by *ritiro*. 'I was sick of sitting around doing nothing,' he once said. 'I was sick of writing letters. I was sick of reading, playing cards or billiards.'

At Elland Road, Charles had not been regarded as an especially enthusiastic trainer. He was last in nearly everything the Leeds players did but the two managers he played for, Frank Buckley and Raich Carter, knew he would deliver the goods on matchday so they left him alone. In contrast, the Juventus players hailed him as one of the keenest trainers at the club. He was the first player to arrive at the Combi and the last to leave. Sivori, on the other hand, was always late for training. 'Where I come from only the chickens get up at this time,' he would moan. This often resulted in a rebuke from team skipper Boniperti. 'I played on the right flank and I had to work hard when John was around,' remarks Emoli. 'He wanted to work all the time. He would shout at me, "Cross Flavio! Cross! Go up, Flavio! Go down, Flavio! Cross Flavio!" It was all right for him because he just headed the ball but it was hard work for me. I could never wait for him to finish.'

On 25 August Juventus arranged a warm-up match with Biellese, a non-league side from Biella, one of Turin's satellite towns, and the good pre-season form continued with the Serie A side winning 5–0. Charles scored with a typical header. After this friendly, *Tuttosport* praised the Welsh international for 'settling very quickly' and identified him as Juventus's key man in the forthcoming *campionato*. 'Charles confirmed he is the ace that frightened the English grounds. He will be the determining factor in the way Juventus will conduct themselves in the championship. He was missing last season. Now he has arrived and he has brought tactical stature and agonistic qualities to the side.'

Juventus were installed as one of the hot favourites to win *Lo Scudetto* in 1957–58 but three days after the Biellese game, the tremendous optimism generated throughout the summer disintegrated on a balmy night in Bologna. In the penultimate pre-season friendly, Bologna, a decent Serie A side, crushed Juventus 6–1 with their left winger Ezio Pascutti – who would go on to play 18 times for Italy – scoring a hat-trick. Juventus fielded their strongest side and the result raised serious questions about their championship credentials. It also left Agnelli questioning the wisdom of his recent acquisitions. 'I remember the Bologna game. It was a terrible match for us,' he says. 'After the game I thought, "Good God, what have I bought!" At that moment I was scared about the season ahead.' The young president was not the only one who had doubts about the quality of Charles and Sivori following this hammering inside the magnificent Stadio Renato Dall'Ara. The players, too, wondered if the two *stranieri* were good enough to play in Italy's top flight. 'A terrible thought crossed our minds after Bologna,' explains Bruno Garzena. 'Were these two players, Charles and Sivori, really great? Had we bought two players who were not compatible with one another?' Says Emoli, 'No one played well against Bologna. Even the two new arrivals had a really bad game and I must confess all of us began to have doubts about the forthcoming season. Everyone was talking about what we had done in Sweden and Bologna was a tremendous downfall.' Bruno Boldi adds, 'We were out of this world in Sweden but after Bologna we weren't sure about ourselves any more. The club was worried about things after that game.'

According to Garzena, the harsh lesson in the Dall'Ara set them up for their championship win in 1957–58. 'That defeat was the best defeat Juventus had had for a long time because after that game we woke up. We went to Bologna and we thought we could play like we did against AIK. We soon realised we couldn't.'

A 4–2 win over Lazio in Rome – Charles, described as *'formidabile'* by the press, scored his side's second goal – in the final pre-season friendly ensured Juventus avoided entering the season on a downer. Their opening-day fixture was against Verona at the Comunale and on 8 September 1957, on a blistering hot Sunday afternoon, a full house saw Charles make his Serie A debut. The stifling heat visibly affected him but on the hour he scored Juventus's third goal in a 3–2 win. A week later, at Udine, Charles scored the only goal of the game. Despite the attentions of his *sentinella* (man-marker), Mario Pantaleoni, he played a one-two with Sivori before beating Fabio Cudicini with a precise shot. Against Genoa in Turin, in what turned out to be one of the most dramatic games of the championship, Charles made it three goals in three matches. The visitors raced into a two-goal lead before Giampiero Boniperti and Sivori pulled Juventus level. Four minutes from the end, Charles forced his way between a couple of Genoa defenders to head the winner. The Welshman later described this goal as his most important of the season. 'I can understand how the opposing centre-halves felt playing against John because I played against him in training and practice matches,' says Rino Ferrario. 'I must admit I didn't enjoy those training sessions because John used to play hard. Can you imagine what it must have been like trying to stop him in a competitive match?'

On 2 October, and after a fourth straight league win at Ferrara against Spal, 'Big John' returned to Elland Road as the Italian club fulfilled its obligation to play Leeds in a friendly, part of the Charles transfer agreement. 'When John walked through the door at Elland Road he looked something else,' recalls his former Leeds teammate Archie Gibson. 'He was tanned and he was wearing a double-breasted coat that you didn't do up with buttons but with a tie-up belt. He looked out of this world.' Jack Charlton adds, 'I didn't know what John was earning in Italy but when he came back to Leeds he was better dressed.' A crowd of 45,000 turned out to see their former idol and with cries of 'Come Back, John!' ringing in his ears he showed them what they were missing, scoring twice in Juventus's 4–2 win.

Then it was back to Serie A duty with *I Bianconeri* beating Padova before facing Torino at the Stadio Filadelfia in the 120th Turin derby. This was dubbed the 'John Charles derby' not only because he scored the only goal of the game (he hailed his goal in his first derby as one of his two favourite goals scored while playing for Juventus, the other was a stunning header against Fiorentina in the 1960 *Coppa Italia* final) but for a piece of sportsmanship that caught the imagination of the Turin public and earned him the nickname *Il Gigante Buono* (the Gentle Giant). Jumping for a high ball with Evo Brancaleoni, Charles caught the Torino full-back in the face in a sickening clash of heads. Brancaleoni slumped to the ground and was close to fainting. While the teams continued playing, Charles, himself concussed, held him in his hands and appealed for a doctor. Writing in *Tuttosport*, Guido Magni described it as 'the most beautiful and humane episode of this last derby'. Shortly before his death in 2002, Ernesto Castano, the left-back in that Juventus side, recalled, 'John was the only player who did these noble things and it was he who started sportsmanship in our league. It was impossible not to love the man. How can you dislike someone who did these things?'

Charles repeated what the Italians refer to as *cavalleresco* (chivalry) in another derby match, when playing in defence. After challenging a Torino player, his opponent was supine in agony. Charles forfeited a great chance to burst through and score by kicking the ball harmlessly into touch so his opponent could receive treatment. That night Torino fans, appreciative of his fair play, visited the Charles residence. 'There was a din outside our villa. Horns going, people shouting,' Charles explained to Ken Jones in an interview for *The Independent* in 1996. 'I looked out and saw this line of cars full of Torino supporters waving their red scarves. When I went and asked what it was all about one of them came forward and said that they wanted to thank me for what I'd done. I invited them in, about 20 all told, and by the time they left in the early hours of the morning they had drunk all my wine.' His first wife remembers the player's nocturnal encounter with these rival *tifosi* but she tells a different story, insisting the Torino fans never entered their home.

'We were in bed when we heard this commotion outside,' Peggy explains. 'It was about eleven o'clock at night. We were a little frightened because we weren't sure what was going on. There were all these cars outside and horns were being tooted. We saw they were Torino fans and we didn't want to go out because we knew they hated Juventus. We thought they were going to lynch us. I remember John going to the window and they cheered before driving away. I don't remember them coming into the apartment. I don't think we would have opened the door to strangers at that time of night.'

Charles's sportsmanship – relinquishing the opportunity of scoring a goal in favour of stopping play for an injured opponent – was unheard of in Italian football, internationally renowned for its win-at-all-costs mentality. 'John kicked the ball into touch quite often. I remember him doing it in a match at Fiorentina when their centre-half, Alberto Orzan, took a knock,' recalls Colombo. 'He was a man of fair play and understanding. What John used to do baffled some people. Some accepted it, some laughed and some would ask, "What the hell are you doing?" Italian players used to feign injury a lot. They pretended to be hurt but John always believed that if a player was on the floor he was genuinely injured. This was part of his nature. I think it must have been something to do with being British because fair play is part of the British way of life.'

Not all of Charles's teammates were as understanding as Colombo. Sivori used to get annoyed at his sporting gestures. '*Che fai? Continua! Continua!*' (What are you doing! Carry on playing! Carry on playing!) he would scream at the 'Gentle Giant' to which Charles would reply, in his poor Italian, '*Lui male*' (He's hurt). Stivanello was another teammate who wished Charles would develop a harder streak. 'I remember one game where two players tried to tackle John as he ran towards the goal,' he says. 'One of them fell down and John saw him on the floor. Instead of scoring a goal he kicked the ball away. I went over to him and said, "Are you mad?" John turned to me and said, "He's injured." I told him, "Yes, but score first, then they can see to the injured player." John did this sort of thing more than once. If I had to find a fault with him it would be he was too nice.'

Stivanello is convinced crafty opponents took advantage of Charles's good nature. 'I remember that game against Torino and I think John was probably conned,' says the former winger. 'John was going forward and the player saw there was a danger of us scoring so he fell to the ground and pretended to be injured, knowing Charles would show no hesitation in kicking the ball into the stand. It was such a nice gesture that you couldn't really tell him off.'

Charles soon encountered the dark side of Italian defending, in a 2–1 defeat at Lanerossi Vicenza in week nine of the 1957–58 championship. Lanerossi's stopper, Remo Lancioni, dished out appalling treatment to the Juventus player, continually hitting him above the jaw. It culminated in Charles being taken to hospital after the game to be treated for concussion. 'Lancioni was a rotter of a player,' recalls Stivanello. 'He hit John so hard in the first half that John fell to the ground. John was saying, "When he comes to Turin I will kill him" and we just laughed at him. "You are going to kill him are you, John?" John wouldn't have been able to kill a fly.' Eight minutes in, Lancioni left the Welshman spread-eagled on the grass after hitting him in the back of the head. Charles rose to his feet and attempted to play but after 40 seconds he fell to the floor, clearly dazed. After treatment with cold water and a sponge, he finished the game but afterwards he was taken to Vicenza's Clinica Elidea for a check-up and stayed there overnight. Emoli, who described Lancioni as 'a nut', remembers this particular match. 'Lancioni was not a fair player,' he says. 'He hit John right, left and centre but always from behind and when he least expected it. He never hit John when he was facing him.'

Another defender who was particularly tough on Charles was Catania's Elio Grani. With the flat nose of a boxer, Grani, known as *Il Mastino* (the Pit Bull) was a typically uncompromising Italian defender and in a match at the Comunale during the 1960–61 season he hit Sivori. Charles witnessed the punch and approached the defender with the bulldog looks, saying in his poor Italian, '*Tu non fare questo*' (You can't do this). Continues Emoli, 'Grani didn't like John interfering and he started to chase after him. He didn't forget what had happened at our place. In the return game in Catania he went after John again but I don't think he had much success. The only times I ever saw John turn nasty were when he saw his teammates getting roughed up. He would protect the teammate who was getting fouled and very often it was Sivori.'

With his imposing frame, Charles frequently found himself defending the man he later described as 'a bit crackers'. 'Every time Sivori was chased around the pitch, because he had just kicked someone, he would run and hide behind John because there he felt so protected,' smiles Bruno Boldi. Charles also protected Sivori from himself. The volatile Argentinian was forever incurring the wrath of referees – during his time in Italy he missed 33 matches through suspension, the fourth worst disciplinary record in the history of Serie A – and in one particular match against Inter, Charles feared Sivori was about to be sent off. 'Sivori was up to his usual tricks. He wouldn't stop complaining to the referee and harassing him,' remembers Castano. 'He was in a dangerous situation and the referee was about to lose his cool. John could see him sending Sivori off.' Charles went up to the inside-forward, slapped him across his left cheek and told him to behave himself. 'It was a spur of the moment sort of thing,' recalled Charles. 'He kicked somebody and I thought he was going to get sent off. I cracked him across the face and said, "Don't do it again."' Sivori remains grateful for Charles's interventions. 'John would always try to calm things down, not just with me but with the other players. On one or two occasions he pulled me out of trouble. He was always there to make peace.'

As leader of the Juventus attack, Charles himself was a marked man to a greater extent than Sivori. To prevent him scoring, defenders would pull his shirt, step on his toes and kick his ankles. 'You don't mind getting kicked when you're on the ball but in Italy they kicked you when the ball was 50 yards away,' explained the former Manchester United and Scotland forward Denis Law, who had a spell with Torino in 1961–62 when Charles was in his final season at Juventus. 'I saw John take some hits and bumps,' says Sivori. 'I saw him get knocked about in more ways than one.' While Sivori would seek revenge against opponents who fouled him or abused him, Charles would simply smile and continue. 'He always contained himself and he never retaliated. It was just as well that he was such a calm and quiet character because I didn't know anybody who would have been able to handle John if he lost his temper,' says Sivori. 'God gave him a fantastic physique and, thankfully, a good temperament as well.'

As hard as defenders tried – and they used all the tricks in the book – they never thwarted Charles. Possibly the most acclaimed goal he ever scored for Juventus – it is certainly the best-remembered – came at Marassi, the home of Genoese club Sampdoria. It illustrated the extent to which Charles's sheer power and athleticism prevailed over cynical defending. Charles was just outside the penalty area, around 20 metres from the Sampdoria goal, when the Italian international centre-half Gaudenzio Bernasconi tried to pull him down by the waist. 'He was around him like a belt,' recalls Garzena. As Charles was falling he stretched out his right leg and whacked the ball into the net. 'He still had the ability to score even though he was falling down,' says Sivori. 'He scored so many goals but that is the one that has stayed in my mind.'

Sometimes his colleagues wished *Il Gigante Buono* would rise to the bait. Castano admitted Charles's pacifist approach irked him. 'If someone hit John he would just smile at them and maybe shake their hand,' said the ex-defender. 'He would carry on as if nothing had happened. It was so annoying. How can someone hit you and you don't say anything? I wanted him to be more aggressive.' In a career that spanned four decades, Charles was never booked or sent off. There were times he wanted to lash out but he kept his temper in check by counting to five.

Sivori often approached his fellow forward and said, '*Ti prendono in giro. Usa la tua forza*' (Don't let them get away with it. Use your strength). Even Agnelli wished he would 'fight back a bit more' but Charles never changed. He was forever the gentleman, refusing to declare war on his markers. When he was a child growing up in Swansea, his father had told him never to hurt an opposing player. 'Don't kick 'em,' Ned would say to his eldest son. 'Just play football.'

In the 2–1 defeat at Fiorentina in December 1957, he collided with Fiorentina's centre-half, Sergio Cervato. Clearly dazed, Cervato dropped to the ground. Seeing him in distress, Charles put his hand under his arm, caressed his cheek and helped him to his feet. 'There were times when I think John didn't even want to score,' says Ferrario. 'He didn't want to score because he took pity on a defender or the team. He didn't want to inflict a heavy defeat on them.'

Opponents who attempted to rile Charles with verbal abuse during matches discovered they were wasting their time. Unlike his surly Argentinian teammate, Charles was seemingly immune to such provocation, a trait illustrated in a match against Inter during his first year in Italy when he came across Benito Lorenzi. The Inter forward – nicknamed *Veleno* (poison) – had a reputation of being one of the dirtiest players in Serie A and he imagined he had come up with the perfect idea for unsettling Juventus's British import. Whenever he came within earshot of Charles during the match he would say, '*La Regina e una puttana*' (Your Queen is a whore). 'John didn't understand what Lorenzi was saying so he called Colombo over and asked him to translate,' recalls Stivanello. 'Colombo told him and we all thought John would lose his temper but John just said, "The Queen isn't my Queen. I'm Welsh." Colombo told Lorenzi what he said and Lorenzi just looked at John and walked away. He didn't know what to say. That incident showed John had a great sense of humour.'

Stivanello recalls one match, against Alessandria in a *Coppa Italia* encounter at the Comunale in April 1959, when *Il Gigante Buono* did lose his temper. 'I don't remember the name of the player involved but he committed a bad foul on John, a terrible foul. John went over to him and said, in a furious way, "*La prossima volta ti picchio*" (Do that again and I'll hit you). The player got the message. He didn't bother John again.' At the end of 90 minutes the score was 2–2 and the tie went into extra-time. 'They had kicked John so much that he started charging people out of the way,' adds Stivanello. 'He scored three goals in extra-time and we won 6–2, so we said to him after the game, "Can you do that every Sunday so we can take things easy?"' Stivanello's recollection corroborates Sivori's opinion of the placid Charles. When a journalist asked him how many goals he thought the Gentle Giant would score if he played aggressively, Sivori replied, 'I think maybe he would score ten in a single game.' Such an approach was never an option. 'If I've got to knock people down, then I don't want to play,' Charles once famously said.

One winter's day during training, Castano also witnessed the Welshman's fury. 'It had been snowing and we were at the training ground playing tennis with snowballs,' he explained. 'This one player – and I don't want to reveal his identity – kept abusing John.

He was throwing snowballs at him and laughing. He just would not stop. John lost his cool. He went over to him, picked him up, took him over to the goal, stuck him against the net and said, "This time I'll just pin you against the net. The next time I don't know what I'm going to do to you." We all saw this and were flabbergasted. One of our players, [Ermes] Muccinelli, tried to pull John back when he picked up this player but John was so strong that he just pulled Muccinelli along with him.' *Il Gigante Buono* had shown there was a line that could be crossed.

On 15 December 1957, Charles played what many of his former teammates believe to be his finest game in the black and white colours of Juventus. It was inside the Comunale and Atalanta were the opposition. Juventus had returned from playing three friendly matches in England, at Sheffield Wednesday, Sunderland and Arsenal, and the players were exhausted. 'We were supposed to fly back from England on the Thursday in time to prepare for the Atalanta match but our flight from London was cancelled because of fog so we came back to Turin by train. We didn't arrive until the Saturday morning,' recalls Stivanello. The toll of travel resulted in a listless first-half display by Juventus and with the score standing at 0–0 Atalanta fancied their chances of returning to Bergamo with at least a point. 'The coach [Brocic] came into the dressing-room at the interval and he knew we were out of form. He said to us, "There is one way to resolve this." He told John to get inside the penalty area as much as he could and ordered the rest of us to pump the ball into the area and onto John's head. He thought that was our only way of winning this match. That's what we did. John got three headers and scored three goals. We won 3–0. That's a game I will never forget.' Emoli remembers it too. 'John won that game by himself,' he adds. 'He was brilliant that day.'

Charles's favourite game in his first season was not his one-man show against the *Bergamaschi* but the match against Lazio in Rome on 6 April when he scored a brace in a 4–1 win. Heading down to The Eternal City, the team stopped at the Adriatic seaside resort of Rimini, a rewarding break for the players' previous good results. 'We stayed in a beautiful hotel and after training I met this woman,' recalls Colombo. 'John knew what I'd been up to because he was sharing the room with me. The Juventus management also knew what I'd been up to, probably because I was late getting up for breakfast! When we arrived in Rome they said I wouldn't be playing. They told me I needed a rest and wasn't in the right condition to play. We won 4–1 and John scored twice. He made me look as if I wasn't needed in the team. "John, I look like a *brocco* (second-rater) because of you!" I told him. Do you know what he said to me? "You carry on with the women. I'll score the goals!"'

Charles had quickly become the idol of the *tifosi* and he had to get used to the fanaticism of the Juventus supporters who lavished him with gifts such as jewellery and suits. Before one match a supporter shouted at Charles, '*Guarda mia moglie!*' (Look at my wife). Charles turned around and watched the man lift up his wife's dress up to her neck to reveal black and white striped underpants and bra. 'If I took Terry to a Juventus game,' recalls Peggy, 'the fans would take him off me and start carrying him on their shoulders. I found that a bit frightening. The Italians are lovely people but I wasn't used to their demonstrative behaviour.'

The 1957–58 season remains one of the finest in Juventus's trophy-laden history. In some style, *I Bianconeri* clinched *Lo Scudetto* for the first time in six years. They finished eight points ahead of Fiorentina in the days of two points for a win. Brocic's men mathematically won *Lo Scudetto* on 4 May, with three matches still to play, when they drew 0–0 with eventual runners-up Fiorentina in Turin. Juventus won 23 of their 34 matches, scoring 77 goals in the process. Bruno Boldi rates this championship as 'perhaps the most remarkable Juventus has ever won' and by 2002, *I Bianconeri* had won a record 26 championships. 'We were scoring three or four goals in every match,' he adds. 'We were too good to describe.'

Garzena insists winning the title in 1958 – the club's tenth – was down to Brocic changing the team's approach in response to the humiliating pre-season defeat in Bologna. 'Brocic was a man of great understanding and sensibility. He made a couple of adjustments to the team after this game. He decided matches had to be won in the penalty area and he had a forward by the name of John Charles who would win any ball that was put into the air. He had two of the most attack-minded inside-forwards in Boniperti and Sivori, who would never dream of going back to help the defence. So Brocic told me, Emoli, Ferrario, Corradi and Colombo to stay inside our 35-metre area, win the ball and just give it to our forwards. We didn't really worry about midfield – we called that "No Man's Land". That's how the championship was won in 1958.'

Of the four men Charles played for during his five years in Turin (Brocic, Renato Cesarini, Gunnar Gren and Carlo Parola) it was Brocic who brought out the best in him. His successor, Cesarini, modelled the team more around Sivori (it was Cesarini who had recommended Sivori to Juventus and Sivori returned the compliment by pushing for Cesarini to replace Brocic). Parola used Charles in defence and the players did not particularly rate Gren as a coach. The Yugoslav polyglot, however, built his team – and strategy – around the Welshman. 'He knew John's potential,' comments Colombo, 'and he exploited that potential to the maximum. John determined our play in 1957–58.' Boldi agrees. 'Although Boniperti and Sivori were both world-class players, I would say 90 per cent of winning that championship was down to Charles. He made things easy for the other players. If they had the ball and they didn't know what to do with it then you could kick it to John because nine times out of ten he would win the ball.' Even a player as egotistical as Sivori credited Charles with bringing *Lo Scudetto* to Turin. If Juventus did not have Charles, he proclaimed, then the championship would have been won by either Fiorentina or Milan.

Il Gigante Buono enjoyed the perfect debut season. Apart from picking up a championship medal he was named Italy's Footballer of the Year and he also won the coveted *capocannoniere* (top goalscorer) award with 28 goals – the first and, to this day, the only Briton to have won this title. He may have scored more goals for Leeds but this was an effort that demanded respect. 'It wasn't easy to score that many goals in Italy because you were severely marked,' recalled Law. 'You had to get rid of two guys, not one. It wasn't creative football, it was purely defensive.'

Charles's forward partner, Sivori, netted 22 goals. 'We had five wonderful years together but that first season at Juventus was the most incredible,' he says. 'John was the decisive player in that championship. He was our ace.' The former Leeds player was sixth in France Football's European Footballer of the Year awards behind the winner Alfredo Di Stefano, Billy Wright, Raymond Kopa, Duncan Edwards and Lazslo Kubala.

Charles and Sivori, the 'Terrible Twins', established themselves as the most prolific and most feared attacking partnership in Serie A. 'John would jump into the air and everyone would think he was about to head at goal,' explains Emoli, 'but then he would see Sivori, turn his head and give him the ball. Sivori was the main beneficiary of John's power in the penalty area. John created more goals for Sivori with his assists than Sivori did for John. He would give the ball to Sivori using his chest and they would play some brilliant one-twos together. On the field, they were an absolute dream, they blended so well. John understood the way Sivori played.' Of the 22 goals Sivori scored that season, Garzena insists at least 15 were down to Charles.

In 12 months Juventus were transformed from relegation candidates to undisputed champions. Only two sides had won the league by a bigger margin since the modern Serie A began in 1929–30 – Fiorentina, who finished twelve points ahead of Milan in 1956 and Torino, who finished ten points ahead of Juventus in 1947. 'A journalist asked Umberto Agnelli how, in just one year, his club had gone from managing to avoid relegation to winning the championship with great comfort,' says Garzena. 'He told him, "The answer is simple. I went to England and bought the best centre-forward they had. Then I went to South America and bought the best footballer available there."' Agnelli admits the club's management had no idea the two players would gel so well and so quickly. 'Marrying Charles with Sivori was not really a deliberate tactical ploy,' he says. 'We were already onto Sivori before we bought Charles. We were just buying two very good players. It just so happened they matched each other so well.'

Away from football, Charles's young family quickly adapted to life in Turin, although his wife was not enamoured of their first home. 'I'd just left a nice house with a garden and now I'd gone to a ground-floor flat which didn't have much of a garden,' she says. After a year, her disenchantment was remedied when the club found them a new apartment, on the Cavoretto hill overlooking the city and boasting stunning views of the Alps. It was a two-storey apartment, split into three sections. 'It was like a huge villa and it was one of three luxury apartments on this hill,' remembers Terry Charles, the player's eldest son. 'It had the most beautiful views of Turin and the mountains.'

Their hillside home was filled with the furniture from their house in Leeds. 'We shipped over most of the furniture because we didn't know what we were going to,' explains Peggy. 'We brought over a big settee and big chairs. We wanted to keep them because they were so comfortable. All the apartments in Italy have marble floors and the settee and chairs had castors on them and I remember us flying across the floor whenever we sat in them. I had to get John to take the castors off in the end.'

The player and his wife bought a property of their own in the summer of 1958, an apartment in the swanky seaside resort of Diano Marina, on the Ligurian coastline, close to the French border. 'Our friends in the British Consulate recommended Diano Marina to us,' adds Peggy. 'They said the sea there was good for the children. When we went to look at Diano Marina we saw some apartments being built and we bought one which would be ready the following year.'

The club endeavoured to help the Charleses settle. The player was provided with a Fiat car, the 1100 Familiare, although Charles initially infuriated the Agnellis by buying a Citroën a day or two after arriving in Turin. 'I didn't think,' said Charles, oblivious to the fact he was, in effect, being paid by Europe's biggest car manufacturer. 'Gianni Agnelli was on the telephone asking what I was trying to do to him.' Peggy was provided with a nanny-cum-cook, a Sicilian woman called Maria, to help her with the domestic chores. 'Umberto Agnelli occasionally deigned us with a visit to see if we were all right,' says Peggy. The club was merely protecting its investment. 'Juventus looked after Charles and Sivori in an admirable way,' says Emoli. 'They were the pupils of the Agnelli family, the jewels in the Juventus crown. The money the club paid for them was frightening.'

After moving to Turin, Charles found himself eating risotto, lasagne verde and spaghetti instead of bacon and poached egg on toast. 'The first time I was faced with a bowl of spaghetti it went everywhere but down my bloody throat,' he later recalled. And instead of bitter-shandy, he was sipping red wine. The Charles family missed bacon and custard and Peggy's parents brought over packets of the custard powder when they flew over to visit. Charles would sometimes disappear into the countryside around Alba, a town south of Turin, with his Juventus teammates to search for truffles. Those discovered in this region are reckoned to be the best in the world.

Charles's two eldest sons, Terry and Melvyn, attended *asilo infantile* (primary school) where they wore the traditional uniform of a black pinafore with a white starched collar. 'I soon picked up Italian and we ate in lovely restaurants,' adds his ex-wife. 'I loved going to the markets. I had never seen things like a pepper or an aubergine. We didn't have those things in England in the 1950s. We had loads of friends but they were nothing to do with football. I honestly don't think I met the wife of another Juventus player while I was there. I also learned to drive in Italy. I had failed back in England but after I had Peter I decided to give it another go and I passed.' Her reward was a little Fiat 500 from Umberto Agnelli.

It was one of many Fiats the Charleses owned. As a match-winning bonus, Agnelli rewarded his Gentle Giant with his company's latest vehicle. 'We had a big garage and it was full of cars and Lambretta scooters,' remembers Charles's second son, Melvyn. 'They were all gifts given to Dad.'

After his exploits of the 1957–58 season Charles found himself one of the main attractions in 1950s Italy. The newspapers printed stories claiming sex kittens Sophia Loren and Gina Lollobrigida were jealous of the attention the Juventus forward was attracting. He had become a national celebrity and this meant occasionally – and reluctantly – abandoning his secluded hillside apartment to mix with Italy's great and good. On one occasion Agnelli insisted that he attend a party because Loren, one of Juventus's most famous fans, would be there and wanted to meet him. Charles declined but Agnelli kept pressing him and in the end he relented. 'What's she like, John?' asked some of his former Leeds teammates when he returned to Yorkshire to see his in-laws. The closest they would ever come to the sultry Italian actress was watching one of her films in the local cinema. 'She's got freckles,' he replied.

Handsome, blessed with a magnificent physique, and Italy's number one football player, it was predictable that companies would seek association with the Charles brand. Litrico, an upmarket men's tailor, wanted him to advertise their suits, so too did another suit manufacturer, Lebole. Juventus, however, would not allow footballers to endorse products. There was even a plan for a comic book character to be based on Charles – he was to be called Dick Fulmine (Dick Lightning) – but this too was vetoed by the club.

He may have been enjoying a millionaire's lifestyle – earning the sort of money he could only have dreamed of while playing for Leeds – but Charles sometimes pined for home. 'John got a little bit homesick now and again,' says Bruno Boldi. 'He got to know this English family who lived just outside Turin and if he was feeling nostalgic he would spend a few hours with them on his days off. John and his family lived quite a secluded life. The only player he really mixed with was Colombo who spoke four or five words of English.'

Charles hankered after the pubs back home. 'You have bars,' he once said in an interview with *Tuttosport*, 'but pubs are more intimate and comfortable. I also miss a social life. Here I have few friends. That's nobody's fault. That's life.' Ferrario, who became close friends with the Gentle Giant, says Charles was unable to hide his bouts of homesickness. 'I did know for a fact that John missed the convivial ambience of Wales and the North of England. He missed going to the pub after a match. I could read him like an open book and I could see he was missing home or thinking of home.'

Chapter Six – Your Country Needs You

John Charles was 18 years and 71 days old when he made his international debut, against Northern Ireland at Wrexham's Racecourse Ground on 8 March 1950. He became the youngest player to wear the red shirt of Wales and his record survived for 41 years until Ryan Giggs was thrown on as a substitute in a 4–1 defeat against Germany, in Nuremberg in October 1991.

The centre-half had yet to complete a full season with Leeds when the selectors who picked the Welsh international side decided to take a look at the Swansea-born teenager who was making quite an impression in West Yorkshire. Some of the selectors had gone to Elland Road to watch Charles in action in Leeds' 3–1 FA Cup win over Cardiff and they were impressed with what they saw. The Home International match against Northern Ireland was an ideal fixture for his international baptism. Defeats against England and Scotland meant the Welsh had no chance of winning the championship so it provided the selectors with a chance to experiment.

Charles was back in his native South Wales when he learned he would be representing his country. Leeds were due to play Cardiff at Ninian Park and Buckley granted the player a few days' leave so he could visit his family in Cwmbwrla. 'I am naturally delighted and honoured at having been picked to play for my country,' the teenager told the *Western Mail*. 'I had been quietly hoping I was in the running for a cap but felt by no means certain.'

The FA Cup defeat at Arsenal freed Charles to play against Northern Ireland. Had Leeds drawn at Highbury then the replay at Elland Road would have taken place on the same day as the Wales match – and Buckley had publicly stated he would not release him for international duty if Leeds had to play a second match against The Gunners. 'I was with John when he first found out he had been picked for Wales,' says his former Leeds and Wales teammate, Harold Williams. 'We were going down to Wales by train because we were playing Cardiff. We arrived at Newport station at about 4.30 in the afternoon and I went onto the platform and bought a newspaper because it said the Welsh team had been announced to play Northern Ireland. And that's how he discovered he was going to play. He didn't get excited. He didn't say anything. It was as if he expected it to happen. In my opinion, John knew he was a good player.'

Charles's debut was utterly forgettable. Overawed by the occasion, the Leeds player froze. Just a year before he had been sweeping the stands. Now here he was, changing in the same dressing-room as the players he worshipped as a boy. There was Tottenham's Ron Burgess, Cardiff's Alf Sherwood, Arsenal's Walley Barnes and the two Swansea players, Roy Paul and Trevor Ford. Charles had cleaned the boots of Paul and Ford while he was a groundstaff boy at the Vetch Field.

For the first and only time in his career Charles was fazed. Recalling his nightmare first match for Wales, he said, 'Sitting in the dressing-room before the game I kept telling myself, "Keep calm, it's just another game." And what happened? I made a complete hash of things. Nothing I did went right and the harder I tried the worse it became. Looking back on it now, it was obvious I was not mentally ready for such an ordeal.'

The result was a goalless draw. Charles had to mark the West Bromwich Albion centre-forward Dave Walsh and he gave the debutant a difficult time. Before the kick-off Charles had a conversation with Richard Ulyatt and he confessed to the *Yorkshire Post* writer that he was nervous. It showed during the game when the usually composed Charles would go in to make a challenge and pull out at the last second. Time and time again his colleagues in defence bailed him out but not everybody noticed the youngster's nerves. 'John didn't play particularly well that day but he never gave me the impression that he was nervous or edgy,' says Williams, who won the third of his four Welsh caps that Saturday afternoon. 'But it was a bloody awful game. Wrexham was a poor ground in those days and the game was dead. You do get games where nothing happens.' Not everyone thought Charles played badly. Bill Shortt, Wales's goalkeeper that day, says, 'I thought he played OK. He didn't appear nervous. He seemed to be in command all the time. He was only 18 but he was an old 18.' Ron Burgess, the Tottenham Hotspur left-half and one of Wales's key players in that era, earmarked the teenager as a future star. 'He played well enough for most of us to say, "He's here to stay!"'

The clash against the Irish was no classic. In fact, it was so dull that the 30,000 crowd could hear referee Arthur Ellis talking to the players because there was so little enthusiasm from the terraces. As one football writer noted, 'The proverbial pin could have been heard to drop.' One newspaper reported that a female spectator fell asleep in the stand while other members of the crowd read newspapers. The *Western Mail* condemned the match as the worst involving Wales since the Second World War. 'To describe it as poor is being too kind.' Cardiff's evening newspaper, the *South Wales Echo,* was just as scathing. The soccer diarist known as Citizen described it as 'the most apathetic game of football I have ever seen on the international field' and 'the worst possible advertisement for association football'. Of Charles's performance the same newspaper declared, 'He was not outstanding and is still cumbersome. He is promising without a doubt, but not an international yet.'

Charles knew he had failed to live up to the pre-match hype and he returned to West Yorkshire wondering if the selectors would pick him again. Major Buckley offered consolation in a heart-to-heart chat with his young star, telling him it was not unusual for players to have a bad game on their international debut and assuring him he would win another cap. Charles had to wait 14 months before that second cap came his way, in a Festival of Britain match against Switzerland, in May 1951. The Arsenal centre-half Ray Daniel was on tour in Brazil with his club affording Charles, who was now being used as a centre-forward at Leeds, another opportunity in defence.

Again, Wrexham was the venue, but this time the outcome was a much happier one. Wales won 3–2 and the press unanimously agreed Charles had a better game than he did against Northern Ireland. The Swiss came desperately close to spoiling his second outing. Wales were leading 3–0 with 20 minutes to go when Charles had 'one of the worst 20 minutes of my life' as Switzerland's centre-forward Alfred Bickel roamed across the pitch, totally confusing Charles. It was Bickel's cross from the right wing that allowed Robert Ballaman to make it 3–1, then Charles Antenen made it 3–2 with ten minutes left, but Wales grimly held on.

Charles scored his first international goal in his third game, against Northern Ireland at Belfast's Windsor Park, in April 1953. Charles was scoring freely at centre-forward for Leeds, something the Welsh selectors could not ignore. Since Trevor Ford had made the number 9 jersey his own, the selectors decided to drop Newcastle's Reg Davies and hand Charles the inside-right position. It worked a treat. In a match that saw three Welsh players win their first cap – Derrick Sullivan, Terry Medwin and Harry Griffiths – and with a forward line of players all born in Swansea, Wales won 3–2 and Charles was named man of the match. He scored twice, both first-half headers, before setting up Ford for Wales's third. 'I remember that game in Belfast because the next day we had to be back in Swansea to play Leeds at the Vetch,' says Medwin. 'We were sailing from Liverpool and the boat was in two minds whether to leave because the weather was so bad. But we got there, won 3–2, had a meal in a hotel after the match, then got back on the boat at midnight and arrived in Liverpool the following morning. John, Harry and myself got on a train and we got into Swansea at 4.15 in the afternoon – half an hour before kick-off! We took a taxi to the Vetch and were changed by 4.40 p.m., then we played another game. We won 3–2 and both John and I scored.'

After his brilliant show in Windsor Park, Charles was never ignored by the selectors again. He was picked for the two May friendlies, against France in Paris and Yugoslavia in Belgrade, but afterwards he probably wished he had been left at home. Wales were crushed 6–1 by the French in the Stade Colombes before going down 5–2 in the Partisan Stadium a week later. Charles played inside-right in both games but made little impression.

Wales were singularly unimpressive in Paris. They took the lead inside a minute courtesy of an awesome 20-yard drive from Ivor Allchurch but at half-time they found themselves 4–1 down with Rheims forward Raymond Kopa, who would later star for Real Madrid, and Sochaux winger René Gardien both scoring twice. Earlier in the first half, as France were turning on the style, Charles had a great opportunity to make it 2–2 when he was one-on-one with the French goalkeeper, Lille's Cesar Rominski, but he uncharacteristically squandered his chance. An exhausting season seemed to have sapped the big man's strength. In the second half France added two further goals, from Antoine Bonifaci and Joseph Ujlaki, and inflicted on Wales not only their heaviest defeat since the 6–0 drubbing at the hands of England at Stamford Bridge 24 years earlier but also their heaviest defeat on foreign soil. Trevor Ford said the French 'made us look like amateurs'. Wales were outclassed in every department and the *Western Mail* described the result as 'a humiliating blow to Great Britain's football prestige'.

After the pasting in the Stade Colombes the Welsh selectors and press, and probably the players, too, flew to Belgrade fearing the worst. There, a member of the British Embassy gave Ron Burgess, Wales's captain, a rundown on Yugoslavia's tactics. A sightseeing tour scheduled for the day before the game was cancelled so the players could properly prepare for the friendly. The selectors kept faith with the same side that lost badly in Paris and they were rewarded with a better display. In fact, Wales might have returned home with a draw had it not been for a disastrous 15-minute spell in the first half that saw the Yugoslavs score four times with Rajko Mitic hitting a hat-trick. The Yugoslav press blamed Wales's goalkeeper, Bill Shortt, for his team's defeat. Mitic's third goal was the result of Shortt allowing a 30-yard shot to squirm under his body.

Wales retained a degree of dignity. The following day *Sport* newsaper said, 'There were times when the Yugoslav victory was in question.' *Borfa* called it 'a beautiful and exciting game' while *Politika* hailed it as the best match seen in Belgrade since the war.

The following October, Wales kicked off the Home International Championship against England at Ninian Park in Cardiff. There was more than usual at stake. With this competition doubling up as a World Cup qualifying group, the top two sides would travel to Switzerland to take part in the 1954 World Cup. With Ford sidelined with a foot injury this was Charles's first outing for his country at centre-forward, with Reg Davies filling the inside-right berth. A crowd of 60,000 watched in amazement as Wales outclassed their more illustrious neighbours but went on to lose 4–1 in what was the first in a series of unlucky defeats against England during the 1950s.

England included Billy Wright, Tom Finney and Nat Lofthouse but Wales, with the majestic Charles tormenting the Blackpool centre-half Harry Johnston, were rampant in the opening 40 minutes – 'a crimson flood swamping through England' was how the *Daily Mirror* described it – but the home side had only Ivor Allchurch's 20th-minute goal to show for their overwhelming supremacy as Gil Merrick, England's goalkeeper, made a series of outstanding saves. 'I was at Ninian Park watching that game,' recalls Alan Harrington, the former Cardiff City and Wales defender. 'John's performance in those first 45 minutes was the best display I've ever seen from a centre-forward. Harry Johnston never won a ball in the air. The problem John was having was that he was jumping so high he couldn't get the balls below the crossbar. The Welsh players were also hitting the ball down the middle to John who would then chest the ball 20 yards away to Reg Davies!'

Roy Clarke, the Manchester City winger, played in this 4–1 defeat. 'I crossed the ball to John and his first header hit the post. I crossed to him a second time. He hit the crossbar. I crossed to him again. He hit the post. Then I put in another cross. He hit the crossbar.' Watching from the stand was younger brother Mel. 'John must have hit the crossbar six times,' he recalls. 'I think that was his best ever game for Wales. Harry Johnston didn't have a chance against John.'

Charles has always said he considered the 1953 match against England as his best performance at centre-forward. 'In the air he was unchallengeable. On the ground he made the English defence panic practically every time he got the ball,' said the *Western Mail* of Charles's display. 'On at least six occasions Charles missed scoring himself by a hairsbreadth margin – not by bad finishing but through 100 per cent bad luck and, of course, Merrick.'

Johnston, a composed and constructive centre-half, was one of the country's most accomplished defenders but he did not know what had hit him that Saturday afternoon in the Welsh capital. 'As for Johnston, poor chap,' said the *Manchester Guardian* in its match report, 'he might as well have been at Palomart Observatory star gazing.' After the mauling he suffered at the hands of the Leeds player, he won only two more caps. This Home International meeting was the first time Johnston had confronted Charles and it was an encounter he never forgot. 'I had never had to play against anyone like him before. To play against him you need a pair of steps,' he remarked in a 1956 interview, when he was manager at Reading. 'The ball is coming straight to you in the air. You get under it and judge it perfectly. Up you go to the ball, right up to it. Then, before you know where you are, there is this big fellow Charles up above you, nodding the ball away six inches from your head.'

The turning point of the contest came just before half-time when Alf Sherwood left the pitch with concussion after colliding with Finney. By the time the left-back returned ten minutes after the break, England had taken advantage of the extra man and scored four goals with three of them stemming from right-winger Jimmy Mullen whom Sherwood was marking. Wolves' Dennis Wilshaw equalised on the stroke of half-time, then early in the second half England scored three times in as many minutes to kill off the Welsh. Wilshaw got his second in the 49th minute, before Lofthouse scored in the 51st and 52nd minutes. A resounding win for England. 'But it was still the best football Wales produced in my time,' said Sherwood.

Charles was back in goalscoring form the following month, against Scotland at Hampden Park. Charles, who received scant service throughout the game, had three chances and scored from two of them. Brown and Johnstone had given the Scots a 2–0 half-time lead but three minutes after the break Charles reduced the arrears. He chested down Bill Foulkes's centre and beat George Farm with a stinging drive. Farm got a hand to the ball but could not stop it flying into his net. Lawrie Reilly restored Scotland's two-goal advantage before Ivor Allchurch made it 3–2 with what Charles considered the finest goal 'Golden Boy' ever scored. Allchurch seemed to overcome the entire Scottish defence before beating Farm from 20 yards. With two minutes remaining Charles snatched a dramatic equaliser. He chased after Ronnie Howells' long goalkick, held off Willie Telfer and shot at Farm. The ball hit the Blackpool goalkeeper and rebounded back to Charles who made no mistake with his second attempt.

Wales had to beat Northern Ireland at least 3–0 in Cardiff to stand any chance of making it to Switzerland but in a match best remembered for two goalkeepers making their debuts – Arsenal's Jack Kelsey for Wales and Doncaster Rovers' Harry Gregg for Northern Ireland – the visitors claimed an unexpected win that meant England and Scotland would represent Britain in the World Cup. Peter McParland scored both of his country's goals with Charles replying 12 minutes from the end. The *Western Mail* was critical. 'John Charles was a shadow of the man who had such grand games against England and Scotland. How could he be expected to achieve miracles when for most of the game he did not even have the opportunity of touching the ball?' The ball Charles loved most was down the middle, as he showed at Hampden Park, but in this game he received only one such pass, from Ray Daniel, and scored from it.

In May 1954 the Welsh flew to Vienna to face a good Austrian side that had qualified for the World Cup. This was not the *wunderteam* that graced Europe's playing fields before the war but they boasted the tall, dark Ernst Ocwirk, long recognised as one of the best wing-halves in world football, and Robert Dienst, a quick, dangerous forward.

Before the game the Welsh party enjoyed their customary city tour, taking in the opera house, St Stephen's Cathedral and the Hofburg Palace. One evening the players visited the British barracks and Charles sang one of Billy Daniels' songs for his audience.

Wales, not surprisingly, lost the match. Austria, who insisted on using the same Swiss football that would be employed in the forthcoming World Cup, were simply too good and ran out 2–0 winners with goals from Dienst and Paul Halla.

Four Welshmen won their first cap inside the Prater Stadium that day – Stuart Williams at right-back, Bill Harris at right-half, Derek Tapscott at inside-right and Cliff Jones on the left wing. But it was Charles, back at centre-half, who stole the headlines with an imperious performance that had even the Austrian crowd applauding. 'He was incredible in that game,' says former Swansea Town and Tottenham Hotspur winger Jones. 'It was the best performance I've ever seen from a centre-half and it was the best performance I saw John give. He was breaking up attacks and running 50 yards with the ball and laying it off to his teammates. They won 2–0 but if it hadn't been for John, and Jack Kelsey who also had a great game, it could have been a lot more.' Austria's press talked about only one Welshman the following morning. *Wiener Kurier* said, 'Austria should have won by four or five goals but the amazing stopper Charles prevented a debacle and a more convincing win.' *Salzburger Nachrichten* compared him to the legendary Austria and Rapid Vienna footballer, Franz Binder. 'The best player on the field was not an Austrian but a Welshman – John Charles. The way Charles treated the ball, his opponents, and the severe way in which he took charge of the situation was a treat to watch.' *Welt Am Montag* added, 'John Charles played a magnificent game and did everything one could expect from a perfect footballer.'

The match was threaded with a spiteful undercurrent which started after Tapscott charged the Austrian goalkeeper, Kurt Schmid, who was left hanging upside down in the net. The crowd was incensed, so too was Dienst who angrily confronted the Arsenal player. At that time, charging the goalkeeper was part of the British game but on the continent it was abhorred. The home side retaliated and Charles was the victim. One of the Austrian players made no effort to play the ball, instead planting his studs on Charles's thigh. 'John,' Kelsey later recalled, 'went down like a log.' When Jack Jones, the Welsh physio, ran onto the pitch to treat the player he saw six black stud marks tattooed on his leg. 'John never said a word to anyone,' added Wales's chain-smoking goalkeeper. 'He just got to his feet, went on playing and never attempted to retaliate.'

Wales played Austria 18 months later at Wrexham. If the first game in Vienna was bad tempered it was nothing compared to the animosity in the second – football's version of a backyard brawl which became known as 'the Battle of Wrexham'. That afternoon the placid Charles lost his temper in front of 25,000 people.

All was calm in the opening 20 minutes as the visitors produced the football that had clinched them third place in the previous year's World Cup. The Austrians quickly established a two-goal lead, first through Theodor Wagner and then Gerhard Hanappi. Thereafter, as Austria coach Herr Moltzer put it, the match 'degenerated into a game of rugby'. Ford and Tapscott's persistent charging of the Austrian goalkeeper, Bruno Engelmeier, sparked the rough stuff. Their actions infuriated the Austrian players and when French referee Louis Fauquemberghe declined to penalise the two Welsh forwards the Austrian players sought their own form of retribution. At the end of the game both dressing-rooms, observed one journalist, 'resembled casualty stations'. Austria's inside-right, Wagner, was stretchered off with a broken shin bone and Wales's Mel Charles was carried off with a leg injury after being scythed down with 15 minutes remaining. 'Two Austrian players went for Mel,' remembers Tapscott. 'They just kicked him and one kick brought him down. John was about 20 yards away and he went running up to this player.' The sight of his younger brother crippled with pain clearly affected Charles. 'John lost a bit of self-control and he grabbed the Austrian by the shirt. It was the only time I ever saw him angry,' remembers Cliff Jones.

Charles was reduced to tears at the sorry state of his brother in the dressing-room after the game. Some of his teammates feared Mel would never play again. Charles later admitted he was close to hitting the culprit but checked his temper. 'He then calmed down but for the rest of the game you could see he wasn't happy,' adds Tapscott. 'He was worried about Mel who had to be carried off the pitch. I've got to be honest, that was the only time I saw John lose his temper and I played quite a few games with him for Wales and I also played with him for a couple of years at Cardiff City. They kicked Mel all over the park that night but quite a few of us got injured, including myself. I had to go to hospital the next day and have an X-ray on my back. It was one of the dirtiest matches I ever played in.'

Mel Charles vividly recalls the incident that led to his older brother shooting upfield to confront his assailant. 'I got kicked from behind and John got hold of him and said, "If you ever do that again to my brother I'll bloody kill you!" It was the first and only time I saw him get nasty.'

Tapscott pulled a goal back for Wales but in a match remembered for its brutal content and forgotten for its result Austria held on to win 2–1. Afterwards Moltzer described the Welsh players as 'really rough' and maintained that his players 'retaliated in kind'. The *Western Mail* labelled the so-called friendly 'a disgrace to national football'. On the subject of the Welsh team, *Bild Telegraf* claimed only Charles and Ivor Allchurch tried to play football while Ford and Tapscott were 'spoiled stars'. *Neues Österreich* described the match as 'a pitched battle'. *Die Presse* blamed Fauquemberghe for allowing the match to spiral out of control. But perhaps the most damning appraisal came from Ernst Ocwirk, one of world football's great players during the 1950s. 'I have played in 57 internationals and seen many more but I've never seen so much vindictive fouling as at Wrexham. It was more like a boxing and kicking match than football.'

Sandwiched between these games with Austria were two epic meetings against England. At Wembley in November 1954, in front of 91,112 spectators, Charles, at centre-forward, gave Wales a 38th-minute lead, turning home Allchurch's centre which had skidded past Roy Wood. However, luck was with the English as it had been a year earlier at Ninian Park.

Minutes after Charles's goal, Wales were down to nine men as Ray Daniel and Derrick Sullivan left the pitch with concussion. Both returned for the second half but neither was the same player. Roy Bentley equalised in the 68th minute, then the same player put England 2–1 up. Charles levelled two minutes later with a superb effort, bursting through the English reguard before beating Wood with a low shot. Eight minutes from time, and after Frank Blunstone created a goalmouth scramble, Bentley got his hat-trick.

Charles scored the only hat-trick of his international career in the 3–2 win over Northern Ireland in Belfast, on 20 April 1955. 'Nine times out of ten when a high ball reached him he would get possession despite the attention of two, sometimes three, Irish defenders,' wrote Dewi Lewis in the *Western Mail*.

The following October, England visited Ninian Park. Wales, looking for their first Home International Championship win over the English for 17 years, had a new team manager. Captain Alf Sherwood, with the help of team trainer Eddie Nash, had replaced

Walley Barnes who quit football to work for the BBC. The switch brought some changes to Wales's pre-match preparations. The team had a pre-match tactical discussion 'for the first time I can remember' remarked Trevor Ford, who had played for his country since 1947. The players were fed a diet of sandwiches and salad and instead of the usual lapping and sprinting the team trained by playing a 90-minute match against Cardiff City.

Charles was back at centre-half to help his teammates repel a formidable England forward line of Stanley Matthews, Don Revie, Tom Finney, Nat Lofthouse and Dennis Wilshaw. Sherwood opted for man-to-man marking. He planned to take care of Matthews with Stuart Williams marking Finney, Roy Paul watching Revie while Charles had to stop Lofthouse. The decision paid off. With Sherwood's pre-match cry of 'Chase until you drop!' ringing in their ears the Welshmen stormed into a 2–0 lead at half-time with two goals in two minutes, first from Derek Tapscott and then Cliff Jones.

Charles was enjoying a magnificent game at the back but six minutes after the interval, to the horror of Jack Kelsey, the Leeds star inadvertently handed England a lifeline by heading a harmless England cross into his own net. With both their sons playing, Charles's parents, Ned and Lily, were among the 60,000 crowd at Ninian Park that Saturday afternoon. Lily was watching her very first football match. Unfamiliar with the rules of the game, she was unaware the two teams changed ends after 45 minutes so when she saw John head the ball into the net she rose from her seat to celebrate, oblivious to the sight of her despairing eldest son, his head in his hands. 'Lily got to her feet and started clapping like mad,' recalled Ned after watching his son score an own-goal. 'I asked her, "What are you clapping for, Lil?" She answered, "Our John has just scored a goal." And I replied, "Yes, but he's scored it for England!" After the match I told John and Mel about it. They thought it was the funniest thing they'd ever heard.'

The pair may not have found it so amusing had it proved the catalyst for an England comeback. Despite a late onslaught by the English, and with the limping Paul a passenger for the last half-an-hour, Wales held on for a famous victory and, inside Cardiff's Park Hotel, the players spent the night celebrating. The Welsh should have gone on to win the Home International Championship that season but a 2–0 defeat against Scotland at Hampden Park in November followed by a 1–1 draw with Northern Ireland in Cardiff five months later meant all four countries finished with three points and shared the championship.

A meaningless friendly between Leeds and Arsenal at Elland Road may well have denied Wales winning the title. The clubs arranged to play this match on 7 November – two days before Wales met Scotland in Glasgow. Leeds insisted on Charles playing while Arsenal announced they would be fielding their Welsh internationals, Jack Kelsey and Derek Tapscott. To exacerbate matters, the train taking the trio to Glasgow after the match left Leeds at 2 a.m. on the Tuesday morning. After the friendly the three players sat in a Leeds hotel and played cards until it was time to leave. Once in Scotland they spent the rest of Tuesday sleeping off the journey so their pre-match training consisted of a few sprints on Wednesday morning. With three key players clearly not at the races it was no surprise to see the Scots – with Rangers centre-half George Young, known as the 'Rock of Gibraltar', outstanding – win by a comfortable two-goal margin. Blame for the first goal could be laid at Charles's door. His poor headed clearance in the 14th minute fell to Bobby Johnstone who beat Kelsey with a low shot. Henceforth, there was only one winner.

Against Northern Ireland, Wales scored a memorable goal. Inevitably Charles was the instigator. In the tenth minute the centre-half picked up the ball in his own six-yard box and ran the entire length of the pitch before passing to Ford. His dummy allowed the ball to roll on to Roy Clarke who slammed the ball past Norman Uprichard. 'I meant to hit it to the far post but it went in at the near post instead,' admits Clarke. 'John ran from one penalty area to the other before passing to me – it was a great goal.' So great, in fact, that the BBC showed it as part of the opening credits to the Saturday night programme *Sports Special*. Winning his first Welsh cap that April afternoon was Alan Harrington and it was the Cardiff City defender who began the move that led to Clarke's goal. 'I got the ball inside our penalty area and I heard John shout, "Give it to me!" So I gave it to John and he ran the length of the pitch and set up our goal,' says Harrington. 'We all lost a gold watch that day.

Had we beaten Northern Ireland we would have won the championship and the Welsh FA had promised every player a gold watch if we did that.'

When Wales opened the 1956–57 Home International Championship against Scotland at Ninian Park on 20 October, the Football Association of Wales (FAW) had, for the first time, appointed a national team manager. His name was Jimmy Murphy, Manchester United's assistant manager. He would combine his role as Wales boss with his duties at Old Trafford. Born in the Rhondda, Murphy enjoyed a successful career with West Bromwich Albion as a right-half and played 22 times for Wales. Known as 'Spud' at Old Trafford, on account of his Irish background, he was manager Matt Busby's ebullient number two and he played a pivotal role in bringing together the players that became known as the 'Busby Babes'.

Murphy's first game, against the Scots, ended in a 2–2 draw but it was a match Wales should have won. Charles, at inside-right, had a hand in both goals, scored by Ford and Terry Medwin, but he created enough chances for Ford to have bagged a hat-trick. 'How often I wished during this game that Wales could have two John Charleses,' lamented Dewi Lewis in the *Western Mail* the following day. 'One to make and the other to take the chances.'

Next came England at Wembley and here Murphy began to make his mark. To prepare for the match he took his squad to train at the Vickers Sports Ground in Weybridge, Surrey, away from the ticket hunters and autograph collectors. The players trained in the morning and afternoon with Murphy talking about nothing but tactics. In the evening, they unwound with a visit to the cinema.

Despite the improved pre-match preparation Wembley remained a bogey ground for the Welsh as history repeated itself. Charles gave them a seventh-minute lead, rising at the far post to head Medwin's free-kick past Eddie Ditchburn. But then, six minutes later, they lost their goalkeeper Jack Kelsey after a collision with 'Gentleman' Tom Finney. Since no substitutes were allowed, Alf Sherwood, playing his last match for Wales, took over the goalkeeping duties. For ten minutes in the first half Wales were reduced to nine men when Mel Charles was stretchered off after a Johnny Haynes drive hit him in the stomach. He returned after the interval along with Kelsey, who was put on the left wing to shadow Stanley Matthews. Visibly in pain, Kelsey was withdrawn after 12 minutes. England won 3–1 with Haynes, Johnnie Brooks and Tom Finney getting their names on the scoresheet. That first Welsh win at Wembley was proving elusive.

Wales closed their Home International campaign with a goalless draw against Northern Ireland in Belfast. This otherwise forgettable match proved significant for Charles, undertaking the role of Wales captain for the first time. Sitting in the Windsor Park stand that day was Juventus president Umberto Agnelli who had flown over from Italy to watch the Leeds player in action. He was thinking of buying him.

CHAPTER SEVEN – TEARS IN GOTHENBURG

After a disappointing Home International campaign, Jimmy Murphy turned his attention to qualifying for the 1958 World Cup in Sweden. In the European section, Wales were drawn in Group Four with Czechoslovakia and East Germany, which meant two trips behind the Iron Curtain. Only the group winners qualified for Sweden and this meant victory over the talented Czechs at Ninian Park in the opening qualifier on 1 May 1957 was imperative.

Murphy's team selection was more complicated since Charles had just signed for Juventus. In this particular era, the turning out of a player for his country – for a friendly or competitive match – depended entirely on his club.

It was never easy persuading British clubs to release players for international duty but now the FAW had to deal with an Italian club – and one which had paid a whopping £65,000 fee for a player was bound to guard its asset jealously. But Juventus granted Charles permission to play against the Czechs and also agreed to release him for the back-to-back qualifiers in Prague and Leipzig later that month. Umberto Agnelli said he would give 'sympathetic consideration' to Charles playing against the East Germans at Ninian Park in September. A delighted Milwyn Jenkins, chairman of the FAW, sent Agnelli a telegram thanking him for his 'fine gesture'. A relieved Charles, whose wife Peggy had recently given birth to their third child, Peter, said, 'I am thoroughly delighted. What a lovely christening present. I wanted to play for Wales in the whole of the World Cup series and now everything is turning out all right.'

As Charles flew from Italy to London, where he caught a train to Cardiff to join up with his fellow Welshmen, it seemed Juventus would not stand in the way of his international ambitions. It was a false dawn. His five years in Turin were marred by arguments with Agnelli over playing for Wales. Juventus frequently refused him leave to play for his country. The decision deeply upset the patriotic Charles who once said, 'I would train in the woods if it meant playing for Wales.' Explains Mel Charles, 'John loved playing for Wales because it gave him a chance to meet up with his old mates. If he was picked for Wales and then Juventus stopped him playing he would get very upset.' Terry Medwin adds, 'John loved coming back to play for Wales. If playing for Wales meant that he had to fly over from Italy at 10 a.m., play at 3 p.m. and then fly back later that night he would do that.'

In his five years at Juventus he played only 14 times for his country and three of those matches came in the South American tour of May 1962 which Juventus allowed him to take part in because they were desperate for him to sign a new contract. 'I lost quite a few caps playing in Italy,' said Charles. 'Juventus wouldn't always let me go. If we were playing just before or just after an international I would have to stay behind. It broke my heart. You can win championships and cups but there's no feeling like playing for your country. I loved playing for Wales. It meant a lot to me.'

The Italians were not always at fault. The majority of international games were played on a Saturday and with Serie A matches taking place on a Sunday it was impossible to release Charles for Wales. His claim was valid when it came to midweek matches but Juventus were not always sympathetic.

The subject of Charles being released to play for Wales is a sensitive issue for Agnelli. 'We never stopped him playing for Wales,' he says. 'We never stopped any player from any country playing for their national team. We might not have been happy about them playing but we never stopped them playing for their national team.' His memory is playing tricks on him. Juventus refused to allow Charles to play in the World Cup qualifier against East Germany in Cardiff, which was a Wednesday fixture, and in the Home International match against Scotland on 13 November 1957, which was also a midweek date.

Charles has remained reluctant to criticise his former club for their possessive behaviour. 'You've got to look at it from Juventus's point of view,' he once explained. 'They paid a lot of money for me and they were worried to death I'd get injured. They were paying my wages so I had to do what they told me. I didn't have the privilege of saying what I could or couldn't do. Sometimes they'd let me go, other times they wouldn't. If it was an important match they tended to let me go. That wasn't always the case with friendlies.'

Against Czechoslovakia, Murphy picked Charles at centre-half. He was filling the void left by Ray Daniel who, the previous year, had been suspended from football for one season for accepting 'under the counter' payments from his club, Sunderland. Charles may have wooed Juventus with his phenomenal goalscoring exploits at Elland Road, but Murphy firmly believed he was the best centre-half in the world and marvelled at the way he could head a ball 40 yards clear. 'I didn't mind playing at the back. I played wherever they wanted me,' admitted Charles. 'I was just pleased to play.'

At centre-forward, Colin Webster, on the fringes of Manchester United's first team, won his first cap. The Welsh may have had home advantage but the Czechs were expected to win. They boasted world-class players such as left-back Ladislav Novak, left-half Josef Masopust and centre-forward Vladislav Bubnik. They also prepared meticulously for the game, arriving in Cardiff three days before the match and insisting on ten footballs for their training sessions which were held, somewhat surprisingly, at Ninian Park itself. The Welsh had to make do with the sports ground belonging to the Guest, Keen and Nettlefolds steelworks. The Czech trainer even tested the temperature of the bath water inside the Ninian Park changing-rooms before the players jumped in. Wales won with a strike from Blackburn's Roy Vernon seventeen minutes from time with Jack Kelsey performing heroics in the final ten minutes as the Czechs laid siege to his goal.

Charles had an outstanding match in defence but midway through the second half there was an anxious moment for his chaperone, Gigi Peronace, the Italian who had brokered his move from Leeds to Juventus a few weeks earlier. After going into a tackle

Charles fell to the ground and, clutching his leg, rolled over. Peronace feared a broken leg, which would have ended the £65,000 transfer. From his seat in the stand, the portly Calabrian jumped to his feet and shouted, 'Oh, my Johnny! What's happened to you, my Johnny!' To his relief, Charles was soon on his feet and thwarting the Czech attackers. After the final whistle the crowd invaded the pitch and mobbed Charles as he headed for the tunnel. Britain's most expensive footballer required police assistance to reach the dressing-room.

Wales's fate would be decided in the next two games, against East Germany in Leipzig and the return game against Czechoslovakia, in Prague. First came the East Germans. From London Airport the Welsh squad flew to Berlin via Hamburg and were then bussed, along a dreary autobahn, to Leipzig where they stayed at the Astoria Hotel, in the heart of the city centre. Charles, who had been involved in a tour of Holland with Leeds, made his own way to Leipzig via Amsterdam and Frankfurt and arrived two days before the game.

Respected football writers Willi Meisl and Erich Chemnitz both predicted a Welsh victory. So too did East Germany's Hungarian manager, Janos Gyarmati, who announced, 'We are amateurs playing against professionals.'

Charles was again picked at centre-half with brother Mel replacing the unimpressive Webster at centre-forward. Just before kick-off, Charles was caught up in an embarrassing situation. As skipper he was supposed to swap a bouquet of flowers with his opposite number but, as they exchanged pleasantries over the centre-spot, Charles found himself empty-handed. 'I was coming out of the dressing-room and someone gave me this bunch of flowers. They should have been given to John but obviously they mistook me for him,' recalls Mel Charles. 'After the national anthems were played I turned to my teammate, Dave Bowen, and said, "Dave, what do I do with these?" He told me to throw them into the crowd, which is what I did. Then John came over and started effing and blinding at me. Apparently he had to give the flowers to the East German captain and he'd spent five minutes looking for the flowers I'd thrown into the crowd. But at least I won us a bit more support.'

The match was played at the Zentralstadion, a vast, open-air concrete bowl which was built using bomb debris from the Second World War. The players and the match officials reached their changing-rooms by lift and this added a further ten minutes to half-time.

A capacity crowd of 110,000 watched the World Cup qualifier. The late Jim Hill, who reported on the match for the *Daily Express*, remembered the first time Charles touched the ball. 'He headed it from inside his penalty area to the halfway line and you could hear 110,000 people gasping in awe.' Charles was, however, outplayed by East Germany's one-armed forward, Willi Troger. Mel Charles gave Wales a sixth-minute lead but the East Germans came back, first through Gunther Wirth and then Troger, who had lost his right arm in an industrial accident. Recalling this game, and specifically his encounter with 29-year-old Troger, Charles said, 'When I saw him [Troger] I thought, "Bloody hell, he's only got one arm!" I didn't want to hurt him. I remember feeling sorry for him and maybe I shouldn't have done.'

Under Murphy's orders, the Charles brothers switched roles with 15 minutes left, Mel going to centre-half and his older brother moving to centre-forward, but to no avail. East Germany won 2–1. Wales were a huge disappointment. 'We were delighted to win but how Wales shocked us by their poor form. They appeared to be without fight,' said the *Sportecho Berlin* newspaper. In the *Western Mail*, the pipe-smoking Dewi Lewis was disappointed by Charles's display. 'Even John Charles seemed to be affected by the spiritless play of many in the team and I can't recall him being so slow in the tackle,' he wrote.

Defeat against the Czechs seven days later would mean the end of the Welsh World Cup dream. Murphy and his players flew, rather nervously, from East Berlin to Prague in a 48-seater Dakota aeroplane. After they arrived in Czechoslovakia, the Welsh selectors were punished for their short-sightedness. Incredibly, only twelve players were taken for these two qualifiers behind the Iron Curtain, compared to ten selectors. It would have been eleven but Milwyn Jenkins, chairman of the Welsh FA and a solicitor, had High Court commitments. With Dave Bowen and Derek Tapscott injured in the East Germany match and Reg

Davies bedridden with a sore throat, Murphy was left with only nine fit players to face the Czechs, so centre-half Ray Daniel and Swansea Town's centre-forward Des Palmer were flown over from Britain. 'There were more selectors than players,' said Charles. 'It was crazy. You've got to put the players first but with Wales it was the selectors first and the players second. One time we were playing abroad and we were one seat short on the aeroplane. In the end it was one of the players who had to stay behind, not one of the selectors.'

In the Czech capital, known as The City of a Hundred Spires, Charles and his teammates were given a tour of a chocolate factory and, in the evenings, they watched the European Boxing Championships since Prague's cinemas were booked up six months in advance. They also met the world-famous runner, Emil Zatopek, who had won three gold medals in the 1952 Olympics in Helsinki. Like the Welsh party, Zatopek was staying in the Hotel Paris.

Murphy, realising he needed Charles more in attack, used him as a centre-forward for this second game against the Czechs. Daniel played at centre-half with Palmer, who arrived in Prague on the day of the match, at inside-right. How Wales paid for their shambolic preparations. Inside Dukla Prague's Stadion Juliska, the Czechs tore them apart. They won 2–0 but as Mervyn Thomas said in the *South Wales Echo*, it could so easily have been 6–0.

Jack Kelsey had never seen Charles so ineffective for his country as he was in these two matches. 'I can safely say these were the two worst games I have ever seen the big fellow play for Wales,' the goalkeeper later admitted. It seemed the much-publicised transfer, coupled with travelling to Holland with Leeds and flying to Italy to undergo his Juventus medical, had worn out 'Big John'.

Wales's final qualifier, against East Germany in Cardiff, came four months after the Prague debacle. Czechoslovakia topped the group after beating the East Germans both home and away. This match was now purely academic and it came as no surprise when Umberto Agnelli told the FAW he would not be releasing Charles. The striker had scored in Juventus's first two games of the 1957–58 season and desperately wanted to play for his country but Agnelli refused to budge. 'We have plenty of goodwill for Wales and if circumstances were different John would be playing back home,' said Agnelli, five days before the East Germany clash. 'Unfortunately, we have so many new players in our side that they have not yet knitted together and it is essential they have plenty of practice before meeting the stronger clubs in the league.'

Wales did not miss their Gentle Giant, soundly beating the East Germans 4–1 on a wet evening at Ninian Park. Palmer, who replaced Charles in the Welsh attack, scored a hat-trick.

Two months later Wales, along with the rest of the teams that finished second in their group, were handed a dramatic World Cup reprieve by FIFA. Due to the Arab–Israeli conflict, the Asia–Africa qualifying section was plunged into disarray because the Arab nations refused to play Israel. FIFA demanded that Israel play some sort of qualifying match if they wanted to take part in the World Cup and decided they would meet one of the runner-up teams. In a low-key draw in Zurich on 15 December 1957, the names were put into the Jules Rimet Trophy – Wales, Holland, the Republic of Ireland, Bulgaria, Poland, Romania and the runner-up from the still unfinished Group Eight, either Italy or Northern Ireland. The team that was drawn to face Israel in a two-legged play-off was Wales.

Tel Aviv would host the first match on 15 January 1958. The return would be in Cardiff on 5 February. For Jimmy Murphy there was more good news, this time from Turin. Juventus would release Charles for both matches. With the ubiquitous Peronace at his side, Charles made his own way to Tel Aviv and arrived on the Sunday, three days before the match and a day ahead of his Wales teammates. The Juventus player, wearing a smart overcoat, was at the airport to greet his colleagues. 'The weather in Britain when we left was bloody awful and we arrived in Israel huddled in our overcoats,' recalls Stuart Williams. 'Then we saw John. He was all bronzed and he was wearing this beautiful, grey, Italian lightweight suit. Obviously the weather had been great in Italy!'

Peronace's constant accompaniment of Charles led one journalist to call him the highest-paid wet nurse in football. Says Alan Harrington, 'I asked Gigi Peronace what he was doing out in Israel. "In case John wants anything," he said. Whatever John wanted, Gigi would get. If John wanted to take us out for a meal

Gigi said he would come with us and pick up the tab.' Stuart Williams likened the Calabrian, who always wore a brown, pinstriped suit, no matter what the weather, to 'a mobile butler' out in Tel Aviv. 'He was running around opening doors for John and pulling chairs from under the table for him,' recounts the former West Bromwich Albion defender. 'He would ask him, "What do you want to drink, John?" John would say, "A cup of tea." And Gigi would get him a cup of tea. I don't think I ever saw John without Gigi at his side. It was amazing. He was like John's valet, a sort of manservant.'

The Welsh players found it difficult to acclimatise. In the space of 24 hours they had gone from cold, foggy Britain to training in sunshine and 80-degree heat.

It proved too much for reserve goalkeeper Graham Vearncombe who collapsed during a training session inside the half-built Ramat Gan Stadium, the venue of the match. The Cardiff City player was carried to the shade of the changing room to recover. 'I remember when we were training out in Israel seeing John lying down in the sun,' says Alan Harrington. 'While we were running and running he was sunning himself in the middle of the pitch. If it had been anyone else Jimmy Murphy would have said, "What the hell are you doing!" but because it was John he didn't say anything.'

Charles was asked to play centre-forward and was expected to bulldoze past his 17-year-old marker, Gideon Tisch. Wales were comfortable 2–0 winners, although Charles had a subdued game. The visitors' star man was Ivor Allchurch, who opened the scoring with a 25-yard shot shortly before half-time. Dave Bowen made it two in the second half.

The return at Ninian Park three weeks later was a formality. Wales, again with Charles spearheading the attack, dominated just as they had in Tel Aviv but Yaacov Chodoroff, the acrobatic Israeli goalkeeper dressed in black, prevented his side losing by a cricket score. Chodoroff was keeping a clean sheet until he collided with Charles while the pair jumped for a high ball with 20 minutes to go. Charles was unhurt but Chodoroff suffered concussion, a broken nose and a sprained shoulder. He was forced to carry on and Wales took advantage of his dazed condition, scoring twice through Allchurch and Cliff Jones. Afterwards the semi-conscious goalkeeper, unaware the Welsh crowd gave him a standing ovation as he left the pitch, was taken to nearby St David's Hospital. Banging into the colossal Charles clearly affected Chodoroff. In the hospital he spoke to the nurses in Hebrew because he believed he was in his native Israel. He also thought his side had lost 4–0 and not 2–0. As for Charles and his teammates, they celebrated World Cup qualification at the Park Hotel, not with champagne, which the FAW could not afford, but with beer.

Charles would be present at the 1958 World Cup yet for several weeks it appeared Wales would be without him in Sweden. When Italy failed to qualify for the competition, the Italian Football Federation had decided, after a 14-year absence, to resurrect its domestic cup competition, the *Coppa Italia*, which would start during the summer while the World Cup took place in Sweden. Juventus told Charles he would not be released because he had to play the early round matches against Pro Vercelli, Biellese and Torino.

Charles, who described the *Coppa Italia* as 'a run-out for the reserves', was incensed, especially when the other Italian clubs such as Milan, Inter, Lazio, Padova and Atalanta, released their star imports for World Cup duty. 'Different clubs had different rules and at Juventus we were always challenging for something so the club wanted to keep its best players,' explained the Welshman.

A cynic would conclude the Turin club was using the *Coppa Italia* as an excuse to prevent Charles playing for his country in Sweden. Four days after the first-leg win in Israel, Charles played for Juventus against Roma in Rome and was anonymous as *I Bianconeri* crashed to a 4–1 defeat. Umberto Agnelli blamed his lacklustre display on the trip to Israel. Three months later, Agnelli stopped Charles playing in a friendly against Northern Ireland in Cardiff. The decision provoked an angry response from the player. 'I'm far from happy about it,' he said. 'I've never felt so down in the dumps.'

There was better news on 24 April. With the World Cup opening ceremony just six weeks away, Juventus agreed to release Charles for the World Cup. 'Charles fully deserves the honour of playing for his country,' said Agnelli. The word in Turin was that this was a 'thank you' present for him doing so well in his first season. The championship was almost in the bag and with five Serie A matches remaining he was *capocannoniere* (top scorer) with 27 goals.

'Agnelli gave me his word of honour that if Wales beat Israel I could play for them in this World Cup,' Charles later revealed. 'When I reminded him of his promise he said I could go.'

Before the player had time to toast the news another, more worrying hurdle was thrown in his path. The Italian Football Federation said Charles could not play in the World Cup because 'insufficient notice' had been given for his release. While the FAW and Juventus argued his case, Charles was grounded. This spoiled Jimmy Murphy's pre-tournament preparations as the forward missed five days of training with the Welsh squad in London. He was also a conspicuous absentee when the Welsh party arrived at Stockholm's Bromma Airport on 2 June. 'If we were to have a chance we needed John,' said former Wales inside-right Ron Hewitt before his death in 2001. 'We had two wingers, Terry [Medwin] and Cliff [Jones], but without John our system was useless.' Mel Charles adds, 'Without John we didn't have a chance of reaching the quarter-finals. He was such an important player for us.' In the foyer of the Welsh squad's hotel, the luxurious Grand Hotel in Saltsjobaden, a high-class resort 20 miles from Stockholm, the Wales manager cut an anxious figure. 'How can I plan anything without knowing whether John Charles will turn up or not?'

Wales's opening match, against 1954 World Cup runners-up Hungary, was only 96 hours away when the Italians gave Charles the green light to fly to Sweden. 'I was beginning to feel very downhearted,' he recalled. 'It was a relief when I was told I could go. I mean, how many times does a player get to play in the World Cup?' He arrived at Bromma Airport, via Copenhagen, at three o'clock in the morning on 5 June. The plane was supposed to have landed four hours earlier but it was delayed in Copenhagen because of mechanical trouble. There was no one at the airport to meet him. One of the selectors, Fred Dewey, went to collect Charles and bring him back to the Grand Hotel, but he left Bromma at midnight believing the player was not going to turn up. Just as Charles was preparing to sleep on the airport's seats he was rescued by football journalist Dewi Lewis, in Sweden covering the World Cup for the *Western Mail*. Lewis drove Charles to Saltsjobaden.

Later that morning, as Charles walked into the dining room for breakfast, he received a surreal reception. As his younger brother recalls, 'I'll never forget it. John walked in. He looked like a Greek god because he was so tall and bronzed. The selectors saw him, threw down their knives and forks, stood up and started singing, "For he's a jolly good fellow."' The players, too, were delighted the team's star man had arrived. Derrick Sullivan went up to him and said, 'John, you're the greatest thing that's arrived in Saltsjobaden since sliced bread.' Explains Stuart Williams, 'John arriving from Italy was a big boost for us. That really lifted our spirits. He was such a vital part of our team.'

While the other Welsh players wore black blazers specially made for the World Cup by Simpson Ltd of Piccadilly, Charles had to stick with his normal attire. The fiasco over whether he could participate in Sweden or not had meant the Juventus player was absent when the squad were measured up for their blazers in London a few days before flying to Stockholm. The selectors had gambled and ordered one for Charles without the tailors knowing his exact requirements, but the blazer was too small. 'The sleeves were halfway up my arms and it didn't cover my bottom,' he explained. He ended up 'borrowing' clothes from reserve goalkeeper Ken Jones. 'John came only with a small attaché case while I brought a massive bag of clothes with me,' recalls the former Cardiff City and Scunthorpe player. 'He looked at my trousers and said, "These will be all right." I told him to give them back and do you know what he said to me? "Well, take them off me then." He was a huge bloke so I let it go.'

Wales were drawn in Group Three with Hungary, host nation Sweden and Mexico. The selectors were pessimistic about their team's chances and had booked the flight home after a week, when the first-round games finished. The first match was against the Hungarians in Sandviken, an industrial town 330 miles from the Arctic Circle, at the 20,000-capacity Jernvallen (the Iron Ground). With a team that became known as the Magical Magyars, Hungary had reached the 1954 World Cup final where they surprisingly lost to West Germany. The 1958 team was nowhere near as strong. Following the bloody Hungarian Uprising in 1956, most of Hungary's best players, such as Ferenc Puskas, Sandor Kocsis and Zoltan Czibor, exiled themselves and never played for their country again.

There were three survivors from the wonderful 1954 team in Lajos Baroti's side – goalkeeper Gyula Grosics, wing-half Jozsef Bozsik and the deep-lying centre-forward Nandor Hidegkuti. Grosics and Bozsik were both 32 while Hidegkuti was 36 and overweight. Still, the Magyars were expected to beat the Welsh but Baroti, with good cause, feared Charles. When he heard Juventus had released him for the tournament he told the press, 'This will make our task much harder.'

Hungary had a distinct advantage over their opponents. They were based in Sandviken while the Welsh, down in Saltsjobaden, had to endure a three-hour bus ride. Charles remembered the journey 'went on and on'. When they arrived they saw the Hungarians warming up on the pitch. 'With us it was a case of getting off the bus and getting changed for the match,' said the Juventus star. On a sunny evening Hungary took the lead after four minutes through Bozsik's 15-yard drive.

Charles was heavily marked. His reputation preceded him and every time he received the ball two Hungarians closed in on him. They reckoned that if they removed Charles from the match they would stop Wales. In the opening minutes the striker was cut down at the ankles by Lajos Tichy, the first of a barrage of fouls on the forward. 'I remember jumping for a cross and one of the Hungarians put both his hands around my neck,' he said. Yet he rose above the constant fouling to head the equaliser in the 26th minute. Charles soared above everyone in the penalty area to head Cliff Jones's corner past Grosics. 'John bulleted the ball into the net,' says Jones. 'You could hear the thump as he headed it. It was a real thump.' It would be the only goal Charles scored in Sweden. 'John used to cause panic in the penalty box,' explains Terry Medwin. 'He could jump way above the defenders but he never used his elbows or pushed. He was very clever. He would jump just before they did and he would just lean on them to stop them getting that extra two or three inches.' The match ended 1–1. The Stockholm daily, *Tidningen*, was in no doubt as to who was the star of this game. 'John Charles was gigantic' it said.

Three days later Wales faced Mexico, beaten 3–0 by Sweden in their opening game, in Stockholm's Rasunda Stadium. Jimmy Murphy's men were expected to win comfortably. Charles recalled his manager's pre-match talk inside the dressing-room. As usual, it lacked political correctness. 'He was calling the Mexicans "ranchos" and said they were only good for riding horses, not playing football.' Murphy had watched the Mexicans lose against the Swedes. 'This lot are rubbish!' he told his players. How the Latin-Americans were to prove him wrong. Wales were hopeless, although Ivor Allchurch put them ahead after 12 minutes. In the last minute Mexico snatched a deserved equaliser when Jaime Belmonte headed past Kelsey. Charles had one of his worst games for his country. His contribution amounted to four harmless headers as Jorge Romo, Mexico's unknown centre-half, marked him out of the game. 'Everyone played badly in that one, even John,' says Cliff Jones. The press was scathing the following day. 'WELSH DISPLAY WAS SHOCKING. DRAW WITH MEXICO MAY MEAN EXIT FROM EVENT' said the *Western Mail*. 'NO ALIBIS FOR WALES. EVEN CHARLES FLOPPED AGAINST FIGHTING MEXICANS' was the headline in the *South Wales Echo*. Its football correspondent, Mervyn Thomas, wrote, 'I have seen Wales play some bad internationals. This time they were so downright disappointing that few of them deserve one halfpenny of the fifty pounds they each picked up for playing. In fact, I have suggested to them that they should donate their fees to some worthy charity.'

Wales's fate would be decided in their final group match, against Sweden in the Rasunda Stadium four days later. There was encouraging news for Murphy. The Swedes had already qualified for the quarter-finals after winning their first two matches and their English manager, George Raynor, decided to rest some of his key players such as Nils Liedholm, Gunnar Gren and Kurt Hamrin. A Welsh victory would guarantee a date against World Cup favourites Brazil in the last eight. A draw would probably mean a play-off against either Hungary or Mexico to decide who joined Sweden in the quarter-finals since goal difference did not count in 1958.

Murphy went for a goalless draw. Charles was asked to protect his brother, Mel, who was Wales's first-choice centre-half in the competition. By pushing Charles into a defensive role Murphy denied the public a fascinating duel between the Juventus forward and the Swedish centre-half, Julli Gustavsson, who played for Serie

A club Atalanta. The pair had some titanic battles in Italian football but on this occasion Gustavsson had nothing to worry about and what was arguably the dullest match of the series ended 0–0. The Welsh players were jeered off the pitch by the 30,000 crowd and afterwards Charles admitted he 'felt sorry for the people who paid to see it'. Dewi Lewis, writing in the *Western Mail*, said watching this game was like being 'at a Sunday afternoon tea party'. The Swedish press was more critical. Journalists had marvelled at Charles's displays during Juventus's pre-season tour of Sweden the previous summer, yet here he was being used – or, as they saw it, abused – by Murphy's negative tactics. 'What Are Wales Doing To John Charles?' cried *Aftonbladet* while *Dagens Nyeter* branded him the 'flop' of the World Cup so far. Raynor felt Wales 'could and should have won' and was surprised his opposite number opted for safety first.

Charles, who never had a bad word to say about anyone, refused to condemn Murphy's negative tactics. 'If we stopped Sweden scoring then we would stay in the World Cup. I think Jimmy did the right thing. We couldn't score a lot of goals so he concentrated on defence.' As for the selectors who had booked their flight home after the first week, they had to fly to London and come straight back.

As the Hungarians thumped Mexico 4–0 later that evening, it meant a second contest with Lajos Baroti's side in Stockholm two days after the Sweden match. The evening sunshine lit up the virtually empty Rasunda Stadium. A crowd of only 2,832 turned up for this play-off, the lowest gate in a World Cup since the first tournament in 1930. They watched the Hungarians inflict a series of violent fouls on Charles which went unpunished by referee Nikolai Latychev. The Russian was a controversial choice for this match. Here we had an Iron Curtain referee officiating a game involving an Iron Curtain team. The Welsh were worried Latychev would favour Hungary and their worst fears were soon realised. In the first half he refused to award them two blatant penalties, both involving Charles. First, he was hauled down at the waist by Antal Kotasz. A minute later, he was shoved in the back by Sandor Matrai.

Against the run of play Lajos Tichy put Hungary ahead in the

33rd minute. Charles, who was being hacked down at every turn – particularly by the burly Ferenc Sipos – was denied a third penalty early in the second half. As he tried to reach Terry Medwin's corner, Sipos held him down by his hips. 'Sipos was at John all the time, right from the first whistle,' recalls Cliff Jones. 'All the Hungarian defenders were having a go at him, elbowing him and giving him a dig.' In the face of provocation the forward created Wales's equaliser. Just seconds after limping back onto the pitch after being fouled by Kotasz, he picked out Ivor Allchurch who beat Gyula Grosics from 25 yards. After a shocking tackle from behind Charles spent the last 20 minutes hobbling around the pitch like Long John Silver. 'Out of all the games I played in, in England, Italy and for Wales, this one was the worst,' said Charles. The Hungarians inflicted so much damage on him that he was forced to miss the showdown with Brazil. 'They kicked hell out of me and the referee didn't give me any protection. They never stopped kicking from start to finish. The Hungarians used such tactics because, I suppose, they wanted to win and they were prepared to do anything to win.'

The Juventus man played an indirect role in Wales's 76th-minute winner. Terry Medwin capitalised on a mix-up between Grosics and Matrai and sprinted towards the Hungarian goal. Charles's presence in the penalty area caused Grosics, who thought Medwin was going to pass to him, to leave a gap at his near post which the Tottenham winger exploited. 'Hungary kicked John all over the park,' recalls Medwin. 'They went for him right from the start yet John never moaned or retaliated. He just got up and carried on.'

Later that night the Welsh players celebrated in the smart Copacabana Club inside the Grand Hotel. Here Charles's peacemaking skills were once again deployed. A drunk Colin Webster headbutted one of the club's waiters, Verner Felt, after he tried to chat up Felt's girlfriend. Felt ended up in Charles's lap. The former Leeds player rose to his feet, grabbed hold of Webster and, according to Medwin, 'lifted him a foot off the ground and carried him out of the club'. Ken Jones, Webster's friend, was also inebriated, and he shouted at Charles, 'Put him down, John, or I'll land one on you!' The manager of the club threatened to call the police and there was talk Felt would bring an assault charge against

Webster, but Charles organised a whip-round to compensate the waiter who lost three teeth in the incident, with each of the 18 players chipping in two pounds of their spending allowance. The whole affair was swept under the carpet.

The following day the Welsh squad left Saltsjobaden for Gothenburg, the venue for their quarter-final against Brazil. There was one question everyone was asking – would Charles be fit in time to play after the pummelling he took against Hungary? Murphy set the masseurs to work on his bruised body as soon as they arrived at their base in Kungälv, just outside Gothenburg and the player himself told the press, 'It will take an army to stop me turning out against Brazil. I am doing everything possible to be fit enough to play.'

Murphy and the team doctor, Bill Hughes, tried to raise the player's spirits. 'You'll be fit, John! Don't worry, you'll be fit!' ranted Murphy. Not everyone shared his optimism. 'John's legs were so swollen they looked like tree trunks,' says Mel Charles. 'It was clear on the day of the match that there was no way he could play.' The forward took part in a training session but even though he could run without any problem, he was unable to turn on his right leg. He also found he could not do a running jump. Jack Jones rubbed hard at the problem leg but it failed to improve. 'I was thinking during the Hungary match, "If we win this I won't be playing in the next game." I was in a hell of a lot of pain,' said Charles.

The final decision on whether Charles should play against Brazil was left to the player. Before informing Murphy of his decision, he confessed to his younger brother that if he did play he would only let the team down. 'I told Jimmy I couldn't play, that my legs couldn't do it. If I did play, and I suffered another injury during the game, I would have been out altogether and we would have been down to ten men. It was better that someone who was 100 per cent fit should play.' The selectors turned to Colin Webster who, the day before, had been told he would never play for Wales again following the disgraceful scenes in the Copacabana Club.

On 19 June, two days after their play-off with Hungary, Wales walked out into the futuristic Nya Ullevi Stadium for the biggest game in their history and without their most feared player. 'You would never see John upset but he was down before the Brazil game,' says Terry Medwin. 'His eyes were a bit watery. That was the only time I've ever seen him upset.' Murphy told Charles he could fly home to Italy if he wanted, but the player decided to stay in Gothenburg and he watched this epic quarter-final alongside Murphy on the bench. 'Brazil were over the moon John wasn't playing because they were no good in the air,' comments Mel Charles.

Brazil were most people's tip to win the trophy. They were littered with world-class players. There was Didi, their midfield general who was known for his *folha secca* (falling leaf) free-kicks. Garrincha, the 'Little Bird', terrorised left-backs on the right wing. Left-back Nilton Santos had perfected the overlapping run and goalkeeper Gilmar was one of the best in the world. At centre-forward there was the 19-year-old José Altafini for whom Milan had just paid £80,000. His partner in attack, Pelé, was even younger at 17. Pelé was introduced in the final group match, the 2–0 win over the Soviet Union, and kept his place.

Brazil, whose World Cup preparations embarrassed the Welsh – they brought with them a dentist, a psychologist, chefs and their own food – were overwhelming favourites to win this quarter-final. Charles provided his teammates with a cash incentive to beat the South Americans. 'At Juventus John was earning much more money than we were,' says Cliff Jones. 'Before the game he said to us, "If you win today I'll give each of you ten pounds." That was a good amount in 1958. It was a nice gesture but we nearly fainted because John was never forthcoming with money!'

Perhaps spurred on by the thought of an extra tenner, Wales started brightly and after five minutes Charles watched Webster squander a great chance. Cliff Jones crossed into the penalty area for the Manchester United forward but with just Gilmar to beat he missed the target. Sitting alongside Murphy, Charles turned to his manager. 'I would have scored that,' he said. That was the end of Webster, who was eaten alive by the Brazilian centre-half and captain, Bellini. After 20 minutes Brazil took control but the *selecao* were denied by the brilliance of the Welsh defence and goalkeeper Jack Kelsey. Murphy's side, with wingers Terry Medwin and Cliff Jones enjoying a fruitful time against the Brazilian full-backs, also looked threatening on the counter-attack.

Wales's resistance lasted until the 73rd minute when Pelé's mis-hit effort took the slightest deflection off Stuart Williams' boot and rolled past the helpless Kelsey. It was his first World Cup goal and it was enough to win this quarter-final. What would have been the result had Charles played? Murphy, who died in 1989, always maintained Wales would have progressed to the semi-finals had the Gentle Giant played in that match. 'With John Charles fit,' he later said, 'I think we could have beaten Brazil.' Many of the 1958 squad agree. 'Terry [Medwin] and I had probably our best games of the tournament against Brazil,' says Cliff Jones. 'We got a lot of good crosses in. No disrespect to Colin but he wasn't John Charles. I'm certain that had John played that day he would have got on the end of those crosses and made them count.' Mel Charles adds, 'I'm not being biased because I'm John's brother but I think we would have beaten Brazil had John played. We would have gone all the way to the final.'

The Welsh players returned home gallant heroes. All four British sides had qualified for the 1958 World Cup but the Welsh had been the most successful. Scotland were eliminated in the first round, England fell in a play-off with the Soviet Union while Northern Ireland reached the quarter-finals but were swept aside 4–0 by France. One person dared to criticise Wales's approach to the World Cup. Sweden manager George Raynor claimed Murphy had wasted Charles's attacking talents and 'threw away the one man who might even have got them into the semi-final'. He added that, had Charles 'been used properly' in the group matches, Wales might not have needed to play Hungary in a play-off, the match in which they lost Charles. A straight-talking Yorkshireman, Raynor said, 'Having persuaded Juventus to release Charles, the world's number one centre-forward, Wales proceeded to waste him in all but the first match. Instead of using him as a centre-forward, and what a match-winner John Charles can be, he was used defensively.'

For Charles, the tournament was an anti-climax. The top scorer in Serie A failed to live up to the hype surrounding his arrival in Sweden. It was his younger brother Mel who stole the limelight, for once emerging from John's shadow. Mel was named in the 1958 World Cup XI while Pelé hailed him as the best centre-half in the competition. 'I didn't have a great World Cup, just a decent one,' admitted Charles. 'I had a couple of good games and a couple of bad ones as well. I was a marked man and the Hungarians kicked me to pieces in the two games we played against them.'

Charles was forced to wait until November 1959 for his first post-World Cup international, against Scotland at Hampden Park. Again he fought with Juventus to be released. With less than a fortnight to go before the match the Italians, who valued Charles at £280,000, had not given him their blessing. The player, who claimed there was a clause in his new two-year contract saying he could play midweek matches, was furious and threatened to quit Italian football if Juventus stopped him travelling. 'I am sick and tired of being let down,' he said. 'Unless Juventus release me to play for Wales against Scotland, I want to be released from playing in Italy.' One morning Charles failed to turn up for training, the first time he had missed a session since arriving in Turin two years earlier. When the club asked him to report to their headquarters in Piazza San Carlo to explain himself later that day he failed to turn up. The rebellious behaviour eventually paid off. Charles, at centre-half, played in the 1–1 draw in Glasgow and scored with a well-taken free-kick. 'Yesterday I spent 20 minutes practising free-kicks 30 yards from goal. It was certainly 20 minutes well spent,' he said after the match. 'I felt rather strange at first back in the red jersey of Wales but I soon settled down to enjoy myself.' The Scottish FA were glad Charles won his battle with *I Bianconeri* as his presence ensured a further £10,000 in gate receipts.

Charles was not always victorious against Juventus. The Italians refused him permission to play in the two World Cup qualifiers against Spain in the spring of 1961 even though they sent FAW secretary Herbert Powell a letter declaring Charles could play against the Spaniards at Ninian Park on 19 April. Charles's name appeared in their 22-man squad list for that game but Juventus then changed their minds and also said the player would not be available for the return match in Madrid on 18 May. Juventus were on top of Serie A, just two points ahead of Milan and three ahead of Inter, and within touching distance of a twelfth *Scudetto*. They could not afford to part company with their player. 'It would be absurd for us to do without Charles's invaluable support in even a single league match, and to let him run the risk of being injured in an international,' explained Juventus's vice-president, Remo Giordanetti. His absence in those back-to-back qualifiers arguably cost his country a place in the 1962 World Cup in Chile. Ken Leek played centre-forward in both games. A dependable striker for Birmingham City, Leek was no John Charles. Wales lost 2–1 in Cardiff and drew 1–1 in Madrid. Spain went on to play – and beat – Morocco to book their place in Chile while the Welsh reflected on what might have been had Juventus released their best player.

Charles's second international since the 1958 World Cup came the following October when he was released to play in the 1–1 draw against England at Ninian Park before Juventus took the hard line regarding Wales's three-match tour of South America in May 1962. The Italian club blocked him travelling with his teammates until the issue of signing a new contract for the 1962–63 season arose. Juventus wanted him to stay, Charles was talking about returning to England. In a bid to keep him in Turin they reversed their decision and allowed Charles to take part in the tour, which involved two matches against Brazil, in Rio de Janeiro and Sao Paulo, and one against Mexico in Mexico City. Charles did not get the all-clear from his club until midday on 11 May – the day before the first friendly against Brazil. He rushed to Genoa, south of Turin, for his visa, before driving east to Milan to catch the plane to Rio. He arrived at Malpensa with minutes to spare. FAW officials were unaware Juventus had changed their mind and there was no one to meet him at Rio's Galeao Airport. Memories of Sweden 1958.

According to newspaper reports the Welsh players, stripped to the waist while they trained inside the 200,000-capacity Maracana Stadium, were 'astonished' when Charles appeared unannounced. His presence, said the *Western Mail*, 'sent morale soaring'. Brazil won the first game 3–1 in front of a 100,000 crowd. According to Charles, who played at centre-half, the *selecao* were a better team than they had been four years earlier. Garrincha and Coutinho gave the Brazilians a 2–0 lead at half-time. After the break Ivor Allchurch showed a touch of Latin flair by scoring with a 25-yard shot before Pelé, the man who sank Wales in the 1958 World Cup, put the game beyond Wales's reach. Brazil repeated the result in the second match inside Sao Paulo's Pacaembu Stadium four days later but Wales gave them a much harder game. Ken Leek cancelled out Vava's opener and Wales were level until the 82nd minute when the Brazilians scored twice in sixty seconds, first through Pelé and then Afiaris.

Next it was Mexico City, where Wales lost a bad-tempered match against the Mexicans. The bad feeling from the 1958 game obviously lingered. Welsh winger Cliff Jones was sent off while two Mexicans, Jesus Del Muro and Antonio Jasso, were also dismissed. Charles was switched to centre-forward for this final friendly and he scored his team's goal in the 2–1 defeat. 'John Charles showed why he and Omar Sivori are the golden couple of Italian football,' said *La Aficion* newspaper.

In November 1962, Charles signed for Roma. With the club versus country wrangles at Juventus fresh in his mind, he insisted on a clause in his contract allowing him to play for his country whenever he wished. The FAW was unaware of this and when they cabled Roma asking if he could play against England at Wembley and received no reply, Herbert Powell assumed Roma had refused the request. The Italians failed to respond because they were cabled at the weekend when no one was present at the club offices. 'I did not realise for one moment that Wales did not know I was available,' said an upset Charles. 'If I had, I would have sent a cable or telephoned them.' He did not miss much – Wales were thrashed 4–0.

He could have played in the European Championship qualifier against Hungary in Budapest earlier that month but Roma had a Fairs Cup match on the same night, against Turkish side Altay Izmir, and having just signed for the club he made a political decision to stay in the Italian capital.

Charles won 38 Wales caps, surprisingly few considering he is the greatest footballer the principality has ever produced and that his international career stretched over 13 years. Playing in Italy had a price. His last cap came in May 1965, on a wet afternoon in Moscow against the Soviet Union. Wales lost this World Cup qualifier 2–1 and Charles, now playing for Cardiff City, was blamed for the first Soviet goal. Playing at inside-right he lost possession near the halfway line. Roared on by the 105,000 crowd inside the Lenin Stadium, the Soviets broke away and Valentin Ivanov flicked the ball past Tony Millington. Charles recovered and his performance drew praise from the Moscow evening newspaper, *Vechernyaya Moskva*. 'John Charles may not have been as fast as he used to be but he certainly showed us that he still has great ability.' It was a dignified farewell to the international scene.

CHAPTER EIGHT – *LA FINE*

I f Charles's first season at Juventus was a glorious triumph, the second was an anti-climax. Despite fielding exactly the same side that demolished all opposition in 1957–58, Juventus were never really in the championship race, finishing fourth, ten points behind champions Milan. 'Our bellies were full,' explains Bruno Garzena. 'We felt satisfied with what we had done in 1958. Brocic should have been harder with us but he wasn't one for wielding the stick.' The Charles–Sivori tandem did not click as it had the previous season with Charles scoring 19 and Sivori 15. The opposition had got wise to the way Brocic's side played and plotted their tactics accordingly. In a candid interview with *Tuttosport* in 1960, after Juventus had just won *Lo Scudetto* for the 11th time, Sivori reflected on the disappointment of the 1958–59 campaign. 'Our first championship was won because teams did not understand John's play. We put the ball to his head, he would jump and score. Simple. There has never been a player who can head the ball like him. But we abused John really and the second season we were made to pay. The defences learned how to stop him, fairly and unfairly, and he didn't score as much.'

As if providing a lame defence of their crown was not bad enough, Juventus's first crack at the European Cup proved a disaster. As champions of Italy they were expected to give the holders, Real Madrid, a run for their money and *I Bianconeri* were handed a reasonably gentle first-round draw, against Austrian champions Wiener Sportklub. The Turin side made hard work of the first leg, winning 3–1 at the Comunale courtesy of Sivori's hat-trick. In the second leg, in the Prater Stadium a week later, and on a cold and windy night in Vienna, Juventus suffered what remains the heaviest defeat in their history. They were crushed 7–0. According to Charles, the Serie A aristocrats were overconfident going into the return leg. 'We thought the second leg in Vienna was a formality,' he confessed afterwards. 'We thought Wiener Sportklub couldn't give us a two-goal start *and* a beating, not even at their ground. That's where we came unstuck.' Juventus's record in the European Cup during the Charles–Sivori era was pretty dismal. They were involved again in 1960–61 but once more fell at the first hurdle, this time against the Bulgarian champions, Sofia's Army team, CDNA. They won the first leg in Turin 2–0 but, just as had been the case against Sportklub, they capitulated in the away leg, losing 4–1. It was only at the third attempt, in 1961–62, that Juventus put on a respectable show in the European Cup, reaching the quarter-final and forcing Real Madrid, five-time winners of the trophy, into a play-off before losing 3–1 in a brutal and controversial match in Paris.

The Juventus players blame their lacklustre performances in the European Cup on the fact that the competition, then in its embryonic stage (it was launched in 1955–56), was not high on the Turin club's list of priorities. 'I know it sounds very strange but in those days the players did not really believe in this competition,' explains Umberto Agnelli. 'Winning Serie A was by far our most important objective.' The players viewed French journalist Gabriel Hanot's brainchild as a nuisance and an unwelcome diversion. 'We treated it as just another competition and that's why we didn't do much in it,' says Giorgio Stivanello. 'We didn't have any ambitions to win it. We never valued it as a competition. All we wanted to win was our own championship.' Flavio Emoli echoes the view of his ex-colleague. 'In those years the competition was not like it is today. It was not a glamorous competition.'

However, these views sit uncomfortably with two facts. Firstly, the players of Fiorentina and Milan, who were involved in the European Cup prior to Juventus, evidently took it seriously, both reaching the final and losing – in Milan's case after extra-time – to the all-conquering Real Madrid of Di Stefano, Kopa and Gento.

Secondly, the massacre in Prater led to the demise of Juventus coach Ljubisa Brocic which begs the question: why sack a championship-winning coach for losing a supposedly unimportant match?

Whenever quizzed about Juventus's woeful results in the competition's early years, Charles has always reiterated what his former colleagues have said. 'We always got knocked out quickly in the European Cup,' he recalled. 'The European Cup had only just started and Juventus didn't really worry about it. It was always the championship. The club liked to show how many titles they had won.'

After that 7–0 caning at the hands of Wiener Sportklub in November 1958, Charles endured his most frightening experience in a career that spanned four decades. As he lay in the Molinette Hospital, he overheard doctors discussing the amputation of his left leg. Charles, not for the first time, had been identified by the Viennese as Juventus's most dangerous player and to eliminate him from the game the Austrian defenders, in particular their international stopper Leopold Barschandt, kicked the forward from start to finish. 'I complained to the referee,' said Charles after the game. 'He said he didn't see anything wrong.' After the match Charles limped back to the dressing-room. The following morning, after the team returned to Turin, he was sent to hospital. 'I got a swelling on my groin the day after the match, then I broke out into a fever,' he said. He remained in hospital for four weeks, receiving injections of penicillin every two hours to relieve the pain. 'The doctor in charge said he was in two minds whether my left leg might have to come off. Time passed and I somehow got better. But I'll never forget that match.'

Another game that raised concerns for Charles's well-being was the clash against Fiorentina in Florence during his first season in Italy. In the first half Charles went to head the ball towards the Fiorentina goal but, as he tried to reach it, his chest smacked into one of the posts and the player bounced backwards. For several seconds, as his huge figure lay motionless on the ground, the crowd held its breath. 'We heard this noise – it was a crack – and we all rushed over to John to see what had happened to him,' explains Rino Ferrario. Agnelli was watching the game from the VIP box. 'I thought, "My God, he has killed himself!"' he recalls. And Emoli adds, 'He hit the post with such force that we all thought he was dead. He was foaming at the mouth.' But Charles rose to his feet, lifted up his shirt and rubbed his chest before telling his colleagues he was all right. '*Io buono, io buono*,' he said.

Apart from a sore, red chest, he was unhurt. 'I looked at the post after Charles got up and it was still shaking!' says Ferrario. During the break Agnelli rushed into the dressing-room to see if his prize asset was badly injured. 'He was behaving as if nothing had happened,' Agnelli remembers. 'Anyone else would have been killed but he was so strong.'

In the dressing-room, when Charles took off his jersey, a horrified Gianfranco Leoncini caught sight of the haematoma on his chest. 'Yet he had the strength to go back onto the field and play as normal,' he says.

Brocic was replaced by former inside-forward Renato Cesarini, an Italian who had emigrated to Argentina but returned to his native country in the 1930s to play for Juventus. He was close to Sivori and made him the team's *uomo decisivo* (key player). Umberto Colombo believes Sivori assuming the role of top dog at the Comunale was one of the reasons Charles ended his love affair with Juventus in 1962.

The winning of the *Coppa Italia* provided some consolation for the Welshman following the disappointments in both the league and in Europe in 1958–59. Inter were beaten 4–1 at San Siro in the final with Charles scoring twice. 'I remember one of John's goals,' says Colombo. 'Boniperti was calling for me to give him the ball but I didn't pass to him. Instead I hit a long ball for John who headed it past the Inter goalkeeper, Giuliano Sarti. Boniperti then started moaning at me. "Why didn't you give me the ball?" John went up to him and said, "Boni, I scored. What are you complaining for?"'

The following year Juventus reasserted themselves as Italy's number one team, winning *Lo Scudetto* in the same fashion as they did in 1958, finishing eight points ahead of second-placed Fiorentina. Once again Charles and Sivori scored 50 goals between them, but this time Sivori was *capocannoniere* with 27 while

Charles bagged 23. Sivori would win the award for a second time the following year.

The newspapers started to talk of a rivalry between the two men, but Sivori insists there was no bad feeling between himself and the player Boniperti described as 'the Norseman'. He says, 'There was never ever rivalry between John and me. The newspapers kept saying there was a fight between us for the *capocannoniere* award but that was not the case. It never bothered me when John won the award and I'm sure John was not bothered when I won it. I was pleased when John finished top scorer in his first year. Whether I was *capocannoniere* or John, it didn't bother me. We were both playing for the same club and we became great friends. He was such a nice person. He was as nice off the pitch as he was on it. He was always there to help people and he was the peacemaker at the club.'

Sivori has long disliked talk of a silent war between himself and *Il Gigante Buono*. There would be no better story than the club's two star players being involved in a dressing-room feud, but after he and Charles won their second championship Sivori took great lengths to dismiss such gossip. In an interview with *Tuttosport* – the bible for the Juventus *tifosi* – he said, 'I would like everyone to understand what John means to us and to me more than the others. He is unique, inimitable. You will never find a man better than him, more honest than him, more sober than him. He who does not agree with John is a bad man. I say that I am his friend, and his friend I am. Before I think of him as a footballer, I admire him as a human being.'

Visiting his best man and former housemate in Turin during the 1961–62 season, Charles's last with Juventus, Peter Harrison saw no evidence of bad blood between the two forwards. 'We were driving around Turin in Sivori's sports car. There was Sivori and John in the front and I was in the back with Sivori's girlfriend,' he remembers. 'I wasn't sitting on the seat, I was sitting on the back of the car. John saw police ahead and he told me to get down because they'd pull us over but Sivori's girlfriend said to me, "If the police say anything tell them to fuck off." John started laughing. Apparently he had been teaching her English. That was the English he had been teaching her! The police did see us but they didn't do anything because they recognised the two players.'

Sivori was one of the most influential players in the Juventus dressing-room, along with captain Giampiero Boniperti. When Boniperti retired in 1961, the former River Plate man emerged as the dominant figure. 'Sivori scored brilliant goals for us but John helped him to score those brilliant goals,' said Ernesto Castano. 'Sivori was very grateful to John and even today he speaks of his gratitude to John, and Sivori is not the sort of person who finds it easy to show reverence to any other player.'

The 4–1 win over Lanerossi Vicenza – a match in which Charles scored twice – at the Comunale on the opening day of the 1959–60 *campionato* set the tone for the rest of the season. A 4–0 win at Padova followed, and three weeks later came the 7–0 hammering of Alessandria in Turin. On 6 December 1959, they lost at Napoli but their next defeat did not come until 28 February 1960 when they were surprisingly beaten at home by Atalanta. During that period Cesarini's side won nine of their ten league fixtures, among them a 6–3 win in Ferrara against Spal where Charles, despite some rough treatment by Valeriano Balloni, scored the third and final hat-trick of his Juventus career.

For Christmas, the club allowed Charles a week-long break in Leeds with his family, to visit his in-laws. There was a proviso. Charles had to train in order to stay at 90 kilos, his optimum weight. When they returned to Italy Peronace picked them up at the airport. 'Have you trained, John?' he asked. 'Every morning,' came the reply. Cesarini later checked his weight on the scales. It showed 90 kilos but Cesarini was not convinced he had been training. With a wry smile, he said, 'You eat so bad in England that you don't have to train not to put weight on, eh, John?'

The coach had every right to fear the player piling on the pounds while he was on holiday in West Yorkshire since the Welshman was blasé about diet. Before one match a gobsmacked Garzena saw him devour a *bistecca alla valdostana*, a heavy dish which consists of a large steak with melted cheese on top, cooked with onions and potatoes in a red wine sauce. 'That meal would have been like eating a brick soaked in water, but believe it or not the coaching staff let him eat it!' says the former full-back. 'We did not have dieticians who cared for us. All that counted is what you did on the pitch, and because John was doing the business they did not mind what he ate.' After another game the players watched in amazement as Charles guzzled down three bottles of *aranciata* (orangeade) one after the other.

For a time Fiorentina pushed Juventus hard for the 1960 championship and after beating *I Bianconeri* 1–0 in Florence on 27 March they were just two points behind their arch rivals from Piedmont. The following week Charles and his teammates faced Bologna at home and the man who would mark Charles, Giovanni Mialich, was in a confident mood. 'As small as I am a lot of people ask me how can I handle him [Charles] efficiently,' said the Bologna defender. 'I would tell a lie if I said John Charles is not a great player, but the fact remains he has never intimidated me and I'm not scared of him. I have already played against him three or four times and managed not to look a bad player.' Mialich must have regretted those pre-match remarks. Despite the visitors playing a five-man *catenaccio* defence, Juventus won 3–0 with Charles – whom Eugenio Fascetti, Bologna's young inside-forward, hailed as 'unique' – scoring twice. '*Niente crisi*' (no crisis), said Cesarini afterwards. He was right. Juventus blew Fiorentina away by winning six and drawing one of their next seven games.

During this period Charles the pop star was born. A proud son of the Land of Song, Charles fancied himself as a crooner, as he demonstrated before Wales's World Cup play-off match against Israel in Tel Aviv in January 1958. Charles, along with his brother, Mel, and team captain Dave Bowen, were invited to make an appearance at a five-star hotel where an Anglo–Asia conference was being held. 'It was full of Muslims, hundreds of them, and they were all kneeling down,' says Mel Charles. 'The announcer said, "We have three distinguished guests with us today and one of them is the greatest footballer in the world, John Charles. He is also a good singer." He then turned to John. "Mr Charles, would you give us a song?" So John walked up and said, "I'm going to sing a little Welsh number called 'That Old Black Magic'."' The song was actually sung by the American Sammy Davis Jr. 'Dave and I couldn't believe what he was doing because nearly everyone in the room was black!' adds Mel. 'I'm sure John didn't realise what he was saying but we ran out of the place and left him on the stage. We found out later that they had clapped John like hell after he finished singing.'

The Juventus players soon discovered Charles's musical streak. Leoncini recalls, 'Every time we were travelling on the team coach John would start singing.' Emoli adds, 'John was a good singer. He would sing at the club, at parties, at every occasion. I liked singing as well and sometimes [Gino] Stacchini and I would be his chorus.' Stivanello remembers Charles *il cantante* (the singer). 'Every time the club had a party he would get up and sing. A party would not be the same if John did not sing. He was a real entertainer – he would get everyone to clap their hands and make them sing as well.'

His favourite song was Tennessee Ernie Ford's 'Sixteen Tons'. 'All it took was for one player to start singing "Sixteen Tons", whether it was at a party or on the coach, and up John would get to finish the song off,' says Castano.

Charles was 'spotted' by a talent scout while singing with his Juventus teammates at La Capannina nightclub in Alassio, a seaside resort near the French border. This was a favourite haunt of *I Bianconeri* players and where some of them would enter the *Angelo d'Oro* (Golden Angel) singing competition. 'If John Charles makes records he will sell only eleven copies – the players will buy ten and Cesarini the other one,' joked Sivori. After the club gave its blessing, Charles recorded four tracks with the record company, Centra-Fonit. Along with 'Sixteen Tons', they included 'La Fine', 'I Left My Heart In Portofino' and 'Non Dimenticar'. The forward was coached by light music conductor William Gallasini who said, 'Charles has an astonishing sense of swing and a tremendous feeling for rhythm.'

All four of his songs were played at the Comunale before the 3–1 win over reigning champions Milan on 15 May 1960. 'We were out in Turin to play Juventus in a friendly,' recalls the former Tottenham Hotspur and Wales left-back Mel Hopkins. 'John had made two records at the time – "I Left My Heart in Portofino" and "Sixteen Tons" – and whichever bar you went into they were playing either one or the other.'

Charles appeared embarrassed by his second career. He did not tell his family in Swansea of his foray into the music industry. 'John flew over to see me a fortnight ago when I was ill but he did not say a word about this lark,' moaned father Ned. Charles was evasive when journalists quizzed him about it at the training ground. At the outset, he denied knowledge of the records. 'I swear on the head of my best friend Colombo,' said Charles when pressed by journalists. 'Don't bring me into this!' snapped back Colombo. 'I swear on the head of Cesarini,' to which the coach replied, 'I don't want to die!' Now red with embarrassment, he admitted to putting 'something on a cassette'.

Sivori playfully predicted the records would flop but 28-year-old Charles's numbers were well received by the Italian public. He made an appearance alongside Nat King Cole on RAI's Saturday night television show *Il Musichiere*. 'And John was on *after* Nat King Cole, not before,' remembers Peggy. In the summer of 1960, to satisfy demand in nightspots, Charles set out on a tour along La Versilia, the stretch of coastline along the Gulf of Genoa, taking in high-class resorts such as Alassio and Viareggio. Peggy was unimpressed with her then-husband's singing abilities. 'I used to get embarrassed because I didn't think John could sing, he just had a deep voice. The whole thing was just a gimmick. He did it to make money but I don't think he made any money from those records. As for "Sixteen Tons", I hope I never hear that song again.'

Juventus sealed the domestic double in 1959–60 when Fiorentina, getting used to their role as bridesmaids, were defeated 3–2 in an exciting *Coppa Italia* final in Turin. Charles scored twice and he cited his second as his most treasured Juventus goal. 'We were trailing 2–1 when I went for a cross, cushioned the ball softly on my forehead, then nodded it over the goalkeeper [Giuliano Sarti] as he came off his line.' Charles's equaliser forced extra-time with Dante Micheli's own-goal settling the tie.

The following year Charles won his third championship medal with Juventus and this *Scudetto* was the most dramatic and unexpected of the three. Both team and player began the season indifferently. A 4–3 home defeat at the hands of Milan in week six, which came seven days after a 3–0 drubbing in Florence, marked the end of the Cesarini era. The reins were temporarily handed to his number two, Carlo Parola, like Cesarini a former

Juventus player. He reverted back to his post of *allenatore in seconda* when Gunnar Gren slid into the Juventus dugout on 21 January 1961, the day before a home match against Padova. Known as 'the Professor', Gren was a famous midfielder for Sweden and had spent most of his playing career in Italy with Milan, Fiorentina and Genoa. As a coach he did not command the same respect. 'He was an excellent player and an excellent person,' says Colombo, 'but as a coach he was pretty mediocre, even though he won a championship for Juventus. The championship was won by the players, not by Gren. He was always wearing civilian clothes, he never put on a tracksuit.'

The performances remained erratic following Cesarini's departure and after a 3–1 reverse against Inter at San Siro in December 1960 the Italian press criticised Charles for the first time since his arrival in 1957. The Welshman, who had scored only three times since the season began on 25 September, had a poor match. '*CHE COS'HA CHARLES?*' (What's wrong with Charles?) asked *Tuttosport*, which blamed his poor form on his escapades at La Versilia the previous summer. The press said he was enjoying too much of *la dolce vita* (the good life) which resulted in journalists phoning the Charles residence to ask if Peggy thought her husband's singing was affecting his football.

'I am disorientated,' confessed Charles after the Inter defeat, a loss that saw *I Bianconeri* slip four points behind leaders Roma. 'The more I try to do good things, the worse it gets. I go onto the pitch with lots of ideas but then my mind becomes cloudy and uncertain.' Uncharacteristically, he criticised the way the team played at San Siro. 'We played very defensively. I had two high balls all game. I don't know what's happening.'

Charles found the net in the next fixture, a 3–2 win at Sampdoria on Christmas Day, but Inter, who had knocked Roma off the Serie A summit, looked to be running away with *Lo Scudetto*. In a bid to release Juventus's grip on the championship, and to secure their first title since 1954, the Milanese had invested heavily in the summer of 1960. They hired a new coach, Helenio Herrera, who had recently been sacked by Barcelona. On a salary of £50,000 a year, Inter made him the highest-paid coach in world football. An Argentinian who was born in Casablanca, Morocco, Herrera was an authoritarian and a disciplinarian. On arriving at San Siro he hung up two signs inside the Inter dressing-room. Both summed up his philosophy.

CLASSE+PREPERAZIONE+ATLETICA+INTELLIGENZA=SCU DETTO
(Class+Preparation+Athleticism+Intelligence=Championship)

DIFESA: Non piu di 30 gol! ATTACCO: Piu di 100 Gol!
(DEFENCE: No more than 30 goals! ATTACK: More than 100 goals!)

Angelo Moratti, Inter's oil tycoon president, paid Barcelona another world record fee of £210,000 for their brilliant Spanish international inside-forward, Luis Suarez. At £150 a month Suarez was also the highest-paid footballer in Serie A. When his salary was made public in the Italian press it caused a stir, not least in Turin. Sivori was incensed that Suarez was getting better money than him so he confronted Umberto Agnelli at the club's offices in Piazza San Carlo and demanded a pay rise. He talked Charles into going with him. Agnelli would surely pay up, thought Sivori, if both Juventus's star players threatened to revolt. 'He [Sivori] asked for his contract and tore it up,' recalled Charles. 'Agnelli just smiled at him and said, "Here's your new contract."' Charles, however, left the office on the same money. Unlike Sivori, he declined to push his president for a fatter pay-packet. 'I was never one for making trouble.'

Following a disappointing 2–2 home draw against Napoli in mid-January, Juventus were five points behind Inter. No one envisaged Herrera's mean machine throwing away such an advantage. After his side lost 5–1 to Charles and company in Turin, Udinese's coach Luigi Bonizzoni remarked, 'Juventus are strong but Inter are something else.'

Gradually Juventus cut back Inter's lead. At Lazio, Charles scored twice in an impressive 4–1 win. Watching that game inside the Stadio Olimpico was Mr Universe and *Hercules* actor, Reg Park, who was in Rome filming *Hercules the Avenger* at Cinecittà studios. The American complimented the forward after the game. 'Bravo, John, you were wonderful,' said Park, hitting Charles on the shoulder. A phenomenal run of 11 wins in 12 matches saw Gren's men overtake Inter at the top, but on 30 April, Inter returned to the summit after they beat Spal and Juventus lost to Sampdoria. Charles was rested for that 3–2 defeat in Genoa because he complained of a light pain in his right leg that had been bothering him for the last two months. At Lecco he was back at full strength, scoring with two headers in a 4–2 victory that saw Juventus leapfrog Inter with just five games remaining.

I Bianconeri slipped up at Padova losing 1–0, but three wins, one draw and one defeat from their last five matches were enough to secure the title for the 12th time in the club's history. For many the 1960–61 championship was, controversially, decided off the pitch when La Commissione d'Appello Federale (Italian football's appeal commission) wiped out the two points awarded to Inter after their crunch match at Juventus on 16 April. The game was abandoned after half an hour when a section of the crowd spilled onto the pitch, the result of the Turin club allowing too many people inside the Comunale. The referee, Carletto Gambarotta, had no alternative but to abandon the *Scudetto* showdown. Inter claimed in such circumstances they should be awarded a 2–0 win and the Italian Football Federation agreed, but Agnelli appealed. The Juventus players waited for the commission's verdict at their training headquarters, Villar Perosa, playing cards beside a telephone.

When a Juventus director relayed the news – that Inter had been deducted the two points and the match would be replayed in Turin at the end of the season – they celebrated with a bottle of red Chianti. The players knew the pendulum had swung their way. Before the hearing both sides were sharing the lead with 46 points. Now Inter had dropped to second with 44 – and they still had to visit Turin.

The Milanese were furious with the commission, believing it virtually handed their rivals the league title. An outraged Herrera showed his contempt for the ruling by fielding his youth team for the replay at the Comunale on 10 June, a move he could afford since his side were out of the championship race. Juventus won 9–1 with Sivori scoring six of the goals. Charles's two-year contract expired at the end of this campaign but he renewed it for another year, not for two as expected.

By now he had a share in a high-class restaurant in Turin named after him, King's, which opened in May 1961 (apart from *Il Gigante Buono*, the Italians also referred to Charles as 'King of Soccer'). Located on the first floor of a building on Via Goito, close to Turin's main railway station, Porta Nuova, the restaurant had previously been used as a dance hall and below it was the Metro e Cristallo cinema. King's was decorated in the baroque style, with gold chandeliers, high-back chairs and mirrored walls, and it specialised in Piemontese cooking such as *brasati* (braised meats), *risotti* (rice dishes) and *agnolloti* (filled pasta). Launching the restaurant was the idea of Umberto Colombo, who convinced Charles to become involved. He knew the project would have a better chance of success if one of the biggest names in Serie A could help promote it. The players were two of four partners – the others were a maître d' and a property developer – with each owning a 25 per cent stake in the business. The menu was expensive in order to attract, in Colombo's words, 'the good people of Turin'.

King's turned out to be the first of the many failed business ventures that ate away at Charles's earnings. Described by Colombo as 'an error of great proportions', the restaurant closed after little more than a couple of years. It cost Charles thousands of pounds. 'I didn't get involved with the restaurant and I don't know what John contributed to it financially,' says Peggy Charles. 'I do know it was Umberto Colombo's idea. It was so easy to talk John into something. He was so easily persuaded.'

Some of the Juventus players frequented King's but the cachet of dining with Italy's top footballers was not enough to secure its survival. 'Thinking about it now,' says Colombo, 'the fact it was on the first floor was the biggest drawback.' The idea that he and Charles would be present to promote the restaurant was scuppered just a month after the restaurant opened. In June, Juventus transferred Colombo to Atalanta, which meant a move from Turin to the picturesque Lombardy city of Bergamo. 'Getting sold to Atalanta was such an inconvenience,' he explains. 'The restaurant came about at the wrong time. It should have been opened with both of us in a prominent position at Juventus but that did not happen. I had to go to Atalanta and John could not care less about the restaurant. There has always been this thing at the back of my mind that Walter Mandelli, who was then managing director at Juventus, transferred me to Atalanta to make things difficult with the restaurant,' continues Colombo. 'I don't know this for sure but I believe to this day that was the thinking behind me going. I got the impression from Mandelli that he thought, "You are a footballer, why do you want to open a restaurant?"'

Bruno Garzena ate at King's 'a couple of times' and says he was not impressed. 'The way the restaurant was set up it was destined to fail,' he adds. 'A restaurant has three focal points – the kitchen, the customer and the till. Those two [Colombo and Charles] did not have a relationship with any of these three things. Why they wanted to open a restaurant I will never know.' Peggy occasionally visited King's but she never saw the restaurant full. 'It was a beautiful place but I think it was too expensive and too opulent.' Rino Ferrario found it too old-fashioned. 'It was not suitable for a city like Turin, it was too English-looking. They got it wrong in a big way.'

The club used King's for various occasions but its first-floor location alienated potential customers. 'It was a very elegant, high-class place,' remembers Giorgio Stivanello. 'The food was good and the service was excellent. It was one of the "in" places to go in the city. John was supposed to be the front-man but he was never there.'

The 1960–61 championship marked the end of an era at the Comunale. The team Charles had been introduced to slowly began to break up. Apart from Colombo's departure, Giampiero Boniperti, the team's heartbeat for more than a decade, announced his retirement at the age of 32. New faces appeared at the club – Giuseppe Vavassori in goal, the stopper Giancarlo Bercellino and the Italian international winger Bruno Mora, the latter signed from Sampdoria.

Juventus were bidding to become the first Serie A club to win three consecutive titles since Torino, who won the championship from 1947–49. The biggest threat would come from the two Milanese clubs, Milan and Inter, who had finished second and third respectively in the previous *campionato*.

Charles was heading a sizeable British contingent in Serie A. Before his arrival Italian clubs had never viewed Britain as a hunting ground, preferring to import players from Sweden and South America, but the impact he made in Turin made British players fashionable and Italy's wealthiest clubs cast their eyes across the stretch of sea they called *La Manica* (the Sleeve – the Italian term for the English Channel). Milan paid Chelsea £80,000 for striker Jimmy Greaves. Inter signed his partner in the England attack, Gerry Hitchens, from Aston Villa for £60,000, Torino signed inside-forward Denis Law from Manchester City for £100,000 and centre-forward Joe Baker from Scottish club Hibernian for £80,000.

None of the four hit the heights of Charles. Hitchens came closest, spending six years in Serie A, playing for Torino, Atalanta and Cagliari as well as Inter. Greaves had the talent to be a success in Serie A and scored nine goals in fourteen matches for Milan, but he hated the discipline of Italian football, fell out with his coach, Nereo Rocco, and was transferred back to Tottenham seven months later. Law and Baker also failed to adjust. Like Greaves they detested the enforced monastic lifestyle but did nothing to endear themselves after crashing their car into a Turin fountain early one morning. Living in the same city, Charles tried to help and advise Law and Baker, but they lasted only one season. Law returned home secure in the knowledge he won over the Torino *tifosi* with several brilliant displays.

'The trouble with Denis and Joe was that they were single men,' recalled Charles in an interview in 1999. 'I was lucky enough to have a family with me but they were single and I don't think they knew what to do with themselves.'

Colombo agrees. 'John was a married man, a family man. Law and Baker were single men when they came to Italy and that made a big difference,' says the former Italian international. 'They suffered because in England footballers had more time off, more of a private life. When they came to Italy all that changed. They were told what time to go to bed, how long they could stay out. That could be unnerving if you were a single man and used to doing your own thing, especially if you enjoyed going out at night to discos.'

Hitchens and Greaves were both married but Charles was unimpressed with Greaves' behaviour at Milan. After publicly stating he wanted to return to England so soon after moving to

Milan, Greaves became an unpopular figure in Italy. Charles felt his unpopularity might rebound onto the other British imports, particularly Hitchens who also lived in Milan. Charles believed Greaves and Law (not Baker whom he thought was too much of an English-style centre-forward) would have been a huge hit in Serie A had they acclimatised to the Italian way of life. 'It's no good going out there and hoping someone speaks English. You must learn the language,' explained the Welshman. 'The big problem is homesickness so you've got to put yourself about and meet people.'

The British players found the attentions of *Guerin Sportivo* (now a well-respected glossy magazine but back then a newspaper with a spiteful gossipy streak) unwelcome. Charles had been one of *Guerin Sportivo*'s victims. According to the publication, he had a fling with an 18-year-old blonde during his first season at Juventus. It was one of many untrue stories that offended the player and upset his wife. Charles spoke to the British Consulate about suing the newspaper for libel but was told to ignore the contents of *Guerin Sportivo* since in Italy it would take about eight years to bring a libel action. 'Oh, forget it,' replied Charles in his typically laid-back fashion. 'I'll be back home long before then.'

Peronace, who took Law, Baker and Greaves over to Italy in that busy summer of 1961, said the trio failed in Serie A because they were 'not mature'. He told the British press two years later, 'The change was too big and too quick for them. Do you hear of Gerry Hitchens arguing with his club? Did you ever hear Tony Marchi (the former Tottenham player who played for Lanerossi Vicenza from 1956–59) complain of being a soccer slave? Has John Charles attacked us in your Sunday newspapers? Of course not.'

Umberto Agnelli says Charles adapted to his new environment because he had a 'good character'. He explains, 'John liked everybody, and everybody liked him. That is the secret in life. He was a good character. Denis Law, for instance, was a fantastic player but he was a difficult character. John mixed well with the other players. He had difficulty with Italian to begin with but at the end he spoke it very well.'

As expected, the 1961–62 championship was dominated by

the Milanese with Milan, despite the Greaves fiasco, pipping Inter by five points for *Lo Scudetto*. Juventus's defence of their crown was pitiful. They finished 12th and a whopping 24 points behind Milan. Gren and Juventus parted company after the second game of the season, a 2–1 defeat at Padova, the Swede leaving 'for family reasons'. Parola returned to steady the ship. A former defender himself, Parola recognised Charles's defensive qualities and, unlike his predecessors, had no hesitation in playing him in defence. Bruno Nicolé, often forced to play on the wing because of Charles's brilliance at centre-forward, could finally play in his favourite position.

Juventus's first win of the season came in week five, a 1–0 home win over Roma. Charles played at centre-half and was man of the match, despite playing the entire second half with an eye patch after a clash with Roma's left winger Giampaolo Menichelli.

The following week Juventus visited Ferrara to face Spal. Serafino Montanari, Spal's coach, made no secret of his hope that Parola would keep Charles in defence. 'I don't know if he's going to be at centre-forward or centre-half but I would like him to play at the back because for us to get a result Juventus must not score, so we do not want Charles up front.'

Milan's Nereo Rocco shared Montanari's view. Before his side's date with Juventus in Turin, Rocco admitted he would 'sleep better' if *Il Gigante Buono* played in defence. 'We hope that John Charles stays away from our penalty area.' Parola, however, played him at inside-right on that occasion and Charles scored, although Milan won 4–2.

Against Spal, Parola did play Charles at centre-half but he still managed to score Juventus's first goal in their 3–0 victory. '*CHARLES IPNOTIZZA LA SPAL*' (Charles hypnotises Spal) wrote *Tuttosport*. There the revival ended. Parola's men won just one of their next seven fixtures. There were defeats against Torino (0–1), Inter (2–4) and, worst of all, Milan (1–5).

The Welshman missed a big chunk of this forgettable championship with an injury to his left knee, picked up in the win against Spal. He continued to play and aggravated the problem. The frivolous fixture in which an Italian League XI took on a Scottish League XI in Glasgow proved a game too far. Charles played only the first 45 minutes after damaging the knee as he went to stop Ralph Brand. Parola tried him for the game against Milan at San Siro but Charles was a bystander in the rain as Milan swept the reigning champions aside.

He was sidelined for the next three league games, against Fiorentina, Sampdoria and Lanerossi Vicenza and on 6 December he was sent to the Vendone Clinic in Lyon, France, for an operation on his knee. The clinic guaranteed the operation for five years. At the Vendone he was fed a diet of paté, meat, chips and salad. He drank mainly coffee and water but was occasionally allowed half a beer. He refused cheese and dessert for fear of putting on weight. 'To walk without a ball at my feet is a terrible thing,' he moaned. His aim was to be back in time for the European Cup quarter-final first leg against Real Madrid on 14 February 1962. 'Those are the sort of matches you remember for the rest of your life.'

Charles was back for the Turin derby ten days before the Real Madrid game. His impact was instant. Juventus won 3–1, with Charles putting his side 2–1 ahead in the 64th minute, guiding Bruno Mora's cross past Lido Vieri. 'He was good but he will get better,' said Parola after this win. 'Against Real Madrid he will be an important player. He played well today – he created one goal and scored another. I'm happy for him.'

A capacity crowd of 71,000 filled the Comunale to watch the showdown against Real Madrid. It seemed Juventus had finally started to take the European Cup seriously. They had disposed of Greek champions Panathinaikos in the first round, drawing 1–1 in Athens before winning 2–1 in Turin. In the away leg, Charles was used in defence, although Parola would have pushed him up front if needed. He was Juventus's best player in that first leg. *Tuttosport* likened his performance to 'a pilot flying a plane'. Outside the Olympic Stadium around 100 Panathinaikos supporters waited to compliment the Welshman. Next came Partizan Belgrade. He missed the 2–1 win in Yugoslavia with his knee injury but played in the home leg which Juventus easily won 5–0.

The result was a quarter-final date with the team that had dominated the competition since its inception six years earlier. Many felt that Real, coached by Miguel Muñoz, were now past their peak. Bill Nicholson, whose Tottenham side reached the semi-finals that year, watched Real's second leg against Juventus. He commented, 'They [Real] were not the side they had been and I came back thinking if we could get past Benfica, we would beat Real in the final.'

Alfredo Di Stefano and Ferenc Puskas, the two geniuses who had helped Real to dominate European football, were both 35. They still had Francisco Gento, the lighting-fast winger they called *La Galerna* (the Gale), and the brilliant inside-right, Luis Del Sol, who would join Juventus the following year. In defence they had the formidable Uruguayan stopper José Santamaría, known as *Il Muro* (the Wall).

Parola vowed to play an attacking formation but, before the kick-off, he gave the Spanish champions a boost by putting the player they feared most, Charles, at centre-half. What happened? Real won with Di Stefano scoring the only goal of the game in the 69th minute. The following day Parola was heavily criticised in the press for his negative approach. 'Why didn't Juve attack?' asked the Madrid daily, *El Alcazar,* whose opinion was shared by most other European newspapers. 'What is Charles doing in front of a goalkeeper?' It declared Mora, Juventus's only class forward apart from Sivori, 'played like a full-back'. Emil Osterreicher, Real's technical director, rubbed salt into the wound. 'When I heard John Charles was playing at centre-half,' said the Hungarian, 'I could not believe it. When it was confirmed, I felt more relaxed. I don't like to talk about the tactics of other teams but that, to me, was blatantly self-defeatist.'

Juventus were given no chance of overturning the one-goal deficit inside the Bernabeu Stadium. Real had never lost a European Cup match inside their own magnificent theatre. Out of 19 they had won 18 and drawn once, against Barcelona the previous year.

Charles, who was asked to play at right-half in Madrid, declined to take a nap before the second leg. 'Before a match I've slept only twice before,' he explained. 'At Bologna in a pre-season friendly and in Vienna in the European Cup. We lost those games 6–1 and 7–0 so from now on I stay awake!' His superstition paid off. Parola's side silenced the 80,000 crowd by recording an unlikely 1–0 victory courtesy of Sivori's 38th-minute strike, which was created by

Charles. Muñoz, like his counterpart in the first match, had got his tactics wrong, opting for caution instead of attack. The Italian press hailed Charles's performance in the second leg, describing it as '*gigantesco*' (gigantic). In the Spanish capital, the Welshman sampled the other, darker side of Real's game, a side that would shamelessly reveal itself in the play-off seven days later. Charles was forced to leave the pitch for five minutes after Antonio Ruiz, Real's left-half, caught him on his troublesome left knee. Maurice Guigue, the French referee known as 'the Gendarme of Marseilles', was self-critical of the way he officiated this all-Latin contest. He felt he had not given Charles – 'the most correct player in Europe' – enough protection. He considered retiring from football after this match but was persuaded to change his mind.

The Parc des Princes in Paris was chosen to stage the play-off between the two sides. Not surprisingly, Parola picked the same team that won at the Bernabeu with Charles at right-half. The game was a malicious and badly refereed affair. By the end, Charles was unable to stand upright in the bath because of a thigh injury and Stacchini was nursing a bad leg. Both were taken to hospital.

To quash Charles and his teammates Real decided to unsheath the broadsword and French referee Pierre Schwinte took a lenient view of some of their challenges. The first controversial decision came after 15 minutes when Santamaría floored Charles inside the penalty box. It should have been a penalty but Schwinte ordered a free-kick outside the box. While Charles was on the ground, Rafael Felo, replacing Ruiz, kicked him in the ribs. The same player gave Real the lead a quarter of an hour later. He fooled the Juventus defence by changing positions, ghosting from right-half to left, before he was picked out by Puskas's glorious pass.

Parola now brought his contingency plan into operation. Charles moved to centre-forward, Nicolé went to inside-right and Bruno Mazzia took over at right-half. It delivered an equaliser within five minutes, Sivori again the scorer. The Real players, whose fouls went unpunished by Schwinte, continued to hammer away at Charles, reducing him to a limping passenger. 'Yes, Real were a truly great team, make no mistake about that. But they could dish out the hard stuff, too, especially Santamaría,' said

Charles, reflecting on the encounter. 'People gloat about them and say they never kicked anybody. Well, they certainly kicked me.'

Real ran out 3–1 winners with Del Sol and Justo Tejada netting in the second-half. '*SCANDALO A PARIGI*' (Scandal in Paris) ran the headline in *Tuttosport*, which blamed Juventus's defeat on Schwinte. 'To have an idea of the sort of violence the Spaniards used all you have to do is look at the condition of Charles and Stacchini when they come back from hospital, not to mention Sivori who ended up with both of his legs bruised,' proclaimed the newspaper. 'John Charles was walking as if he was in two pieces, like a half-bent knife. For the first time in five years we can see from his face that he is in pain.'

An incensed Umberto Agnelli said he would like his side to meet Real again, but next time Juventus must be allowed to finish the game with eleven players and not nine. 'If John had to lose his cool that day he should have lost it with the referee,' says Agnelli. The eminent English referee, Arthur Ellis, watched the play-off on television from his home in Halifax and was disturbed by Real's assassination of Charles. 'When I saw the most honoured club in Europe chopping Charles down so brutally I realised the convictions I had about the European Cup when I was refereeing in it myself were being proved correct,' he said. 'The competition was getting out of hand. The will to win had become the predominant factor and the financial incentives for players were almost making it a matter of life and death.'

Benfica's whipping of Real in the Amsterdam final should have provided the aggrieved *juventini* with some consolation. 'That game in Paris was like a fight,' recalls Flavio Emoli, who missed the play-off with a knee injury. 'Santamaría fouled John but the most blatant fouls on him were committed by two other players, [Enrique] Pachin and Felo. Those two were fighting more than playing football. Real really wanted to win that game.' The physical beating he sustained in the French capital meant he missed the next Serie A match, at Bologna. 'My saddest memory of John during his time at Juventus was that play-off against Real Madrid,' added the late Ernesto Castano. 'As soon as the match started they hit John. He took punches. Santamaría went after

John the entire game but other players were fouling him as well. Real Madrid were masters of not only playing football but fouling as well.'

The Paris defeat triggered an alarming slump in their league form. Parola's men lost all of their seven remaining matches and Juventus ended up sharing twelfth spot with Venezia. Not an ideal way for Charles to say farewell to Turin.

CHAPTER NINE –
RETURN OF THE PRODIGAL SON

As early as 1958, at the end of his first year in Italy, Charles had talked about going home. With Juventus's *Scudetto* celebrations still in full swing he said, 'I have a contract with Juventus for another year. I love my club but I want to go back to England to finish off my career, possibly with Leeds.' Manchester United were supposedly ready with a £75,000 bid to bring Charles back to English football when his two-year contract with Juventus expired in 1959, but Charles decided to stay in Italy for a further two years.

In 1961 he agreed only to a one-year extension and talk of quitting Serie A once again resurfaced. 'This is definitely my last season and I hope that we will all be settled in England or Wales next summer,' Charles told Pat Searle of the *Western Mail*. He had decided to end his five-year love affair with *I Bianconeri* for his family's sake. Peggy wanted their children to be educated in England. Because there was no English-speaking school in Turin, Terry – at seven the eldest of his three sons – had already been sent back to Leeds where he lived with his grandparents. Melvyn was now six and Peter four, and for both Italian was their first language. 'I was the one who wanted to come home,' admits Peggy. 'I felt the boys should go to school in England.'

Not many British clubs would be able to meet Juventus's asking price of around £50,000–£60,000. Of those who could, some might be reluctant to fork out such a sum on a player who was 30 and had recently undergone a major knee operation. Two interested clubs were former employers Leeds, now managed by Don Revie, and, not for the first time, Cardiff City. Leeds, said Charles, was his favoured destination. 'With my wife coming from there and in view of the fact Leeds released me to come to Juventus, I must give them every consideration.'

Charles was adamant the 3–0 defeat at Venezia on 15 April 1962 would be his last game in a Juventus shirt. At the King's restaurant he held a farewell cocktail party. '*Ma perche te ne vai? Perche non ti fermi ancora un po?*' (Why are you leaving? Why don't you stay a bit longer?) asked the guests. Charles replied, 'My wife is English, my children are English. They were born in England. Their future is where they were born.' He even had a pamphlet printed – called '*Quello Che Non Vorrei Scrivere*' (That I Would Never Want To Have Written) – which explained his reasons for leaving. Apart from thinking about his children's education he also wanted to spend more time with his own parents. 'My father wrote to me the other day. My mother and father are getting older and they would like to spend a few more years with us. That's another reason why I am leaving,' wrote Charles. 'I would like to stay amongst you forever, you understand. But I can't.'

Juventus harboured ambitions of keeping Charles. 'It won't be easy to replace John,' said Remo Giordanetti, Juventus's vice-president. During the 1961–62 season, Agnelli was reluctant to discuss the subject of his sale to a British club. '*Parleremo domani*' (We'll speak tomorrow) he would say whenever Charles raised the topic. '*Sempre domani*' (Always tomorrow) a frustrated Charles would respond. The newspapers were full of talk that Agnelli, in a bid to hold onto Charles, was about to make him an offer he could not refuse. 'It would have to be a fabulous offer for me to even consider it,' said the player who, at the end of June, showed Juventus how serious he was about returning home by selling the furniture in his hillside apartment.

Some would say Juventus's offer was indeed fabulous. To sign for another year Charles was offered a £14,000 signing-on fee on top of a £120-a-month salary and the usual bonuses. Juventus would also finance his children's education at an English-speaking school in Milan and, as a final incentive, the apartment on Cavoretto hill would be transferred to his name. To keep him sweet while he made up his mind, Charles was even allowed to take part in Wales's tour of South America. The player still turned down Agnelli's offer. 'Juventus asked me to speak to John about staying and I left Bergamo to go and see him in Turin,' explains Umberto Colombo. 'All he said was, "I want to go home." He was having problems at home. He wanted to keep his family together and he thought getting away from Italy was the best way of doing that. He wanted to start afresh, but once the cracks appear it's difficult to put it back together again.'

Leeds eventually agreed a club record £53,000 fee for Charles and the Prodigal Son was on his way back to Elland Road. 'I think John did not want to go into decline at Juventus,' answers Agnelli when asked why Charles insisted on leaving Turin while still at his peak. 'Like Boniperti, who retired at 32, he wanted to leave the club at his height although I think he would have been quite useful for us for another year or two.' Flavio Emoli believes Sivori taking over from Charles as Juventus's key player was the reason *Il Gigante Buono* quit the Comunale. Sivori was crowned European Footballer of the Year in 1961, the same year he won the *capocannoniere* award for a second time. With a monthly salary of 250,000 lire (£150) he was also the highest-paid player at Juventus and, in his case, the club relaxed its stance on players advertising products. Sivori was permitted to put his name to a brand of football boots and footballs. 'After three or four years Sivori's star rose above John's. But he should never have left Juve,' says Emoli. 'That was the biggest mistake he made in his life. He was so well liked there, so loved.' Colombo, too, is convinced that Sivori's success at that time bothered his friend. 'In 1962 John was not the star of Juventus like he had been in the past. Sivori was the rising star while John's star started to descend. When I was at Atalanta I spoke to Agnelli many times and he said he was doing everything possible to convince him to stay at Juventus. John felt being in Sivori's shadow was not for him. John was such a gentleman he would never have said this publicly. It was just a feeling I had. This, plus his family situation, is what made John leave.'

The signing of Charles mirrored new Leeds manager Don Revie's ambitions for the club which had slumped back into Division Two.

His purchase of the Gentle Giant was his second audacious move. Since taking over the managerial reins the previous year he had already changed the club's colours, an all-white strip inspired by Real Madrid replacing the blue and gold.

The Charles plan proved a disaster. After eleven games and three goals he was transferred to another Italian club, Roma, just three months after shaking hands with Revie. As Jimmy Dunn, a full-back who served Leeds for 12 years says, 'Leaving Leeds in 1957 was the best thing he ever did. The silliest thing he ever did was to come back.'

During his remarkable 13-year reign at Elland Road, Revie proved a master in the transfer market. When he left his beloved Leeds to take the England job in 1974 he could look back on a number of brilliant acquisitions. Bobby Collins, Johnny Giles, Mick Jones, Allan Clarke, Joe Jordan, Gordon McQueen – each one had been a tremendous success. Charles was the one black mark in his copy book.

Revie became friends with Charles during the Welshman's first spell at Leeds. He was captain of Sunderland when the Wearsiders visited Elland Road in April 1957 for what was Charles's final game for Leeds before he moved to Juventus. The former Leicester City, Hull City and Manchester City inside-forward took control of the Yorkshire club in March 1961 following the resignation of Jack Taylor. Revie joined Leeds as a player in November 1958 and his ascension to player-manager is one of the club's legendary tales. Harry Reynolds, then a director, was penning a letter of recommendation to Bournemouth who wanted Revie as their manager. As he was writing, Reynolds realised Revie was the man to replace Taylor so he tore up the letter and persuaded the rest of the board to promote the former England player. Once 'one of the lads' and still in his early thirties, Revie now distanced himself from the players. He told them they were not to call him Don, nor did he want to be referred to as Mr Revie. Instead, they were instructed to call him 'Boss'. During Revie's lengthy reign at Elland Road only one player broke this rule – John Charles. It happened on the Leeds coach, on the way to an away match. Charles asked the manager a question and called him by his first name. Realising what their teammate had done, the rest of the players went quiet, expecting an outburst from Revie. He did not rebuke Charles but neither did he respond to his question. The 'Boss' remained silent as if Charles had never spoken.

The club was in a desperate state when Revie was appointed. Relegated from Division One in 1960 they narrowly avoiding dropping into Division Three the following season. The home gates were so low – on occasions they dipped below the 10,000 mark – that not all the turnstiles were opened on matchday. Leeds had finished the 1961–62 season in a lowly 19th place and Revie knew he had his work cut out if he wanted to build a team capable of winning promotion. To kick-start his revolution he made two signings. The first was the small, Scottish inside-forward, Bobby Collins, from Everton. The second was the towering Charles.

Charles was seen as the big signing. Leeds not only paid a club record fee for his services but his transfer dominated the pages of the Yorkshire newspapers for weeks. Revie thought he would score the goals that would take the club back into the top flight but Charles floundered on his return to the English game. It was Collins, signed for a more modest £25,000, who ultimately transformed Leeds from a poor Second Division side into a First Division force.

Revie had fought off the attentions of Division Two rivals Cardiff City to bring Charles back to West Yorkshire. The Cardiff board sanctioned a 'concrete offer' of £35,000 in April 1962 when they learned the player might be available but the action heated up during the summer. 'I can assure you we are determined to make an all-out effort to sign John for whom we have the highest regard,' said the Welsh club's chairman, Ron Beecher. 'Our offer will be as high as we can possibly go but it is difficult not knowing the fee Juventus want.'

Bill Jones made contact with Juventus's general manager, Felice Borel, while the former Juventus and Italy centre-forward was in London trying to sign Tottenham Hotspur winger Cliff Jones. When the Cardiff manager discovered Borel did not speak a word of English he whisked Nora Carpanini, the 22-year-old daughter of Italian restaurateur Vittorio Carpanini, whose family ran The Louis restaurant in Cardiff's city centre, to Ninian Park to translate the telephone conversation for him. Borel told Cardiff's makeshift interpreter, 'I cannot tell you what Leeds have offered or what price we want. Cable your offer to Turin.' The following day Cardiff's three directors met and shortly after 8 p.m. they wired Umberto Agnelli their offer. The exact amount was never made public, but Juventus revealed it was more than Leeds' £53,000. The Italian club chose the Leeds bid because it was the club Charles himself preferred to join. He had promised his wife they would return to her home town.

On 2 August 1962, with a smiling Revie looking over his shoulder and 'to background music of clicking press cameras, shutters, the whining of TV cameras and tape recorders', a bronzed Charles signed a two-year contract. Time and again the photographers asked him to write his name so they could capture the right image. 'He was writing for so long,' wrote Richard Ulyatt in the *Yorkshire Post*, 'I thought he was starting the opening chapter of a new autobiography.' There was no one happier at Charles's return than the club's vice-chairman, Percy Woodward, who said, 'I had the unhappy experience of watching him sign for Juventus five years ago. Now I am highly delighted to witness the accomplished fact of his signing to become our player again.' Charles told reporters he could play at centre-forward for another two years and that playing in Serie A 'was terrible at times' because of the defensive nature of the Italian game. 'All I want to do now is get started. Let's get on with it and win a few matches.'

To celebrate his return his former teammate, Harold Williams, threw a party in Beeston, at his pub, The Railway Inn. Charles's former colleagues, such as David McAdam, Len Browning and Jimmy Dunn, were invited along with their wives and they dined on sandwiches and fish and chips. 'About nine or ten of us turned up,' says McAdam. 'It wasn't anything posh, just a get-together. It was a lovely evening.'

The club had changed dramatically in the time Charles had been away. He returned to a new manager and a new chairman. Harry Reynolds, a self-made millionaire and managing director of H.L. Reynolds Engineers and Steel Erectors, had succeeded Sam Bolton in December 1961. There were unfamiliar faces waiting for him in the dressing-room, too. Charles knew just two of the current squad, defenders Grenville Hair and Jack Charlton, the only survivors of the 1956–57 side in which Charles last played.

The Welshman was not the only Briton to end his exile in Serie A in the summer of 1962. Denis Law and Joe Baker had both left Torino. Law joined Manchester United for £116,000 while Arsenal paid £70,000 for Baker. According to Fulham and England star Johnny Haynes, Charles was the one who would find it hardest to re-acclimatise to the English game. 'It will probably take him longer to adjust himself to conditions he has almost forgotten,' commented the Fulham and England star. Eyebrows were raised at Arsenal paying such a large fee for Baker, but Haynes added, 'In a way Leeds have gambled almost as heavily as Arsenal.' His words were to prove prophetic.

Jim Storrie, a Scottish forward Revie signed from Airdrie for £15,650, says, 'One of the reasons I went to Leeds was because they had signed John Charles.' Storrie arrived at the same time as the Wales international. 'I had no particular desire to go to Leeds because they were in the Second Division but Revie told me they had got Bobby Collins and John Charles and all of a sudden the package looked pretty impressive. To be playing alongside someone like Charles persuaded me to go to Leeds.' Revie had a batch of young players at the club and they were thrilled at the thought they would be sharing a dressing-room with one of the world's most acclaimed footballers. 'When John came back I went into the dressing-room to see him,' remembers former Leeds stalwart Norman Hunter, then an 18 year old still to make his senior debut. 'I remember him taking off his shirt for training. It went on and on and on because he had this large physical frame. What a physique he had.'

The world of English football was surprised the Division Two club, attracting pretty poor crowds, had come up with the hefty sum of £53,000. It soon became clear who would be paying for the Charles transfer – the Leeds supporters. Season ticket prices rose by 45 per cent from seven pounds seven shillings to ten pounds, while entry to the ordinary enclosure for the first two games of the season, against Rotherham and Sunderland, rose by a staggering 150 per cent, from three shillings to seven shillings and sixpence. Haynes said 'an unnecessary burden has been placed on his [Charles's] strapping shoulders'.

The board issued a statement explaining the policy. 'So many people have offered numerous sums to help pay for the transfer fee that it was felt by the directors that all our supporters should help and not just a few.'

Watching Leeds had suddenly become an expensive pastime and the unexpected hike in admission prices incensed the public. The 'everyone pays' scheme also backfired as only 14,119 – 1,000 more than the previous season's average – watched the Rotherham match. 'The Leeds public disgust me,' snapped a furious Reynolds after the game. A disappointing 17,753 turned up to see Sunderland three days later. The club denied a drop in season ticket sales in the wake of the 45 per cent hike. Leeds general manager and secretary Cyril Williamson said there had been 'scores of inquiries' for season tickets with applications from people living as far away as Durham and Tyneside.

The local newspapers were inundated with hundreds of letters from Leeds supporters furious at the board's decision to increase admission prices. In the *Yorkshire Post* 'an ex-United fan' of Wrightington wrote, 'They did not reduce the prices when they sold Charles for £65,000 and brought in a £12,000 replacement.' A letter signed by 22 fans who worked at the Leeds Corporation described the rises as 'an outrage' and added, 'We have no intention of paying these exorbitant charges.' Another, signed by ten supporters who worked for a printing firm in the city, said, 'We would like to thank Mr Reynolds and his directors for bringing Charles back. What a pity we can't afford to watch him.' Mr L. Palmer, of Seacroft, Leeds, wrote, 'Have Leeds United forgotten theirs is only Second Division football? Have Manchester United put up their prices to buy Denis Law?' Another letter, signed 'Disgusted' of North Park Avenue, Roundhay, said, 'After 40 years I find myself watching the old blue and white stripes of years ago – but this time Huddersfield Town.'

Price rises aside, the return of 'King John' captured the imagination. The *Yorkshire Post* published a special John Charles edition with the blazing headline, 'HE'S BACK AGAIN. 1956 . . . DIVISION ONE, 1957 . . . ITALY, 1962–63 . . . ?' The same newspaper even organised a competition asking Leeds fans to send in a 25-word 'welcome home' message for Charles. The winner received two guineas.

Referring to the club's contentious decision to raise ticket prices,

Mr B. Armer, of Hull, earned himself a runners-up guinea with:

> Tha'rt costing us varry dear,
> Aye, US – WE'RE carrying t'load,
> But if tha shoves us up next year
> Tha'rt more na welcome at Elland Road.

Leonard Bryden, of Aberford, near Leeds, also won a guinea for this effort:

> Oh thou footballer complete,
> With head or feet,
> Welcome back to Yorkshire's Dales,
> Soccer Prince of Wales!

The winner was Mrs A. Sunderland, of Leeds,

> Come four divisions of the League in arms,
> We shall shock them, naught shall make us rue,
> If Leeds United to King John be true!

Charles returned to his adopted home with 24 suits, half of them given to him by Juventus supporters. He was without his family who were enjoying the sunshine of Italy when he signed on the dotted line at Elland Road. Ten days after he became a Leeds player for the second time in his career, Peggy and the children arrived at Manchester Airport, along with several trunks of Italian clothes and shoes Peggy had amassed during her five years in Turin. It was at that point Charles's first wife regretted swapping Italy for England. 'As soon as we landed at Manchester I realised we had made a mistake,' she explains. 'It was awful. It was gloomy and the weather was bad. I looked around and thought to myself, "Here we are again." I was missing Italy straightaway. John and I both loved Italy very much.'

The Peggy who returned home from Turin was unrecognisable from the frumpy, dowdily dressed woman who waved goodbye to England in 1957 when she and her husband flew to Italy to start a new life. 'When I think of how I dressed five years ago . . . it makes me shudder,' she told a local reporter. 'The Italian women dress so beautifully. Their clothes are very simple and very attractive. I have definitely been influenced by their fashion sense.'

Charles and his family stayed with Peggy's parents at their home in Middleton Park Grove until the club bought them a luxury £8,000 property overlooking the River Wharfe in Collingham, ten miles outside Leeds. The Croft was a stone-built detached house with a three-car garage and boasted stunning views of the Wharfe Valley. Inside was a huge kitchen with an automatic waste disposal system and the 20-ft-long lounge came with its own alcove bar. The main bedroom had fitted wardrobes and dressing table as well as its own washbasin.

Despite the fine surrounds Mrs Charles was unable to readapt to life back in England. 'Leeds bought us a lovely house but I was homesick for Italy. We loved the Italian lifestyle,' she adds. 'Personally, I thought we should come back so the children could go to an English school. There was no English school in Turin and we both felt they weren't speaking enough English. Now I know we were wrong. Juventus said they would let us have the apartment if John stayed. How could we have been so stupid! They said they would put the apartment in our name. I could shoot myself now.' There was so much she missed about Italy – the weather – 'all the time I was in Leeds I wasn't once able to wear any of my pretty summer clothes' – the food, the wine and the al fresco lifestyle. She recalled visiting a nightclub in Southport. 'There were six tiny tables and hundreds of people standing around the walls. It was so sordid. Not like the places in Italy where people sit at tables like civilised human beings.'

Charles's first comeback match was a friendly against Leicester City at Filbert Street. It ended 2–2. Charles had a quiet 90 minutes but Revie said he was satisfied with his performance. Apart from an off-target header and a 40-yard sprint that ended with a glorious flick to Jim Storrie, Charles did little in this entertaining game, prompting the 'ambling giant' description in the *Yorkshire Post* the next morning.

Revie's lieutenants, trainer Les Cocker, a hard taskmaster on the training ground, and coach Syd Owen, who would shout and bawl at players during practice matches, had a challenge on their hands since

Charles was clearly out of condition. He had missed pre-season training and at 14½ st. he was overweight. Cocker devised a solo training scheme for the player which involved tough exercises and a supervised massage course.

Cocker's job was made harder by the fact Charles had grown accustomed to the more sedate Italian methods of training. 'John drove Les and Syd spare in training,' reveals Storrie. 'The training at Leeds was very hard. It was a lot of stamina work and running and the big fella was having trouble with that. John would amble along and Les couldn't handle that. He would scream and shout at John and John would look at him as if he was daft. A lot of the young players like myself accepted it because we were young and enthusiastic but John was in the autumn of his career and he didn't want to go through all that crap.'

Willie Bell, the Scottish left-half who was later converted to left-back, remembers one occasion at training when Charles left Cocker lost for words. 'Les would select different players and take them outside to do a warm-up. On this day he picked John. They went outside and John just stood there, put his two arms out in front of him and started flopping his wrists while the other players were stretching and working. "What are you playing at?" said Les. And John just said, "Three championship medals." Les had no answer to that.'

Charles and his Leeds colleagues kicked off the 1962–63 season against Stoke City at the Victoria Ground on 18 August. A crowd of 27,118 turned up to see what was billed as the battle between Stoke's Stanley Matthews, who was 47, and Charles. In the end neither shone. Matthews was kicked off the park and Charles – who 'was less inclined to trust his feet than his head' – was well policed by Eddie Stuart, the former Wolves full-back who had been changed to centre-half. Leeds won 1–0 with Storrie scoring the only goal of the afternoon. Four days later Revie's men faced Rotherham at Elland Road. Charles got his name on the scoresheet but he could not prevent a 4–3 defeat. It was a breathtaking game. Rotherham stormed into a 3–0 lead but Leeds fought back to 3–3 with Charles hitting the third goal after 80 minutes. For the home crowd the goal was reminiscent of Charles's first spell at the club. Taking a return pass from Storrie he fired a shot from the edge of the penalty box that was too hot for the Rotherham goalkeeper, Roy Ironside, to hold. But with five minutes remaining Ian Butler crossed from the left and Alan Kirkman headed Rotherham to victory.

For the second game in succession, Charles was outplayed by his marker, on this occasion Peter Madden. 'By his own standards,' said Eric Stanger in the *Yorkshire Post*, 'Charles had a modest match until late in the game when he was set aflame by the spark of the Leeds rally. To that point he had been outjumped and outfought on the ground by Madden.' Continued Stanger, 'Of Charles himself, perhaps too much is as yet expected of him. He was not last night the Charles of old, no doubt he will be with a few pounds off as the result of some hard training.'

Charles knew he was not living up to the pre-season hype. Occasionally he would drop in at The Railway Inn where his old friend Harold Williams offered him a Welsh shoulder to cry on. 'Leeds had a few Scottish lads playing for them at the time and John seemed to think they were keeping the ball away from him,' says Williams. 'He wasn't pleased with them, I can tell you that.' The former Newport County player has his own opinion as to why Charles flopped in his second spell at the club. 'He had put a lot of weight on. I had difficulty trying to explain that to him.'

After the Rotherham setback, Leeds beat Sunderland thanks to a goal from Revie's young Scottish midfielder Billy Bremner. It should have finished 2–0 but Albert Johanneson, the black winger imported from South Africa, missed a penalty. The fact Johanneson had been assigned the task of taking penalties and not Charles, who was renowned for his awesome shooting power, raised a few eyebrows at Elland Road. As for Charles's own display, he had lost his personal duel with Sunderland's Charlie Hurley. 'I don't think John was happy when he came to Leeds,' observes Bobby Collins. 'I don't think he was enjoying his football. He certainly wasn't the John Charles I had seen play for Wales against Scotland at Hampden Park. We were all waiting for him to do well but it never happened. Maybe there was something bothering him but he never said anything to us.'

The Welshman scored his second goal of the season in a 2–1 defeat at Rotherham, a match best remembered for a half-time bust-up in the visitors' dressing-room. Revie blamed Jack Charlton for allowing a Rotherham player to head a corner past goalkeeper Tommy Younger. Charlton thought Younger should have saved the header. It ended with Charlton throwing a teacup against the wall, missing his manager by about a foot. Revie then walked out of the dressing-room. 'I remember John looking around with a "What have I come back to?" expression on his face,' says Jim Storrie. 'There was shouting and bawling. It was pandemonium.'

He scored his third and last goal for the club in a 1–1 draw at Huddersfield in the West Yorkshire derby, a match that saw him struggle to get the better of the home side's centre-half, John Coddington. The press were beginning to ask questions. 'Charles has not been the football giant he was five years ago,' said Richard Ulyatt after the match at Huddersfield. 'Charles realises as well as those of us who have watched him play in five matches for Leeds United that he has a long way to go before he becomes the man who can lead the team to promotion.' Revie was not unduly worried. He knew Charles was still overweight and would be properly match-fit by mid-October. The supporters, he said, were warned not to expect too much too soon. 'All footballers are fallen idols at some time or other,' responded Revie. 'John is no exception.'

In the next game, at home to Bury, there was more woe for Charles. He became a hobbling, redundant figure after 20 minutes when he injured his back and spent the rest of the match on the left wing. Leeds lost 2–1. He missed the trip to his native Swansea – a game where goalkeeper Gary Sprake, defenders Paul Reaney and Norman Hunter, and centre-forward Rod Johnson made their debuts – but the team coped perfectly well without him, winning 2–0. Charles was back for Chelsea's visit to Elland Road and Johanneson stole the show, scoring both goals in a 2–0 win. For the first time in his glorious career, Charles was fretting about his form. 'I haven't told anyone this before but never in my life have I been so worried,' he told Alan Hoby of the *Sunday Express*. 'Normally I never worry. But night after night I've lain awake unable to sleep trying to work out what is wrong, why I should feel like this, why my confidence seems to have gone, why my form has been so disappointing.' He admitted he missed the atmosphere of Italian football, the 'excitement and electricity which crackled in the air before a big match'. Denis Law and Jimmy Greaves, playing for

Manchester United and Tottenham Hotspur respectively, had found their feet in English football after playing in Serie A. Why had they adapted and not him? 'Greaves and Law were in Italy less than a year. I was there for five years.' Charles vowed to give it a go at Elland Road. 'I owe it to the Leeds directors who spent so much getting me back and to the manager, Don Revie, who understands my problems.'

In this dire second spell at Leeds his best display came in a 1–1 home draw against Southampton on 29 September. He began the match at centre-forward but swapped places with Jack Charlton after the centre-half suffered concussion. In the position where he made his name 13 years earlier, Charles was outstanding. One newspaper went as far as to describe it as 'a world-class display'. Hunter remembers this game. 'Southampton had this striker called George Kirby and he had already sorted Jack out. He was giving all of us a bashing but John came back into defence and that was the end of Kirby. He was heading the ball away before Kirby had got off the ground. I was a very young man at the time and I remember John telling me, "Slow it down." He was telling me what to do and what not to do. It was a defensive display I'll never forget. I'd have loved to have played more games with him.' Revie might now have been tempted to use Charles at centre-half, but he had signed him as a forward and a forward he would stay. 'Don Revie told me my position was safe after he signed John,' recalls Charlton. 'I said to him, "Thank you very much!" He said if John can't make it up front he won't be taking your place at the back.'

After the Southampton game Roma declared an interest in signing the former Juventus player. They wanted to approach Charles about a move back to Serie A but at a board meeting on 1 October, the directors 'unanimously agreed' that Charles was not for sale. Revie said he was 'over the moon' at the board's stance. 'I have no doubt John will find his true form and I think he gave one of the finest exhibitions at centre-half play I have ever seen in Saturday's match against Southampton.' Charles attended the meeting and at the end he shook hands with Harry Reynolds. The message was clear – Leeds were standing by their big summer signing. 'I was a bit worried that I was not doing my stuff,' Charles told reporters. 'They [the directors] have surprised me because they told me they are quite satisfied with me. That leaves me very satisfied.'

Against Middlesbrough on 6 October, Revie played Charles at right-half and an Elland Road crowd of 28,222 saw Leeds lose 3–2. Charles was never in the match but this time the manager took the blame. 'To play Charles at wing-half,' wrote Eric Stanger, 'is akin to the Old Vic relegating Sir Laurence Olivier to the role of the second gravedigger in *Hamlet*.' The 0–0 draw at Derby proved to be his final game. Charles knew he was letting the side down. 'I have reached the stage now where I can't sleep at nights,' he said after this match. 'This is the first time my football has left me for so long. It was a mistake for me to come back.' It was an utterly forgettable farewell. Back at centre-forward he failed to trouble Les Moore, the Derby centre-half. 'John wasn't the same when he came back,' says Jack Charlton. 'He wasn't as good at centre-forward. Our game was about getting the ball forward quickly and knocking it into the six-yard box. In Italy they played a different style. It was slow, then fast, then slow again. John had become accustomed to that style. I don't think he picked up the pace of the English game when he came back.'

When Charles came back to Leeds after playing in Wales's 3–2 defeat against Scotland at Ninian Park on 20 October he asked the board if they would transfer him to an Italian club. He told them he had been unable to settle into English football and that he was disappointed with his own form. The directors held another meeting, on 22 October, and took the same position as three weeks previously. They agreed the player was staying put. The chairman, Harry Reynolds, and another director, Harold Marjason, were not present at the meeting. Both were away on business but made their feelings known on the Charles issue before leaving Elland Road. The statement issued to the press by the board read, 'We are not prepared to release John Charles. There is no question of the matter being reconsidered.'

Afterwards Charles said he was 'surprised and disappointed' that his transfer request had been refused. His proposal to leave the club was a sign of his deep-rooted unhappiness at Leeds. 'We were a very physical, hard-working and hard-running side,' explains Jim Storrie. 'It was high-pressure football. We had to put the opposition's players under pressure all over the park. We harassed and chased. Revie was one of the first managers to introduce that way of playing. I was a forward and my first job was to defend. That was the mentality. John was like a duck out of water playing that way. Had he been younger he might have adapted. He wanted to play one-touch football and flick the ball here and there. At the time that wasn't Leeds' style. Long balls were played to the corner flag and John was expected to chase after them. At half-time in one game I remember John saying, "I'm not running my pants off for long balls." And wee Billy Bremner said, "You're making that fuckin' obvious!"'

Roma, under coach Luis Carniglia's orders, came back for a second bite at Charles and on 28 October Gigi Peronace arrived in Leeds hoping to push the transfer through. He was convinced the club would part with Charles and 'show a profit on the deal'. Peronace's confidence was justified. The following day the board agreed to release Charles. The directors gathered at Elland Road to discuss the situation and after a 90-minute meeting they released the following statement which Revie read to the press.

> In consequence of John Charles's repeated request for a transfer (owing to John and Mrs Charles not being able to settle in England and their desire to return to Italy) the Leeds board are reluctantly compelled to grant his request for a transfer and are prepared to enter into negotiations with an Italian club. This is a great disappointment to the board and supporters after the efforts to acquire and retain this player but in the circumstances no other course was left open to us.

Torino had expressed an interest in Charles a month earlier but it was Roma who moved first and on 2 November he signed for the capital city club. On arriving at the Leeds ground to conclude the deal, Roma's three-man party of Giovanni Paolillo, Roma's secretary, director Franco Pesci, and Peronace was met by the solitary figure of an embarrassed Revie. The meeting was supposed to start at 4 p.m. but, because their flight from London to Manchester had been delayed, the Italian contingent turned up at 7 p.m. By then all the Leeds directors had gone home for tea.

Finally, at 8.30 p.m., discussions began. Roma agreed to pay Leeds £65,000 plus a further £5,000 which would be generated by a friendly match between the two clubs. By making his club a £17,000 profit Revie had not lost too much face over the Charles venture. Both parties said they were happy with the deal. 'We are well satisfied with what we have got,' said Reynolds. 'We have got the best centre-forward in Italy,' said Paolillo. It also meant another bumper pay day for Charles. He received a £15,000 signing-on fee.

Charles's second stay in West Yorkshire had lasted 91 days. The directors decided to put his Collingham home on the market because they felt no other player would want to live so far from Elland Road. 'I am sorry it has turned out like this because I had looked forward to coming back to Leeds. It proved a mistake,' said Charles after the deal was completed. He denied returning to Italy for the money. 'I am going back because I feel my future as a player lies in Italy.'

Peter Lorimer, another of Revie's exciting youngsters who broke into the first team that season, played one match alongside Charles. It was his debut, the 1–1 draw at home against Southampton in September. 'John found coming back to English football after all that time in Italy not only a football shock but a culture shock as well,' says the former Scotland international midfielder. Lorimer became close friends with Charles after the Gentle Giant returned to West Yorkshire to live in the 1970s. The pair were instrumental in setting up the Leeds United Ex-Players Association. 'John went from working with the ball in lovely sunshine to running on heavy grounds in the English winter. I've spoken to John about his coming back to Leeds and he said in hindsight he shouldn't have done it.'

Considering the steep price increases for the first two home games and the extra 45 per cent slapped onto season ticket prices, the supporters had every right to slaughter Reynolds and the board for the Charles affair. However, the reaction to the player's sale to Roma was philosophical. Herbert Young, president of the 100 Club, said it was not their fault Charles had failed to settle. Eric Carlile, secretary of the Supporters Club, said the club 'have paid £53,000 for a memory' but the board 'did try to give us what we wanted'.

Revie had to rejig his side. He signed right-winger Tommy Henderson from St Mirren and forward Don Weston from Rotherham. Jim Storrie left his inside-forward berth to fill the centre-forward vacancy left by Charles and the team's fortunes on the pitch improved considerably. Indeed, Leeds narrowly missed out on promotion that season, finishing fifth. They won promotion the following season. 'If John had come back to Leeds when we were in the First Division it might have been a different story,' remarks Willie Bell. 'In the Second Division you were mainly playing against guys in their thirties whose only drive was to pick up a salary.'

Norman Hunter felt Charles had used Leeds as a stepping stone to go back to Italian football. The moment Charles arrived in The Eternal City a rumour swept across Leeds that Juventus had refused to sell him to another Italian club, which meant Charles was forced to leave Italy before he could return. 'To me it seemed as if John came back for a purpose,' says Hunter. 'I think he had it in the back of his mind to go back to Italy.'

To toast the deal, Charles took the Roma party to The Railway Inn for brandy and sandwiches. They stayed until the early hours of the morning. Before they left to make their way back to their hotel, The Metropole, Peronace went up to Williams and said, 'Thank you, Harold' before thrusting a ten-shilling note into his hand. The landlord was unimpressed. 'They had drunk my best brandy all night and all they gave me was ten shillings! A pint of beer was at least a shilling a pint.'

Charles arrived in Rome the day before a home match against Bologna. The club provided the player and his family with a £100-a-week apartment just off the historic Via Cassia. It was furnished with damask sofas, a seventeenth-century Dutch bar, a Louis XV table and antique Venetian mirrors. The three Charles boys attended St George's, an English-speaking school run by English staff with English rules. 'A bit of old England' was how Peggy described it. 'It is so English you wouldn't believe it. A lovely place that looks like a medieval mansion.'

Roma were one of Italian football's great under-achievers. It may have been the capital city's main club, but it had won *Lo Scudetto* just once, in 1942. Roma president Conte Francesco Marini Dettina wanted a team that would challenge the domination of Juventus and the two Milanese clubs. Charles was a big piece in that jigsaw.

The Welshman arrived in Rome to the news the club had recently changed coaches. Gone was Carniglia, the man who wanted to sign Charles. He was replaced by Alfredo Foni, a former right-back with hometown club Udinese, Lazio, Padova and Juventus. A former Italy international, he had played 23 times for his country in the late 1930s and early 1940s. He had also – unsuccessfully – coached the national team. It was Foni's Italy that had failed to qualify for the 1958 World Cup. 'It must have been a matter of hours in between Carniglia going and John arriving,' says former Roma defender Giacomo Losi. A Roma stalwart, Losi played for *I Giallorossi* (the Red and Yellows – Roma's nickname) from 1955–68, making a club record 386 Serie A appearances. 'I don't think John was bothered about who was the coach. It made no difference to him whatsoever.'

The question in the Italian capital was whether the new signing would play against Bologna at the Stadio Olimpico. '*Vedremo*' (We will see), replied Foni when asked whether the Welshman would feature against Fulvio Bernadini's talented Bologna team, a team that would be crowned Italian champions the following season. 'We must decide if he is in the right physical shape for the Italian championship.' The real dilemma facing Foni was that he already had a quality centre-forward at the club in the shape of Pedro Manfredini, an Argentinian known as *Piedone* (big foot) because he wore size ten boots. In the end, Manfredini kept Charles out of Roma's first team. The South American finished the 1962–63 season as joint top scorer in Serie A with 19 goals while the Welshman was to become a forgotten man at the Olimpico.

Charles had not played a competitive match for a fortnight. His last game was for his country against Scotland, but he insisted he was fit enough to play against Serie A leaders Bologna. He told Foni he had been doing daily exercises. 'Look at my face,' said Charles. 'I'm lean like a boxer trying to get back into the ring.' He had done enough to convince Foni. Charles played but at right-half, not at centre-forward. That position was filled by Manfredini. 'Whatever Foni wants me to do, I'll obey. In the last few months I have played centre-half, half-back, inside-forward and centre-forward. I know there is Manfredini at centre-forward. I know what the situation is.'

His *Giallorossi* debut was a triumph. In front of 70,000 spectators he scored in Roma's impressive 3–1 win. 'The start of Charles has been our ruin,' quipped Bologna's president Renato

Dall'Ara afterwards. Giancarlo De Sisti, Roma's young midfielder, said Charles was like 'good petrol'. The visitors were packed with excellent players – stopper Francesco Janich, winger Ezio Pascutti, midfielder Giacomo Bulgarelli, German inside-forward Helmut Haller and Danish centre-forward Harald Nielsen – but there was an air of enthusiasm about Roma that Bologna could not withstand.

The former Leeds and Juventus player did well in the opening 20 minutes but then the lack of match fitness kicked in. 'In the second-half he was like a bagpipe because he could not pick up his breath,' said the report in *Tuttosport*. Charles scored his side's first goal, in the 13th minute. Paolo Pestrin centred a delicately weighted ball from the left for Charles to head past Attilio Santarelli. Outside the Olimpico after the game, hundreds of *tifosi* waited for Charles and, according to one journalist, they forced him out of the stadium 'as if he was on a tidal wave'. It needed the intervention of police to rescue the player.

By the time Charles played his second game for Roma, a 2–2 draw against Fiorentina which saw him score again, a header from another Pestrin cross, his family had arrived from Leeds. Charles vowed to stay in Italy forever. 'I'm no longer British in soul, now I'm Italian. From Italy I will not move any more.' Eight months later he would be back in South Wales to sign for Cardiff City.

His time in Rome was a miserable one, although his stint with *I Giallorossi* started brightly enough with Foni deciding to play both Charles and Manfredini by using the former at inside-right. In a 2–2 draw at Genoa he rescued his side with a stunning free-kick from the edge of the penalty box. He scored again in a 2–0 win over Sampdoria at the Olimpico, heading home Manfredini's cross seven minutes from the end.

Many consider the 4–2 win at Real Zaragoza in the Fairs (now UEFA) Cup in December 1962 his best game for the Roman club. Charles scored one of the goals that night. 'I saw Charles moving towards the penalty area,' recalls midfielder Giancarlo De Sisti, who was, at 20, a baby in the Roma side. 'I crossed the ball, John went in and, as if he was kissing the ball, he headed it into the net. It was one of the sweetest goals I have ever seen.'

In Zaragoza Charles's new teammates savoured his sense of

humour. As part of their official uniform, the players wore overcoats with gold rings to hold the belt. Charles thought he looked like a traffic policeman and during a walkabout of the Spanish city he spotted a police officer controlling the Zaragoza traffic. He left his colleagues, approached the policeman, borrowed his hat, stood on his platform and started controlling the traffic. 'John and I used to play about in the dressing-room,' continues De Sisti, who went on to play 29 times for Italy. 'He used to ask me to throw the ball at his chest. It used to bounce off his chest as if it was hitting a wall.'

La dolce vita ceased after a 2–0 defeat against leaders Inter at San Siro. There was talk that the players would be fined for producing such a bad display but in the end only one player, Sergio Carpanesi, had to cough up. Charles was marked out of the game by Bruno Bolchi who had not played first-team football for two months. Bolchi replaced Franco Zaglio who was out with a knee problem.

The dip in Charles's form coincided with a number of newspaper reports that he was spending too much time in Rome's restaurants and eating too much *pastaciutta* (pastaciutta is a dish comprising pasta, tomato sauce and chunks of meat). 'All stories,' snapped an angry Charles, although it was no secret Roma were unhappy with his weight of 91 kilos. 'People have seen me in some restaurants eating with friends and family but I never go over the top.'

For the trip to Bergamo to play Atalanta, Foni dropped Charles for the first time. He did not take the news well. 'I don't see myself as a reserve player.' Roma lost 3–1. Being dropped hurt Charles. For the first time in his career, he was not the first name on the team sheet. 'He didn't like being left out of the starting 11,' says Losi. 'He came as a prima donna player. He expected to be in the first team at all times. He didn't want to be a luxury reserve.'

Charles was back for the home match against lowly Venezia and, in a game that saw the *tifosi* jeer the Roma president, Foni's side could only manage a 2–2 draw against a team third from bottom. After the game Dettina publicly stated he made a mistake in buying the Welshman who was clearly not the player he had been at Juventus. 'The only thing you can blame us for is bringing Charles to Rome.'

In the second half of the championship, Charles found himself frozen out at the Olimpico as Foni chose Antonio Angelillo and Pedro Manfredini as his attacking duo. In fairness to the man from Udine it was a wise move. Roma's results suddenly started to improve. Mantova were crushed 7–1, Modena were beaten 3–1 and Catania were thumped 5–1. All these wins were achieved without Charles. 'Roma,' wrote Clive Toye in the *Daily Express*, 'have reduced King John to the stature of an ailing minor princeling.' The message from Foni was clear. He preferred Manfredini ahead of Charles.

On 17 February 1963, the in-form *Giallorossi* travelled to Juventus but Charles was omitted. 'I'm very disappointed not to play but it is destiny that I don't play against Juventus.' Asked for his prediction of the scoreline, his head said a 2–1 win for Juventus while his heart said a draw. The Turin club won 2–0. Charles waited until 18 March for his next game. It was also his last. In a 0–0 draw at Bologna's Dall'Ara Stadium, Charles played alongside Manfredini. Foni's side may have left with a point but Charles's performance was execrable and the following day the critical Italian newspapers described his display as '*patetico*' – a word that needs no translation – and they wrote of the 'ex-King John'.

At the end of the season Roma announced Charles was for sale. 'In football terms, John was old when he came to us. He joined Roma in the winter of his career,' explains De Sisti. 'Physically, he wasn't at his best. He got bigger and bigger and slower and slower. Also, I don't think the ambience of Rome suited him. One of my regrets is that I didn't play with John when he was at the height of his powers.' Adds Losi, 'I don't really know what went wrong but I got the impression John was a player who had had his best days. To outsiders it looked like he was another player from the past who had come to Roma to finish his career. Rome was a market for clapped-out players. They came to us to die out.'

Roma did have a reputation for signing big-name players who had seen better days. Before Charles they bought the great Swedish centre-forward, Gunnar Nordahl, after he celebrated his 34th birthday. De Sisti, who was transferred to Fiorentina in 1965, is critical of the way Roma was run at the time. 'The club had a habit of buying players who were at the end of their careers. From where

I was standing, that was the problem at Roma. That was the mistake the club was making. It had hopes of winning the championship but it couldn't do that with players at that stage of their careers.'

There was one taker for Charles. Somewhat predictably, it was Cardiff City, the club that had tried to sign him on so many occasions in the past. 'I thought John was going to do well with us,' continues Losi. 'I played against him when he was at Juventus and he always played well, but we never saw him play for Roma like he did for Juventus.'

Away from football, Charles's life in Rome was anything but serene. His marriage to Peggy was experiencing difficulties. She failed to settle in the Italian capital, found few friends and spent most of her time hundreds of miles away in Diano Marina, at their seaside apartment. 'Life in Rome was awful, just awful,' recalls Peggy. 'The apartment had a tiny little kitchen which didn't have any windows. I wasn't used to that. Rome wasn't a very nice place to live. It was very oppressive. I remember going out onto our veranda and feeling really hot. The traffic was absolutely horrendous. It's a lovely city to visit but not to live in. Turin was nicer. I went back to Italy thinking it was going to be wonderful, but it wasn't.'

Peggy was spending little time with her husband because of his football commitments. In one fortnight spell, she claims she saw John for a total of 50 minutes. The children were also unhappy in Rome and Peggy never liked living in an apartment, preferring a house. She missed having a garden and disliked the fact the city was filled with tourists. 'Every opportunity I had, I'd go to Diano Marina.'

The situation deteriorated to a point where, after Charles had agreed to leave Roma for Cardiff City, Peggy left her husband. She disappeared for two weeks and Charles spent five days looking for her before finding his wife on a beach in San Remo, on the Italian Riviera, not far from Diano Marina.

Charles returned home and began divorce proceedings in Leeds. The marriage had been in trouble for a year and he had hidden his bitterness for months. After signing for Cardiff City he made the hour-long drive west to visit his parents who were still living in

Alice Street, Swansea. Within 24 hours Peggy arrived at the terraced house with their three children. After five hours of talks, and while Terry, Melvyn and Peter slept upstairs, they were reconciled and Charles scrapped his divorce plans. 'We have agreed to start from the beginning again and forget the past,' said Cardiff's new signing. The following day they went on a family outing to nearby Rhossili beach on the Gower. Charles played cricket with his three sons while Peggy watched proudly. 'I cannot bear to think of life without John and the children,' she said. 'I think I would die.'

They were ready to start a new life in Cardiff. Peggy was homesick for Italy when they returned to Leeds but now she never wanted to go back there. Italy, she said, 'is not the gay and glamorous roundabout that people think it is'.

CHAPTER TEN – BACK HOME

Throughout the 1950s Cardiff City tried to sign Charles. When he decided to finish his love affair with Juventus in 1962 the Welsh club made another strong move to sign the player but Leeds won the race for his signature. In the summer of 1963, the Welsh international was being offered to them on a plate. When Roma president Francesco Marini Dettina decided to cut his losses and offload their Wales international, Gigi Peronace, the agent acting for the Serie A club, approached Cardiff and told them Charles was keen to move to Ninian Park. The Italian knew full well that after a dismal season, first at Leeds and then at Roma, the 32 year old would not interest clubs in either Serie A or the English First Division.

Peronace first contacted Cardiff chairman Ron Beecher, a butcher, in the first week of July. 'I would certainly like to see John Charles in the Cardiff colours and we will do our best to get him *if* the transfer figure is to our satisfaction,' said Beecher. Relegated from the First Division the previous year, the Ninian Park gates had started to dip under the 10,000 mark. The Bluebirds were in need of a big-name signing, not only to build a promotion-challenging team but also to attract the crowds back to Ninian Park where Charles's brother, Mel, was now playing. Signing the Roma player looked to be the answer. 'I don't know how it came about but Ron Beecher rang me and said, "We can sign John Charles. Are you in favour?"' explains George Edwards, at the time one of the club's three directors. 'I couldn't say no to that. If I did I would have been hounded out of Cardiff. We had to try and sign him.'

On 10 July, while Charles was on holiday with his family in Diano Marina, Peronace arrived in Cardiff for talks with Beecher, his fellow directors, Edwards and Fred Dewey, and Bluebirds manager George Swindin, the former Arsenal goalkeeper. After three days of discussions, Peronace flew back to Italy with an offer of £22,000. 'I'm going back to Rome in a far happier frame of mind and I think there is a chance the Roma president will agree to the Cardiff offer,' he told reporters. When Charles learned of Cardiff's 'very fair offer' he said, 'I want to finish my soccer days in Wales. Roma have told me they will not ask too much for me and I expect them to keep their word.'

Peronace was back in Cardiff on 18 July with bad news for Beecher. Dettina turned down their £22,000 bid and said he wanted £30,000. Peronace told Cardiff's directors that Roma, who paid Leeds £65,000 for Charles only nine months earlier, were going to make a huge loss on the player but they were unmoved. 'Under no circumstances will we increase our offer,' Beecher told Peronace. The deal stalled. After speaking to Dettina, and despite telling him Cardiff's offer was the most he could reasonably hope for, Peronace left for London with the two clubs at loggerheads. 'I am not trying to conduct an auction for John Charles. My instructions are to sell him for £30,000,' he said. 'If Roma's tag is not met then they will be happy to keep him and transfer him in Italy. Even if they don't they would rather keep him than accept under £30,000.'

Meanwhile, Cardiff's Division Two rivals Huddersfield Town were said to be 'deeply interested' in buying the Roma player so Peronace headed north to Yorkshire to see if they were willing to meet Dettina's asking price. Talks with Huddersfield lasted an hour and a half and they agreed to pay Roma £30,000 – but only if the team won promotion the following season. Peronace's response was typically dry. 'If I knew you would definitely get promotion we would want £50,000 for John!' he told the club's chairman, James Chadwick.

On the day negotiations with Huddersfield fell through Charles telephoned Peronace from Leeds, where he was visiting his in-laws, and reiterated his wish to join Cardiff. The Italian reopened talks with Beecher who said Cardiff's final offer was £22,500 and that he wanted an answer from Roma by 10 a.m. on Tuesday, 23 July. 'It's getting like a TV serial,' quipped Beecher. 'It's time we had a final answer to our bid. This is our deadline and we are sticking to it.'

With no other offers on the table, and none forthcoming, Peronace telephoned Dettina and, after five hours of trying to contact the Roma president, advised him to accept Cardiff's offer. After more than a fortnight of talks the two clubs reached an agreement. Cardiff would pay £22,500 and fly to Italy at the end of the season to play Roma with the Serie A club keeping the proceeds. Charles was obliged to interrupt his holiday in Diano Marina to discuss personal terms with the Cardiff directors. Peronace told them Charles would arrive in Cardiff from Rome – via Paris – at teatime on 25 July. The club's officials, along with an army of journalists and photographers, waited for him at Cardiff Airport, in Rhoose, on the outskirts of the city. The plane landed but there was no sign of Charles. A seat was booked for him but he had failed to arrive at the airport. Peronace made enquiries and discovered Charles was still in Diano Marina packing. He arrived in the Welsh capital three days later and held formal talks with the club on 30 July. Inside the Royal Hotel, they shook hands on the deal.

For the all-important medical, Cardiff sent Charles to Dillwyn Evans who was based in Cathedral Road, a grand and leafy Victorian terrace near the city centre. His report, dated 30 July and addressed to Beecher, made interesting reading. 'Orthopaedically speaking he is by no means out of the top drawer,' concluded Evans. He informed Beecher that Charles had had a cartilage removed from each knee 12 years earlier. There had been 'a recurrence of trouble' in the left knee in 1961 and a pulled muscle on the front of the right thigh sustained the previous year as well as osteoarthritic changes on the inner side of his left knee. Beecher was warned that either the right thigh or the left knee could cause Charles to break down 'but this is only a possibility'.

Despite these observations Evans did not advise against signing the player. 'His brother, with much worse knees, has lost only one game in the last two years and for all I know John may do just as well . . . there is a very good chance that he has two or three years of good football left in him and, indeed, it may be that some part which is now normal will give trouble before either of the parts that are vulnerable.' The final hurdle was cleared. The club that had been trying to secure Charles's signature since 1951 finally got their man, albeit past his prime.

The Second Division club agreed to pay Charles £40 a week, making him Cardiff's highest earner, along with Ivor Allchurch. The pair were considerably ahead of their teammates with the second largest salary being paid to Barrie Hole, who took home twenty-five pounds and ten shillings.

The £22,500 fee was a considerable amount for Cardiff, who raised most of it by selling two of their promising young players, centre-half Frank Rankmore to Peterborough and inside-forward Alan Durban to Derby County. Both went for £10,000. There were concerns about Charles's age and fitness but Peronace insisted Cardiff had landed themselves a bargain. 'With John in a happy frame of mind I am convinced he can remain a great player for several seasons.'

Cardiff, who signed the player primarily as a centre-half, hoped the transfer would be interpreted as evidence of their ambition to get back into the top flight. The 1962–63 season had been mediocre for The Bluebirds. They finished a disappointing tenth in Division Two but, worryingly for the board, a crowd of only 8,943 turned up to watch their last home game of the season, a 3–0 win over Huddersfield. 'We are trying to show the Cardiff public that we are determined to have a good side at Ninian Park next season,' Beecher told the *Western Mail*. 'Our finances are not such that we can splash out money readily, but nevertheless we are showing that if an opportunity occurs we will not be afraid to go out for the men we want.'

On 9 August, after an exhausting journey which involved a 16-hour train ride from Rome to Nice where he caught a flight to London, a tired Charles signed Football League forms for Cardiff City inside the Ninian Park boardroom, watched by George Swindin. Charles said he had come home to Wales 'for good'. At the press conference he told reporters, 'There was only one club I wanted to join and that was Cardiff City. The negotiations have been long and drawn out and for most of them I have been waiting in Italy wondering what was going on. From now on my sole ambition is to help put Cardiff City on the upward path once more.'

Charles bought a house in Rhiwbina, a suburb in the north of Cardiff, Peggy took a job in the tax offices in the city, and the three children attended Llanishen Fach Primary School.

After signing for The Bluebirds he was introduced to his new teammates. The young Scottish defender, Don Murray, vividly recalls his first meeting with the Welsh international. 'George Swindin brought him into the dressing-room. I just stood back in awe. He was wearing a grey mohair suit, he had a suntan and there wasn't an ounce of fat on him. He was an Adonis of a man. I was a 17 year old who had come down from Scotland and here I was, in the same dressing-room as one of the great players in world football.'

Swindin was all smiles as he posed with Charles on the pitch for the photographers but behind closed doors the Cardiff manager had opposed his signing. The former goalkeeper was against the idea of bringing ageing Welsh footballers to Ninian Park. The club already had on its payroll, Ron Stitfall (37), Ivor Allchurch (33), Derek Tapscott (31), Alan Harrington (29) and Charles's brother Mel (28). Now he had the other Charles brother who would be celebrating his 32nd birthday in December. Cardiff were the Dad's Army of Division Two.

Swindin made public his feelings on the Charles transfer in an interview with the *News of the World* in August 1964, not long after he was sacked by Cardiff. 'I didn't want any more veterans, whatever their nationality,' he said. 'Big John is a great player but I needed youngsters. My plans were centred around youngsters and I said that I didn't want old Welsh internationals coming home to Cardiff to grass.'

The former goalkeeper claimed that when the club started negotiating Charles's transfer from Roma in April 1963 the fee was pitched between £5,000 and £10,000. Swindin said £10,000 was his 'ceiling price' and that Charles would be 'a justifiable gamble' at that amount. 'John had such a standing in Wales that I believed he would boost the spirit of the team and reawaken the fervour of Ninian Park fans,' he explained.

He described the £22,500 the club eventually paid for Charles as 'a ridiculous fee, especially when we had only £25,000 in the transfer pool to rebuild the team'. Swindin wanted to sign a goalkeeper, a full-back and at least two forwards, notably an outside-left. With Charles eating up the lion's share of the transfer kitty Swindin sold Rankmore to raise a further £10,000. He also claimed he was excluded from the negotiations with Peronace and had no say in the personal terms offered to Charles.

Although George Edwards, a former Cardiff and Wales player himself, backed the decision to bring Charles to Ninian Park, he admits he shared Swindin's concerns about signing Welsh veterans. 'George thought what I thought, that we had too many old players in the team,' says Edwards. 'Maybe we should have got rid of at least one of them before we signed John. I was concerned we had too many old stagers at the club but once the John Charles story was leaked to the newspapers there was no way we could say no. George accepted the deal but he wasn't happy about it. But I think he knew if we said no to signing the best player Wales had ever produced we would have been hounded out of the city.'

The departures of two young players, Rankmore and Durban – who both went on to play for Wales – to make way for an old player like Charles must have infuriated Swindin. 'I can't say I was particularly thrilled about signing John Charles,' admits Edwards. 'At the time £22,500 was a decent sum of money. We could have got four or five youngsters for that amount. Perhaps that was what George felt at the back of his mind. I was of the opinion John would do well for us for a season or two.'

Edwards was keen to follow the example of Charles's former club, Leeds, who would win promotion to Division One that season with a team built entirely around hungry, ambitious youngsters such as Gary Sprake, Paul Reaney, Norman Hunter and Billy Bremner. 'We had to get back into the First Division and I wondered whether buying old players was the right way to go about it. Looking back, we had just gone down and we should have built a younger team to get back into the First Division. Instead we signed people like John, Ivor Allchurch and Mel Charles. We wasted three years.'

Charles's arrival at Ninian Park prompted a cynical article in the *South Wales Echo* from journalist Gareth Bowen, a lifelong Cardiff supporter. Bowen, who week after week came home from Ninian Park 'cursing the team up hill and down dale', wrote, 'What we hope is that you can do for City what Stanley Matthews has done for Stoke. He's led a fighting comeback to Division One and filled the terraces at the Potteries ground.' Bowen was to be a disappointed man. When Charles left for Hereford in 1966 Cardiff was still a run-of-the-mill Second Division club.

The players, however, thought capturing the former Leeds and Juventus star was a real coup. 'Personally, I thought it was a huge boost for everyone at the club that it could attract the services of someone like John Charles,' says Don Murray. 'Not only would he give us an extra dimension on the field but the signing excited the soccer public of Cardiff.'

On 14 August, in the humble surroundings of Twerton Park, Charles wore the blue shirt of Cardiff for the first time, in a pre-season friendly against Bath City. It was a surreal start for the former Juventus player whose presence attracted a 5,000 crowd and ensured Bath donated one hundred guineas to the Red Cross Society Centenary Appeal, which the non-league club had promised to pay if Swindin's new signing played. Picked at centre-half he had little to do against the Southern League outfit. On the few occasions he was called upon Charles coped effortlessly. But in the 72nd minute, after Dick Scott put Swindin's side ahead just after the interval, Charles headed the ball into his own net and Bath earned a 1–1 draw. As he rose to head a long ball, it flicked off the top of his head and over the advancing Graham Vearncombe.

For the embarrassed Charles there were words of consolation from Charlie 'Cannonball' Fleming afterwards. The Bath forward maintained he would have scored anyway if Charles had not got to the ball first. Despite the own-goal it was a satisfactory first game for the player. Peter Corrigan, then football correspondent for the *South Wales Echo*, wrote, 'City's £22,500 import looked a winner in a calm, dignified and nonchalant sort of way.' In the *Western Mail* Phillip Jones wrote, 'One mistake spoiled an otherwise satisfactory return. It was an embarrassing moment for Charles but he revealed the touches, particularly with some splendid head work, which have carried him to the top rank in world football.'

His next appearance for The Bluebirds came four days later, in a public trial match at Ninian Park. This was the public's first chance to catch a glimpse of the Gentle Giant and a crowd of 3,750 watched the kickabout. 'No question, John brought the crowds back to Ninian Park,' says Derek Tapscott. 'He put thousands more on the gate. His arrival made the club look bigger than perhaps it was. I personally thought he would have gone to a bigger club than Cardiff. He still had two or three years left in him. I think he was a hell of a good buy. He was a big, big name and wherever we played there was a decent crowd because people wanted to see John.'

Charles made his league debut for The Bluebirds in the opening match of the season, against Norwich City at Ninian Park on 24 August. He very nearly missed the game. Just six days before Norwich were due in town the Football League blocked his registration as a Cardiff City player because Roma still owed Leeds £9,500 of the fee they had agreed to pay for Charles in November 1962. Cardiff could not play Charles in any of their teams, nor could they pay him wages.

The news hit Ninian Park like a bombshell. Ron Beecher and his directors were hoping the player's presence against Norwich would attract a bumper gate. After weeks of Charles-mania, the curtain raiser was in danger of ending in a huge anti-climax. 'We feel we are being victimised,' was the response from an angry Swindin. 'Not only the club but John Charles as well because from the day the Football League stopped his registration he cannot be paid by us. Therefore he is being held responsible for the debts of his former club. Negotiations for the transfer were started by us weeks ago, yet we received no warning that his registration wouldn't be accepted.'

The £22,500 payment owed to Roma was suspended, Beecher immediately appealed to the Football League and Swindin placed Don Murray on stand-by for Saturday's game. In a forthright leader column on 21 August, the *Western Mail* criticised the Football League for its ruling describing it as 'an affront to natural justice' and saying Charles and Cardiff 'are victims of a kangaroo court'. It continued, 'The player is deprived of his livelihood and the club of his services; it means that the only two palpably innocent parties in the affair have been singled out for punishment.' Alan Hardaker, secretary of the Football League, said he sympathised with player and club but added that if a man buys a car on hire purchase and sells it before he has finished the repayments, it remains the property of the original owner. His argument cut no ice with the *Western Mail*. 'John Charles is not a motor car and it is not part of the League's task to act as a combination of county court judge and bailiff.'

Cardiff had an ally in the FAW. Its secretary, Herbert Powell, said he would do 'everything in his power' to resolve the situation in time for Charles to play against Norwich. While the player ignored the hoo-ha by training with his new teammates at Sully, just outside Cardiff, Powell cabled the Italian Football Federation and asked them to look into the matter. Swindin named Charles at centre-half for the Norwich game and said he would wait until the last minute before replacing him with Murray. 'I just can't bring myself to believe the authorities would wittingly stop us playing Charles in this important first game,' said the disbelieving manager. The day before the match, after a week of doubts and deadlocks, Swindin was told Charles's registration was accepted and the player was cleared to face The Canaries. Cardiff paid Leeds £9,500 as part of the £22,500 fee to Roma.

If Charles had not played against Norwich, the 22,078 crowd that turned up at Ninian Park on a sunny Saturday afternoon to watch the Second Division contest would have been deprived of a goal that has become part of Cardiff City folklore. It came in the 42nd minute. With the score at 1–1, Norwich winger Alistair Miller was penalised for offside. The home side were awarded an indirect free-kick. Charles, 75 yards from Kevin Keelan's goal, kicked the ball 'high, hard and handsome'. It bounced in front of Keelan, struck his shoulder and went into the net. Had the ball not touched Keelan the goal would have been disallowed because an indirect free-kick meant the ball had to touch another player. 'The Norwich goalkeeper was dumbstruck. So too was Charles,' said the report in the *Western Mail*. Cardiff winger Peter King laughed as he went to congratulate Charles. 'We thought he could walk on water after that goal,' remembers King. Barrie Hole adds, 'I don't think John tried to score. He just over-hit a ball into the box and he caught the goalkeeper off his line.' Cardiff went on to win 3–1 and

Charles had a solid debut although he nearly gifted the visitors a goal with a poor back pass. Cardiff goalkeeper Graham Vearncombe bailed him out.

Had Charles brought the crowds back? The Norwich gate was 5,000 down on the first home fixture of the previous season but it was nearly 14,000 up on the last home game of 1962–63.

Charles found the net in his second Bluebirds outing four days later, against Manchester City at Ninian Park. The men from Maine Road were 2–0 up with 30 minutes remaining and seemingly cruising to victory. Ivor Allchurch pulled one back for the home side before Charles, his right leg heavily bandaged after pulling a muscle, back-headed a free-kick for a last-minute equaliser. The 25,532 crowd went wild with hundreds of supporters invading the pitch.

Charles was out for the next game, the arduous trip to Scunthorpe. 'Rotten luck' was how he described his injury against Manchester City. It was only the second time in his whole career that he had pulled a muscle. Swindin's men coped without Charles, returning from North Lincolnshire with a 2–1 win.

As Cardiff supporters wondered if this was going to be their year The Bluebirds were brought down to earth at Maine Road, losing the return fixture against Manchester City 4–0. They slumped to their first home defeat of the season, losing 2–1 against Portsmouth. George Edwards began to have misgivings about the club signing 'old timers' following a 4–1 defeat at Bury on 17 September. 'John played in that game, so too did Mel [Charles], Ivor [Allchurch] and Derek [Tapscott]. After the game I heard their chairman talking on the phone. To this day I remember what he said – "It wasn't much of a victory. They're the worst side I've ever seen here." I knew we had players in the team who were standing and not running.'

Four days after the Gigg Lane debacle Charles faced his old club, Leeds, at Ninian Park. For the first time that season he was put at centre-forward but he failed to puncture the Leeds defence. The match ended in a goalless stalemate. Jack Charlton, marking his former mentor, could not have had an easier match as Charles was forced deep in search of the ball. The press were critical of the two Cardiff wingers, Peter King and Alan McIntosh, for failing to supply Charles with decent crosses. 'Charles did not score the goals when he was with Leeds nine months ago, but he has no chance for Cardiff with their present frustrating forward line,' wrote Huw Johns in the *Sunday People*. 'Either support must be bought for him or he must be returned to the defence. He is wasted in Cardiff's current attack.' The club did not heed Johns' advice.

The Leeds match was followed by a trip to the North East, to Wearside, to face Sunderland at Roker Park. 'John was up front that day and Sunderland had a big centre-half called Charlie Hurley. It really was a clash of giants,' says Don Murray. 'Like John, Charlie was tremendous in the air. That was some battle.' In a match that was described by the *Western Mail* as 'not one for the chicken-hearted', Ivor Allchurch scored a brilliant first-half hat-trick to silence 'the Roker roar' and Charles hit the crossbar with a 40-yard shot. City were leading 3–2 at the break but midway through the second half Sunderland levelled through Hurley. 'The corner came in from the left and Charlie jumped above John and sent a header screaming into the net,' says Murray. 'To beat John in the air took some doing but Hurley could do it on his day. After he scored John turned to us and said, "Blame me lads. I didn't get off my knees." I'll never forget him saying that. Here was the great John Charles admitting he was responsible for conceding a goal.' As Sunderland poured forward looking for the winner they were repelled by a Cardiff side effectively reduced to seven fit men. Gareth Williams, suffering with concussion, was a passenger. Goalkeeper Dilwyn John was hurt and full-back Peter Rodrigues was forced to finish the game on the wing due to injury. The limping Charles had to abandon his post up front to patrol his penalty area. The Bluebirds held on and football writer Malcolm Usher referred to Cardiff's defensive display as 'the greatest retreat since Dunkirk'.

An injury crisis gripped Ninian Park. George Swindin had already lost Alec Milne, Alan Harrington, Trevor Peck and Steve Gammon – all with broken legs – before a ball was even kicked. Now Gareth Williams, Trevor Edwards and Derek Tapscott were on the treatment table. By November Swindin was down to 12 fit professionals yet this skeleton squad won three out of four games including an impressive 4–0 win at Newcastle. Cardiff paid the price for not reinforcing the squad in December with a run of five straight league defeats that saw The Bluebirds concede a staggering 21 goals.

It began with a 3–2 loss at Southampton. Then came a trip to Norwich. Cardiff lost 5–1 and the *Western Mail* branded their performance as 'pathetic' and even Charles – 'not the thrustful leader of recent games' – did not escape criticism. Playing at centre-forward, he was upstaged by another Welshman, Ron Davies, who sunk The Bluebirds with a hat-trick. Norwich's centre-half, Barry Butler, 'had the most comfortable 90 minutes without having to extend himself'. Over the Christmas period Cardiff faced Preston twice, first at Ninian Park and then at Deepdale. Both ended in 4–0 drubbings and the two results, Charles later confessed, 'shattered the team's morale'. In the home game Charles was accused by the press of not showing enough determination and initiative. The defeat could have been far worse. Apart from scoring four times, Preston hit the crossbar and had a blatant penalty refused when Gareth Williams brought down Alec Ashworth. After the match at Deepdale, Cardiff dropped to 18th in the division – their lowest league placing for 17 years.

The 5–0 hammering at Fratton Park on 11 January 1964, at the hands of a Portsmouth team who had not won in six matches, proved too much for the City board. Vice-chairman Fred Dewey, in charge of the club's affairs following Beecher's death from cancer, publicly slammed the team. 'This is the worst Cardiff City side I have ever seen.' Swindin, too, was furious. 'I want a team of 11 men who will go out on the field with one purpose – to win for Cardiff City.' Dewey called an unprecedented 'clear the air' meeting with the players ahead of Friday's home match against Rotherham, summoning the 16 professionals into the Ninian Park boardroom the Monday after the Portsmouth defeat. To allow the players to speak honestly, Swindin was not invited. 'The meeting was well worthwhile. The players spoke freely and what they have said has given us plenty of room for thought,' said Dewey afterwards. 'I feel that on Friday night when we meet Rotherham at Ninian Park there will be 100 per cent endeavour by every player in the team.'

Charles reverted to centre-half for the clash against the Yorkshiremen and the meeting earlier in the week seemed to have done the trick as Cardiff, on a frozen pitch, ended their barren run with a 2–1 win. The victory was more comfortable than the scoreline suggested. An impressive 1–1 draw against Leeds, who were on top of Division Two, followed. Charles was majestic on his return to Elland Road. How the watching Leeds directors must have wished they played him in defence – rather than persisting with him at centre-forward – after signing the player from Roma.

Despite losing four of their last five matches The Bluebirds did enough to stay up, finishing 15th. 'I came to Ninian Park with high hopes of a successful year,' said Charles after the league campaign ended with a 3–1 defeat at Middlesbrough, 'but that long run of injuries, when almost everybody seemed to be hobbling around on a broken leg, shattered the team before it had a chance to get going properly and I think much of the trouble we hit later stemmed directly from that unhappy period.' He added, 'This has certainly been a hard season and I hope we don't have to go through another like it at Ninian Park.'

The tortuous season cost Swindin his job. He took it badly and attacked one photographer and chased another as they waited for him outside the ground after he was told the news by the City board. Says George Edwards, 'Swindin lived on his nerves. He never swore but said things like, "flipping heck" and "Christopher Columbus".' The players were not sorry to see the back of their paranoid manager. 'One day there were four or five regular first-team players talking in the dressing-room,' recalls Peter King. 'We didn't know it at the time but the door was locked. We were probably talking about what was on television the previous night but George Swindin thought we were talking about him and plotting against him.'

Three days after Swindin was shown the door, Charles won a Welsh Cup-winner's medal, his first piece of silverware for three years. The Bluebirds met Bangor City in the final and in the replay at Shrewsbury – Bangor had won the first leg 2–0 and Cardiff the second 3–1 – the Second Division side won 2–0 guaranteeing their place in the Cup-Winners' Cup for the first time.

A couple of days later Charles and his teammates flew to Italy to play three friendlies, one against Roma, which was part of the

Charles deal, and the others against Charles's old club, Juventus, and Latina of Serie C, Italy's third division.

With Swindin gone, directors George Edwards and Viv Dewey took charge of the party with Charles as their interpreter. Team trainer Ernie Curtis, a member of Cardiff's 1927 FA Cup-winning side, was put in charge of team affairs.

Don Murray had never before witnessed the kind of hero worship reserved for Charles when they arrived at Milan's Malpensa Airport. 'People inside the airport were crying when they saw John. They were pulling at his jacket and trouser legs. John towered above them and as he walked past he was patting them on the head!'

The first friendly ·was against Juventus in Turin. 'When we arrived in Turin it got back to me that a few players were going to go into the city to look for girls,' recalls Edwards. 'So I called a meeting and told them that we were in Italy because John Charles had joined the club, that he was a big name in Italy and we had to do him justice. If they treated this trip as a holiday they weren't only letting the club down they were letting John down as well. Anyone messing about would be on the first plane back home.'

I Bianconeri had not forgotten *Il Gigante Buono*. On the day of the game Charles was presented with three gifts. At the club's headquarters at Piazza San Carlo, he was awarded a diamond-studded brooch, a gold medal from Italy-wide Juventus supporters and an inscribed parchment paying tribute to his services to Juventus. It was an emotional occasion and it affected the reserved Dewey. In the dressing-room before the game the director made a rare speech to the players. 'I know it's a busman's holiday,' he told them, 'but when you go out onto the pitch try not to let the big man down.'

They responded to Dewey's plea. At half-time the scoreline read, Juventus 0 Cardiff City 3. Some of the 40,000 crowd were furious and, as a sign of their disgust, they threw the cushions they brought to the stadium onto the pitch. Mel Charles put The Bluebirds ahead after 16 minutes. He smashed the ball past Carlo Mattrel after his older brother outjumped two Juventus defenders. Charles himself made it 2–0 after 34 minutes, rising above three Juventus players to head Bernard Lewis's free-kick into the net. 'All of a sudden,' recalls

Dilwyn John, 'the crowd started shouting "Charlo! Charlo!" It was unbelievable.' Ivor Allchurch made it 3–0 a minute before the break. 'John was trying really hard in this game,' says Barrie Hole. 'I remember him heading the ball against the crossbar and it nearly snapped in half.'

During the interval Charles was presented with another gift in the most extravagant fashion. As he came out for the second half an aeroplane flew low over the Stadio Comunale and dropped an object which was tied to a parachute. It turned out to be a watch.

Juventus scored three times after the break to avoid an embarrassing defeat. Nenè pulled one back from the penalty spot with 20 minutes left before Silvino Bercellino, who appeared to be offside, scored their second in the 81st·minute. With three minutes remaining Bercellino equalised. 'The Juventus fans chaired John off the field and into the dressing-room,' says former Cardiff winger Peter King. Around 2,000 *tifosi* were waiting for him in the Comunale's car park. As Charles left the stadium to board the team coach, they ran towards him. 'They carried him on their shoulders and this went on for quite a while,' recollects George Edwards. 'It must have been quarter of an hour before they let him go.'

Juventus fans in cars and on their scooters escorted the Cardiff bus back to its hotel. 'There were people running alongside the coach shouting John's name,' says Peter King. 'John couldn't go out of the hotel without being mobbed. He was like a film star.' Dilwyn John recalls walking the streets of Turin with *Il Gigante Buono*. 'Restaurant owners and bar owners would try and drag him into their places.'

In Rome, for the second friendly, Charles was still an object of affection despite his lack of success with the club. The Cardiff players decided they wanted to go to the beach at nearby Ostia but not all the players had brought their swimming trunks. Charles took the Cardiff team to a shop he knew at the city's Termine railway station. 'As we were walking along you could hear people muttering "John Charles". They would turn around and follow us,' says Edwards. 'By the time we got to the shop I turned around and there must have been 200 people behind us! They all wanted John's autograph. He signed a few but then I had to move him along.'

Cardiff were nowhere near as impressive against Roma as they had been against Juventus. The sun, spaghetti and Roman heat clearly affected their performance, although the visitors took the lead after half an hour. Charles made the goal, drawing goalkeeper Enzo Matteucci off his line before passing to Bernard Lewis who side-footed the ball into the net. Giancarlo De Sisti levelled before half-time, Angelo Sormani put Roma 2–1 ahead straight after the break before De Sisti got two more for his hat-tick. The Bluebirds lost the final match against Latina 4–3. Edwards concludes, 'That trip proved to me that John Charles was a god in Italy.'

CHAPTER ELEVEN – LISBON LION

The man the Cardiff directors hired to replace George Swindin was former Portsmouth, Newcastle United and Scotland wing-half Jimmy Scoular. One of British football's hard men, Scoular's legs resembled tree trunks and he was known as 'Iron Man'. A month before accepting the Cardiff job he was sacked by Bradford Park Avenue. 'Jimmy was the dirtiest bastard I ever played against and I've got the marks to prove it,' comments George Edwards. 'The reason we went for him was because he had a lot of contacts in the game. He knew everybody. If he wanted to find out about a player all he had to do was pick up the phone.' Like Swindin, Scoular believed a young team would take Cardiff into the First Division and slowly but surely he weeded out the veterans. 'When Jimmy came he said the same thing as George Swindin, that we had too many old players,' adds Edwards.

In his first season there was little transfer movement and a stale dressing-room may have been responsible for the team's woeful start. The Bluebirds had to wait until the twelfth match of the season for their first league win, against Derby County at Ninian Park on 10 October. Scoular's men eventually finished thirteenth thanks to a decent finish which saw Cardiff lose just four of their last fourteen outings.

Charles began the season at centre-half with Scoular's uncompromising style rubbing off on him. In the fourth match of the season, at Preston, Charles was booed by the partisan Deepdale crowd for a series of hard challenges on the Preston forwards. Left winger Doug Holden was sent 'spinning around like a top' after the Cardiff defender lunged for the ball. Holden picked himself up 'and stared in disbelief' at Charles. Brian Godfrey, Preston's centre-forward, kept a safe distance from Charles after a few tackles. Scoular loved it and his faced beamed with delight every time the home crowd jeered Charles. 'When a player is booed like that he must be doing something worthwhile for his side and that was precisely what John was doing,' said the Cardiff manager who kicked lumps out of his own players during training matches. 'He was destroying the opposition but doing it quite fairly and squarely. There was nothing dirty in his play and no one could complain about it.'

After the 1–1 draw at Deepdale Charles admitted he was 'playing it harder this season' but added, 'I have never in my soccer career gone in deliberately to foul a player. I am not doing it now and I never will.'

Don Murray took Charles's place after the former Juventus player was injured in a 3–1 defeat at Huddersfield at the end of September. The teenager impressed Scoular enough to keep the number 5 shirt for the rest of the season with Charles flitting between right-half and centre-forward. The apprentice had toppled the sorcerer. 'John took me under his wing at Cardiff,' explains Murray, who grew up in the Scottish Highlands. 'He was a great talker on the pitch and I learned so many things from him, the little things. I remember a game at Derby. A cross came from the right and I went up to head it away. I headed the ball outside the area but to the middle of the goal. It fell to a Derby player who hit the crossbar when he should have scored. John grabbed hold of me and said, "Don't ever do that again! When you head a ball away, head it back to where it came from." I never forgot that.' Murray recalls another memory of Charles. 'I can't remember who it was against but a corner was given against us. John, who was standing on the penalty spot, jumped in the air, caught the ball on his chest, turned in mid-air and knocked it back to our goalkeeper, Graham Vearncombe. It was an unbelievable piece of skill. A lesser player like myself would have just headed it away as far as possible.'

John Toshack, who grew up not far from Ninian Park, also became his protégé. The scrawny teenager from Northumberland

Street in Cardiff's Canton area idolised Charles and wanted him to teach him everything he knew. Charles's son, Melvyn, claims his father taught Toshack how to head the ball. In the afternoons, after training, Charles would take Toshack aside and they would work together on the Ninian Park pitch. On one occasion the pair spent half an hour heading the ball back to each other. 'Tosh could flick the ball with his head but he wasn't so good at directing them and that's what John worked on with him,' says Don Murray. 'Tosh learned a lot from John.' Toshack, who would sign for Liverpool in 1970, went as far as to say, 'I learned as much from John as I did from years playing the game.' He had a lengthy spell playing alongside Charles in the reserves during the 1965–66 season when his idol was trying to recover his fitness after a knee operation. 'John had a huge influence on Tosh,' adds Peter King. 'John did as much as he could to help him.'

Charles scored just three league goals in the 1964–65 season, his lowest return since 1950–51. Two came in the 5–0 drubbing of Swansea Town at Ninian Park on 6 April 1965. An otherwise nondescript campaign was livened up by Cardiff's performances in the Cup-Winners' Cup. It began with a trip to Esbjerg, a busy fishing port on Denmark's west coast, on 7 September 1964. Factories and shops closed early so the town's population could watch The Bluebirds and in particular Charles. 'Wherever we went in Europe, whether it was Spain, Portugal, Belgium or Denmark,' says Murray, 'you could be sure that John's face would be plastered all over the local newspapers. He was the one player in our side that everyone knew. The rest of us were nobodies.' The 10,000 crowd that gathered inside Esbjerg's modest Idvaetspark saw Charles, at centre-half, help The Bluebirds to grind out a 0–0 draw. Peter King's header won the second leg at Ninian Park three weeks later.

The second draw paired Cardiff with the cup holders, Sporting Lisbon, with the first leg being held in Sporting's Estadio José Alvalade. En route to lifting the Cup-Winners' Cup the previous season the Portuguese outfit had beaten Manchester United 5–0 in Lisbon and eight players involved in the mauling of Matt Busby's star-studded side would start against the Welsh club. Yet this was a good time to face Sporting. They started their championship badly and when Cardiff arrived in Lisbon they were third from bottom in the Portuguese league after a 3–0 defeat against Torriense. Scoular and his players were given another pre-match boost two days before the first leg when the club sacked its French coach, Jean Lucien, and replaced him with Julio Juca, a former Sporting player.

The gruff Scot expected Sporting to pile on the pressure in the Alvalade so he devised a defensive approach that revolved around Charles. It was dubbed 'the Scoular Scheme'. Gareth Williams, an inside-forward, dropped back into defence with Charles acting as a 'sweeper' behind a line of four defenders, Alan Harrington, Peter Rodrigues, Don Murray and Williams. The plan was to keep out Sporting's forwards, notably their Brazilian star Osvaldo Silva, and hit them on the counter-attack. It worked to perfection. The defence, with Charles at his very best, smothered Sporting's raids while Greg Farrell and Derek Tapscott gave Cardiff an astonishing 2–0 lead after 70 minutes. 'John was outstanding in Lisbon,' says Tapscott. 'He had experience of playing on the continent, we didn't. He told us what to expect, that the referee and linesmen wouldn't give us anything, that we shouldn't argue with them, that we should just get on with the game if the Sporting players tried to have a go at us. His experience in Europe was vital.'

Paolo Figueiredo pulled one back for the home side nine minutes from the end but his goal could not prevent a famous Cardiff victory. At the final whistle the Sporting fans threw their cushions onto the pitch in disgust.

In the dressing-room afterwards Scoular shook each of his players by the hand saying they were 'just marvellous'. He told waiting reporters, 'Our lads had fought like Trojans and it would be totally unfair to single out any player for special mention. They are a team of heroes.' Charles was the difference between an expected defeat and a famous victory. 'John gave us the experience we needed in these games because we were so naive,' says Don Murray. 'He told us Sporting would dive and look for free-kicks and penalties, that we had to stay on our feet and not dive in. It was all good advice.' Alan Harrington has never forgotten the way Charles played inside the Alvalade that December night in 1964. 'Whenever we got a corner or a free-kick John would go up for it. As soon as it broke down he was back in defence. To see him running up and down the pitch was unbelievable. He was in his 30s but he never flagged. He was here, there and everywhere. He was telling everyone what to do and if a Sporting player beat you, there was John right behind you. He was absolutely tremendous that night.'

Many of his old Cardiff teammates believe Charles's best performances for The Bluebirds came in the Cup-Winners' Cup. Playing on the European stage, in arenas such as Sporting's Alvalade, probably reminded him of his Juventus days. 'John was a very emotional man and I remember him walking off the pitch after we had beaten Sporting 2–1,' says Harrington. 'He had tears streaming down his face. He was crying. I asked him, "What's wrong?" And he said, "We've won." The big games in Europe were when you really saw John play for Cardiff City. He was really up for it. We trained at Sporting's ground the night before the game. John was never the best trainer but you could see he was really up for this one. His tackling and distribution were magnificent.'

Charles prevented what seemed a certain Sporting goal in the very first minute. 'They had a corner and I foolishly drifted outside my six-yard box,' explains Dilwyn John. 'One of the Sporting players headed the ball down. It bounced over my head and was going into the top corner of the net. John came from nowhere and headed it away. No other player could have done that. He read the situation so well.' It was a crucial clearance and as important as either Farrell's or Tapscott's goals. Had the home side taken the lead that early the outcome of the match might have been very different.

After the game the Cardiff players celebrated in a Lisbon bar. 'The bar staff tried to rip us off,' says Peter King. 'So we called John over. He was a sort of father figure for us and because he spoke Italian there was a good chance the Portuguese would understand him. The waiter started arguing with him and John picked him up with one hand and pinned him against the wall. They sorted the bill out for us in the end.'

Sporting arrived in South Wales for the return leg a week later and were confident of overturning Cardiff's lead. 'Tonight we win 2–0,' said the club's president, General Homem de Figueiredo, on the day of the game. Fernando Mendes, Sporting's captain, warned Cardiff that his side would play better at Ninian Park than it did in Lisbon. The Portuguese were hoping Charles would not be fit for the second leg. He suffered a thigh muscle injury in the 4–0 win over Plymouth Argyle the previous Saturday but recovered in time for the return, allowing Scoular to implement the same strategy he used in Lisbon with Charles as 'sweeper'. In front of a delirious 25,000 crowd, Cardiff ensured their place in the quarter-finals by battling out a 0–0 draw.

Their opponents in the last eight were Spanish side Real Zaragoza, who were sitting in second place in the *Primera Liga* behind Real Madrid when the draw was made. Again, Cardiff were away for the first leg. The 'Scoular Scheme' that had thwarted Sporting was again deployed inside the Estadio La Romareda, this time in a bid to snuff out Real's quick, hard-shooting forward line of Encontra, Santos, Carlos Lapetra, Martinez Marcelino and Juan Manuel Villa, known in Spain as *Los Cinco Magnificos* (the Magnificent Five). Apart from Encontra they were all Spanish internationals. Marcelino was a national hero after scoring Spain's winner in the European Championship final against the Soviet Union in 1962.

The defensive wall that held firm in Lisbon was well and truly dismantled in the opening 12 minutes in Zaragoza. Lapetra put Real ahead with a 20-yard free-kick. Charles – 'the rock', wrote Bryan Stiles in the *Western Mail*, 'upon which wave after wave of Real attacks floundered' – prevented a second minutes later when he blocked D'Arcy Canario's goal-bound shot. Pais doubled the lead with a fierce 35-yard strike after 12 minutes. The partisan crowd expected Real to score a bagful but four minutes after Pais's goal Gareth Williams pulled one back, then Peter King equalised before half-time. City returned home with a 2–2 draw. 'That game in Zaragoza was the best I ever saw John play for Cardiff,' says Murray. 'We were 2–0 down so early on and really under the cosh. Then John actually started playing Real Zaragoza on his own. He was absolutely unbelievable. If it wasn't for him we would've been 9–0 down. He never stopped running, he won everything in the air, he won every tackle. When we were under the cosh he pushed us on. I came off the field totally in awe of him.'

After their comeback in Zaragoza the British press dubbed Scoular's men *Los Once Magnificos* (the Magnificent Eleven). For Charles it was a triumphant return to the stadium where, three years earlier, he had scored twice for Juventus in a friendly against

Real. According to the *Heraldo de Aragon* newspaper, he had played with 'perfect authority'. It added, 'What rubbish for people to say he is finished.' Like Murray, Alan Harrington rates Charles's exhibition inside La Romareda as his finest in the blue shirt of Cardiff. 'John was magnificent against Sporting Lisbon but he was even better against Real Zaragoza. Their football was brilliant. It was a tremendous game, one of the best I've ever played in.'

Charles was touch and go for the second leg a fortnight later. He had missed the two games since the draw in Zaragoza – a 2–0 league defeat at Newcastle and a 3–1 Welsh Cup win over Merthyr Tydfil – with a thigh strain, but two days before the match, and after a strenuous practice match at Coronation Park, he was declared fit to play.

Charles's presence could not stop the Spaniards marching into the semi-finals. With 17 minutes left on the clock Marcelino weaved his way into the penalty box, bamboozled the Cardiff defence and shot past Bob Wilson. Scoular immediately responded by moving Charles into attack and he nearly headed a dramatic equaliser. Charles outjumped the Real defence only to see the ball fly past Enrique Yarza's upright. Cardiff's European adventure died with that effort and Real had made Charles eat his words. 'These continentals have no stamina for a hard battle,' he proclaimed after the 2–2 draw in Zaragoza. In front of a 38,500 crowd at Ninian Park, City's biggest gate for nearly four years, Real rode Cardiff's full-blooded challenges. On a cold February night they won the tie with a magnificently taken goal. A second Welsh Cup success – against Wrexham – meant Cardiff had a second bite at the Cup-Winners' Cup the following season.

In the summer of 1965 Scoular began to weed out Ninian Park's old-timers. Ron Stitfall retired while Derek Tapscott, Mel Charles and Ivor Allchurch moved to new clubs. Charles, who had just started a scrap metal business with his brother, looked like he had also played his last game for the club. He turned down their offer of a new contract after his two-year deal expired. Although Scoular offered him a new 12-month package, the 33 year old was unhappy with the reduced terms. The board offered him twenty-five pounds plus a further twelve pounds in incentives. It was a considerable drop in wages and prompted a bitter response from the player: 'I can earn more working part-time in the scrap metal business.' At the end of May Charles flew to Moscow to play in Wales's World Cup qualifier against the Soviet Union, vowing he would never kick a ball for Cardiff again. 'All I know is that the sooner I'm away from Ninian Park the better.'

On 26 July Scoular received a letter from the player saying he was 'packing up football' to concentrate on his scrap metal business. However, when a local photographer telephoned to ask him to pose for a picture showing him hanging up his boots, he declined. 'If Charles wants to give up the game then there's nothing we can do about it,' said a philosophical Scoular. Five days later Charles unexpectedly turned up at Ninian Park and asked Scoular if he could train with the squad. Scoular said yes and Charles took part in a 90-minute practice match which saw the first team take on the reserves at Coronation Park. He scored a picture-book header that rifled past Lyn Davies, Cardiff's number-two goalkeeper. 'There was unbelievable power in that header. Lyn went white,' says Peter King, who played in that game. 'John was standing on the far corner of the penalty area. He didn't jump, he just threw his head at the ball. I couldn't have kicked the ball harder. John was making a point with that header, that he deserved better than the club was offering him.'

The following week, inside Scoular's office, he signed a new one-year contract. The man who said he was desperate to leave Cardiff was now singing a different tune. 'I'm really looking forward to another season with City,' he told reporters. The reason for his change of heart? 'Football's been my life, I just can't leave it. I had really meant to retire but somehow I can't give up the game.' The real reason was that Cardiff agreed to pay him forty pounds a week plus incentives.

During this period Bournemouth tried to sign him. The Division Three club believed acquiring a player of Charles's stature would increase the gates at Dean Court and revive football in the town. Bournemouth agreed to pay Cardiff a fee close to £10,000 and Charles held talks with their manager, Reg Flewin, at Dean Court. There was a drawback. Joining the Dorset club would mean uprooting his family from Cardiff. He asked Flewin for a few days to think over the move before speaking to him on the phone. Three days later he turned down Bournemouth's offer.

The 1965–66 campaign was a nightmare for Charles, whose season ended after three months with a knee injury. It started so well. Playing at centre-forward in the opening day fixture against Bury at Ninian Park, he headed the only goal of the afternoon after ten minutes. He scored again in the 2–1 home win over Derby County four days later. The Bluebirds suffered their first setback of the season, losing 3–2 at Norwich before Charles made it four goals in four matches by hitting two in the 5–1 demolition of Derby at the Baseball Ground. Peter Jackson, at the time the football correspondent on the *South Wales Echo*, later recalled one of his goals, a free-kick which he corkscrewed around the Derby wall and past their goalkeeper, Reg Matthews. 'Pelé could not have done better.' That was his last goal for The Bluebirds.

In the first round of the Cup-Winners' Cup, Cardiff were drawn against Belgium's Standard Liège. The first leg was played at Ninian Park on 12 September and it was a rough, tough match. Cardiff began brightly and George Johnston put them ahead in the 31st minute. Scoular picked Charles at centre-forward but he was shackled by Standard's towering, Flemish-speaking centre-half Lucien Spronck. Standard won the game after the break. Roger Claessen equalised and Leon Semmeling ensured a 2–1 victory for the Belgian side. For the second leg in the Stade de Sclessin, Scoular based his gameplan around Charles. The Scot believed his side's best chance of success was for the ball to be pumped down the middle for the big striker but Spronck, a Belgian international, mastered Charles in the second leg just as he did in the first and Alan Harrington's own-goal gave Standard a 3–1 aggregate win.

This was Charles's last game for The Bluebirds. In the dying minutes he jarred his right knee after colliding with Joseph Vliers. He tried to shake off the injury but in January 1966, after 12 weeks on Scoular's casualty list, a specialist told him that if he wanted to carry on playing football he would need to have an operation on the knee.

Charles was admitted to the Prince of Wales Orthopaedic Hospital at Rhydlafar, Cardiff, for the 'removal of foreign bodies' from his knee. Around 20 to 30 bits of bone, which the player likened to fish bones, were taken out.

In November 1965, two months before his knee operation, both

Newport County and Plymouth Argyle tried to sign him. Second Division Plymouth agreed a £7,000 fee for Charles and Derek Ufton, manager of the Devon club, lunched with the former Leeds and Juventus star at Cardiff's Royal Hotel. Ufton, however, left the city without Charles's signature on the transfer forms he had brought with him. 'I want more time to think it over,' said Charles. This was not the first time the West Country outfit had tried to prise him away from Ninian Park. In November 1964 Malcolm Allison, then Plymouth's manager, rang Scoular to ask if he would postpone a Wessex League Youth match between the two clubs because he had five players out injured. Scoular agreed. Allison, almost as an afterthought, said, 'I see John Charles is not in your first team. What do you want for him?' Scoular told him £15,000 although whether the board would agree to that amount was another matter. Charles had lost his place in the first team because of an Achilles injury and the excellent form of his deputy, Don Murray.

Allison, who had just spent £45,000 of his club's money on Swansea Town winger Barrie Jones, believed Charles could help The Pilgrims win promotion to the First Division. 'If Charles joins us I will use him both in defence and attack, depending on the opposition. He is still a very fine player and he would do us a lot of good,' he explained. He travelled to Cardiff to watch Charles in a reserve match and from his hotel room he telephoned Scoular and offered £10,000. Scoular laughed but when he realised Allison was serious he took it to his board. Plymouth's offer was dismissed within minutes and Charles stayed at Ninian Park.

Like his predecessor, Ufton failed to land Charles. The player decided to stay put because Ufton wanted to use him in attack. 'I don't want to play centre-forward again,' remarked Charles. 'I want to play centre-half.' He also refused to sign for Division Four club Newport County – according to their chairman John Bailey, a team 'badly in need of a personality' – for the same reason.

The 33 year old hoped to recover from the knee operation after six weeks and vowed to win his first-team place back, but he never regained full fitness before the season finished on 10 May. There was one consolation – he missed the humiliating 9–0 mauling at Preston in the penultimate game of the season, a defeat that prompted Scoular to snarl, 'If I were a Cardiff City player, I'd be ashamed to walk down the street.'

In his final days at Ninian Park Charles could be found in the tearoom, bossing the apprentices around. He would send them to the newsagents on the corner of Sloper Road, which runs along Ninian Park, to buy him a packet of cigarettes or a bar of chocolate. He would also tell them to fetch him a cup of tea or a bacon sandwich. In exchange, he would regale them with stories from his career, particularly about his days in Italy.

In May 1966, after three mixed years at Ninian Park, Cardiff gave Charles a free transfer. His reaction? 'I intend to stay in football if possible but I've not yet decided what to do.' He expected to be released but felt he still had a couple of years of league football left in him. Coaching in Italy crossed his mind but he did not want to uproot his family again. Charles was particularly keen on joining Swansea Town but the club was not convinced of his fitness and decided against an approach. There was plenty of interest from Welsh League clubs. Pwllheli, backed by local businessman Victor Barma, who offered Charles a job as a salesman and a luxury flat if he joined the North Wales club, were keen for his signature. Portmadoc, who had signed his brother Mel the previous year, wanted another Charles on their books while Bangor City were also interested. There was a call from Ireland. Dundalk wanted him as their player-coach and the carrot was a £2,500 salary plus a house and a job in a brewery since the football post was part-time. Bob Dennison, the manager of Southern League club Hereford United, also came forward. Charles flew to his holiday home in Diano Marina to think over all the offers.

CHAPTER TWELVE –
CIDER, COWS AND COCK-UPS

Hereford United showed how determined they were to recruit Charles in the last week of May 1966. One of the club's directors, Harold Rumsey, made what the *Hereford Times* described as 'a lightning trip' to the Italian Riviera to talk to the player about a possible move to Edgar Street. Rumsey was accompanied by Frank Miles, a local businessman and chairman of the Hereford United Supporters Club. 'Harold and I flew to Nice. We hired a car and drove to Diano Marina where Charles was on holiday,' recalls Miles. 'When we found him he was playing tennis and there was a sizeable crowd watching.'

Bob Dennison was supposed to fly out to talk to the former Cardiff player but he was taking a summer break in Majorca. The job of convincing the Gentle Giant to join the Southern League Premier Division outfit was left to Rumsey. 'It went smoothly. John was such a nice bloke. He didn't ask for the sky. Of course he would get more than the other players at the club but he wasn't asking for anything ridiculous,' adds Miles, who later became Hereford chairman. 'One advantage we had was that John wanted to stay in Cardiff and Hereford isn't that far from Cardiff.' The Welsh capital is about an hour's drive from Hereford, although the trip can take longer if tractors are hogging the A49 that leads into the city. Charles made the journey at least twice a week since Hereford trained on Tuesday and Thursday nights, the sessions starting at 7 p.m. and finishing at around 9 p.m.

Charles listened to Rumsey and promised an answer when he returned home from Italy at the beginning of July. 'It's no secret we are interested in signing Charles and that we aren't the only club keen to obtain his signature,' said Rumsey after arriving back from Diano Marina. Dennison was looking for a replacement for striker Ron Fogg who lived in London and who left Hereford because he was tired of travelling back and forth to Edgar Street. Hereford's eagerness to sign Charles could be traced back to two pre-season friendlies between Cardiff and Hereford in August 1965. Cardiff won 4–2 at Hereford with Charles scoring Cardiff's fourth. Five days later The Bluebirds demolished the part-timers at Ninian Park 8–3 with Charles netting a brace. Former Hereford left-back Peter Timms remembers the second encounter. 'Cardiff were murdering us and at half-time Bob Dennison said to Ray Daniel, who was marking John, "Come on Ray, what's going on?" And Ray said, "What do you mean what's going on? Santamaría couldn't get above John to head the ball!"'

On 3 July – a Sunday – the telephone rang at the Royal Hotel in Coventry where Rumsey, a caterer, was working at the time. It was Charles, who told him he would like to sign for Hereford. Rumsey immediately drove to Charles's home in Cardiff with the forms for him to sign. Hereford chairman Frank Spiers was delighted with his latest capture. 'I hope he will be happy with us and we will be more than satisfied if he plays as well as he did in the trial matches against us last season.' Hereford claimed they had beaten a number of league clubs to Charles's signature, including Notts County and Brighton.

Before making his final decision on whether to join Hereford, Charles had called his friend and former Wales teammate, Ray Daniel, who was still playing for the non-league club. 'Ray told me Hereford was the best club he had ever played for and that's good enough for me,' explained Charles. Daniel, incidentally, was released by the club at the end of Charles's first season. Accompanying Charles to Hereford was his 18-year-old nephew, Geoffrey Bowen. He was on Swansea Town's books the previous season and Charles considered him 'an above average wing-half'.

Charles, who confided to friends he was 'bitterly disappointed' to have been released by Cardiff, was one of two big-name signings made by Hereford that summer. The other was the former Middlesbrough, Sheffield Wednesday and England winger Eddie Holliday.

Charles's first job for his new club was to make an appearance at a garden party, held at Spiers's Hereford home, in honour of two of the club's long-serving players, Daniel and goalkeeper Peter Isaac. 'Having someone of John Charles's magnitude playing with us took all the players back a bit,' says Timms. 'But he was very unassuming, as we found out during the first training session he had with us. He was a megastar in football but he blended in with everyone at the club.' Roger Griffiths, then a 19-year-old right-back at Edgar Street, adds, 'John came to Hereford completely out of the blue. It was an amazing signing really. He was such a big man. I found the size of his neck unbelievable. No wonder he could get such power on his headers.'

Hereford was buzzing about Charles's arrival, as demonstrated by the gates for the two pre-season friendlies at Edgar Street, against Jimmy Hill's Coventry City and Swansea Town. A crowd of 4,651 saw Coventry's 5–1 win while 3,341 watched Hereford defeat Swansea 3–1 with Charles scoring his side's third in the 67th minute.

Bedford Town were Hereford's first Southern League Premier Division opponents, at Edgar Street on 20 August. The public responded to the ambition shown by the club during the summer and the 4,863 gate was the biggest since 1953, and 2,000 more than the corresponding fixture the previous season. Dennison's men stormed to a 5–1 victory with Charles finding the net but he was upstaged by another Welshman, Albert Derrick, who scored a hat-trick. 'After training we used to go into the club bar for a pint and there were always supporters inside wanting to talk to John,' continues Griffiths. 'John would come in and he'd always chat to them. They'd ask him questions about his time in Italy and he'd answer them. John used to love all that.'

The Southern League season was barely a week old when Hereford's resolve to keep hold of Charles was tested by Division Two club Bury, who made known their interest in acquiring the player. Bob Dennison was not interested. 'As far as we are concerned John is worth his weight in gold and I shouldn't imagine he is interested in going to Bury. He had plenty of chances to remain in league football but chose to come here.'

Hereford's opening day drubbing of Bedford was a false dawn. After five games Dennison's side had collected a modest five points and following a 2–2 home draw with Nuneaton in September Charles found himself barracked by frustrated supporters who expected more from him. In the *Hereford Times*, Ted Woodriffe leapt to the player's defence. 'Charles only touched the ball effectively half a dozen times yet he scored, hit the post and created a great chance for Derrick.' Later that month he responded to his critics in the best possible fashion, netting five goals in the 6–1 thrashing of Folkestone.

Their title hopes virtually died the following March when leaders Wimbledon beat them 2–1 at Edgar Street, Hereford's fourth home defeat in six matches. The season's end was an anti-climax. The enthusiasm that had engulfed the club following Charles's signing was waning and a crowd of only 2,836 – nearly 1,100 less than the average home gate that season – turned up to watch the April Fool's Day clash against Chelmsford City, which Dennison's side comfortably won 3–0. Hereford finished the season in tenth place, eight points behind champions Romford. 'Signing John created a buzz at Hereford but it also created a buzz at the other grounds where we went to play,' explains Roger Griffiths. 'I think having John in the team had an adverse effect. We used to arrive at away matches and the opposition would be saying, "Here come Hereford with John Charles." They became hell-bent on doing well against us and we found teams harder to beat.'

For Charles, there was an unhappy return to Ninian Park in the Welsh Cup in 1966–67. Hereford, along with border clubs such as Shrewsbury Town and Oswestry, were invited by the FAW to take part in the competition. If they won, however, they were not allowed to take part in the Cup-Winners' Cup because they were English clubs and, according to UEFA rules, clubs could only play in Europe if the cup they won was from their own country. On 8 February 1967, Charles travelled to Cardiff with his new club hoping to prove a point to Bluebirds manager Jimmy Scoular. He endured a miserable 90 minutes as Hereford sank without trace. The Second Division side were 6–0 up after an hour, although the part-timers scored three times in the last half-hour to make the scoreline more respectable.

During his first season at Edgar Street Charles was reprimanded by the football authorities for the first time in his distinguished career. The match concerned was Hereford's 3–2 defeat at Nuneaton in April 1967. The visitors looked set to leave the West Midlands with a point but with two minutes remaining, the home side scored a contentious winner. The Hereford players claimed goalkeeper Peter Isaac was charged in the back before Nuneaton scored but the referee dismissed their protests. Charles waited for the man in black in the tunnel after the final whistle and told him what he thought of the decision. The forward was 'severely censured' by the FA's disciplinary committee and 'warned as to his future conduct'. Charles was not in the country to learn of the FA's decision. He was a few days into his month-long tour of Mauritius and Zambia with his touring team, the John Charles XI.

His manager spoke on his behalf. 'It strikes me as a bit ridiculous that a player should be severely censured for politely but firmly putting his point of view to a referee,' said Dennison. He insisted Charles did not use foul and abusive language in his conversation with the referee and that all he said in his capacity as team captain was, 'That's the worst piece of refereeing I've seen in my life.' Added Dennison, 'I was standing beside John and as far as I was concerned it was fair comment. John didn't swear. That's why I'm very surprised at the FA's decision.'

Overall it was a disappointing campaign for the Southern League outfit but on a personal level Charles delivered, the Welshman scoring an impressive 37 goals in 54 matches. 'Not bad going,' remarked Dennison, 'for a player who a lot of people thought would only play two or three games for us.' The haul meant he once again attracted the attention of other clubs. First, Irish League club Ards, managed by former England international George Eastham, approached him about a move. Charles, who had recently opened his own sports shop in Cardiff, told him it would be 'too much trouble' to move to Northern Ireland. More appealing was the reputed interest being shown by Swansea Town.

His name came up in a telephone conversation between Dennison and Billy Lucas, Swansea's manager, on the eve of the

1967–68 season. Dennison implied that Hereford, who had signed Charles on a free transfer, might let their 34-year-old forward go if Swansea tabled an offer. The previous year, before he joined Hereford, Charles's hometown club had shown interest in bringing him back to the Vetch Field he once weeded as a groundstaff boy, but they were unconvinced about his fitness.

The ailing Fourth Division club desperately needed to sign someone of Charles's calibre and a move back to Swansea appealed to the player who practically made a 'come and get me' plea to Lucas. 'I am now fitter than I was 12 months ago when Swansea Town could have had me on a free transfer,' Charles told Pat Searle of the *Western Mail*. 'I believe I could do them some good, but Swansea must contact Hereford if they are interested at all.'

He did his transfer prospects no harm when the two sides met in a pre-season friendly at Edgar Street and Charles was the architect of Hereford's 4–2 victory. The Swansea directors later held a board meeting but bringing the former Wales international to the Vetch was not on their agenda.

Another year in the Southern League beckoned for Charles. His side began the 1967–68 season well, winning their first two games, both at Edgar Street, against Stevenage Town and Dover Town. Then came a 2–1 loss at Margate – and an approach from Oswestry Town. The Cheshire League club wanted Charles to replace Jackie Mudie as player-manager. Dennison had no intention of losing his star player. 'The trouble with these clubs,' he said, 'is that they want something for nothing. I'm not prepared to let Charles go and I know he has no intention of going either.'

For the second time in his career Charles scored five goals in a single match, this time in the 8–1 thrashing of Mid Wales League outfit Llanidloes in the Welsh Cup. On 11 December his career took an unexpected twist. Dennison decided to give up his position at Edgar Street to become Coventry City's chief scout. Bill Humphries, who succeeded Frank Spiers as Hereford chairman, offered Charles the role of player-manager. A 'thrilled to bits' Charles had no hesitation in accepting. 'Management,' he said, 'is an aspect of the game that has always appealed to me.'

Since joining Cardiff in 1963, he had harboured a desire to move into coaching. Charles applied for the trainer's job at Ninian Park in

1964 when Stan Montgomery left but Jimmy Scoular, believing Charles still had much to offer as a player, preferred Lew Clayton. The ambition to manage a football team never faded and at Hereford he showed his employers where he thought his future lay by attending an FA coaching course. Humphries was confident Charles would be a success in his new post. 'I think it's only fair we give him the chance to prove himself with us. I believe he has the ability and drive to do a good job in Southern League football. He reached the top as a player and now he has the chance to do as well as a manager. If we had to advertise for another manager it would take weeks to find a successor but we think we've found the man for the job on our own playing staff.'

Charles's teammates were not surprised by the appointment. 'John was almost an automatic choice,' says Peter Timms. 'The club had to give him a chance.' Peter Isaac adds, 'John's personality was more player than manager and he was probably too nice to be a manager, but he was the obvious man to replace Bob.'

His first game as player-manager came 48 hours after he was unveiled as Dennison's successor, in a first-round FA Cup tie against fellow Southern League side Barnet at Edgar Street. He enjoyed a winning start as Hereford, roared on by a 6,392 crowd, beat the London side 3–2. It was Timms who got the winner, his first goal for two and a half years. Charles tasted victory again in his second match, a 2–1 win at Stevenage with Les Cocker scoring Hereford's last-minute winner. Then came a 6–2 win over Margate followed by a 1–1 Boxing Day draw at Nuneaton. Humphries' gamble on Charles appeared to be paying off. 'Before John was our manager our training was just lapping around the pitch but John introduced some of the training methods he had been used to at Juventus,' says Griffiths. 'There was more work with the ball and players worked in small triangular groups. There's no doubt he made me a better player.'

After dramatically disposing of Barnet, Hereford were drawn to face Watford at Vicarage Road in the second round of the FA Cup. Around 1,500 Hereford supporters made the exodus to Hertfordshire hoping their side would pull off a giant-killing act. Charles hoped his part-timers 'would be able to pull something out of the bag for them' but the Third Division side had no wish to be the victims of a cup upset and cruised to a comfortable 3–0 victory.

All three goals came in the first 33 minutes. Charles left Vicarage Road nursing a disappointing defeat and a nose broken during the game. After a bright start to Charles's managerial career, the cup exit sparked a decline in results for the club beginning with a 4–1 drubbing at Barnet. Hereford gradually tumbled down the Premier Division table.

In a Camkin Cup tie against Worcester City, Hereford's traditional rivals, Charles made a number of bizarre decisions which culminated in a 3–0 defeat, the heaviest suffered against Worcester since 1939. First he dropped Peter Isaac who was playing well and replaced him with Bob Appleby who had just recovered from an injury which had sidelined him for five weeks. During the first half, Appleby was hurt trying to scramble the ball clear but soldiered on to the interval by which time Hereford were 2–0 down. To the amusement of the 2,703 crowd, Charles appeared for the second half wearing the goalkeeper's jersey. 'I played a few times in goal for Leeds when the goalkeeper was injured and I also had a spell there during the summer when I was on tour in Zambia,' he later explained. By putting himself in goal, Hereford lost the one player who might have rescued the game. As Ted Woodriffe wrote in his match report for the *Hereford Times,* seeing Charles between the posts 'brought some comic relief' to an otherwise depressing game. He failed to stop Gerry Graham scoring a third goal for Worcester and when their winger Eddie Ward was felled inside the Hereford penalty box, even the home supporters screamed for a penalty. They wanted to see Charles deal with a spot-kick but the referee did not oblige.

Off the pitch, Charles upset the Hereford public in a Sunday newspaper interview headlined 'THE FORGOTTEN GIANT'. He called the rural cathedral city 'a soccer backwater' where 'the cows are better known than the people'. He also revealed he received abuse from farmers when the team was not playing well. His remarks irked Edgar Street. One member of the Hereford United Supporters Club threatened to resign unless Charles publicly apologised, which he quickly did in the *Hereford Times.* 'The last thing that was on my mind was to say anything offensive,' he said. 'I appreciate the chance I've been given by Hereford to manage the club.' Charles claimed he was misquoted. 'There is, of course, a big difference to playing non-league at Hereford and the point I was trying to make was that whereas Juventus are known the world over as a football team, Hereford was better known for its white-faced cattle, salmon and cider. Unfortunately, when it went into print only the word "cows" appeared. The general idea of the article was to show how a soccer player's circumstances change in the course of ten years and I am sorry if what was written has offended Hereford supporters.'

Hereford ended 1967–68 in 16th place, 15 points behind champions Wimbledon. They did, however, reach the Welsh Cup final where they faced the competition's hot favourites, Cardiff City. The final was a two-legged affair with the first match staged at Edgar Street. The remote chance Hereford had of winning the trophy disappeared on this May evening with Cardiff winning 2–0. The second leg at Ninian Park ten days later was academic. Jimmy Scoular's men brushed Charles and company aside 4–1.

It was an uncomfortable start to his reign at Edgar Street and Charles's record was far from impressive. In the 37 games he had taken charge of since Dennison left for Highfield Road, the team won only 12, lost 19 and conceded 68 goals. The home gates also slumped. The average for 1967–68 was 2,679 compared to 3,561 the previous season. In his defence, it was not Charles's team. For the forthcoming season he had the opportunity to build a side in his own image.

He released seven players – Bob Appleby, Ian McIntosh, Selwyn Vale, Roy Lambden, David Dodson, Brian Punter and Les Cocker – and brought in five new faces – Alan Scarrott, John Bird, Roy Evans, Lyn Davies and Brian Purcell. Scarrott, a right-winger, was signed from Reading. Charles went to Swansea Town for Bird, Evans and Purcell while goalkeeper Davies came from Cardiff. 'John came to my home in Reading to speak to me about joining Hereford,' says Scarrott. 'I picked him up at the station in my 1958 Ford Prefect. The size of him struck me first and foremost. He got into the passenger seat and filled it. It's only when he got into my car that I realised just how big he was.' Before committing himself, Scarrott and his wife visited Hereford, and they met Charles outside The Red Eagle pub, next to the cathedral. 'He'd obviously seen me cross the ball – I wasn't much good at anything else. But from John's point of view crossing the ball was everything because if you put the ball in the right place you could guarantee he would score. What people perhaps didn't know was that there was a big drop on the pitch at Edgar Street towards the Meadow End and that's where John scored most of his goals because he would come onto the ball after running down a slope.'

The 1968–69 season had its high points. It saw the opening of the new £25,000 Grandstand and a memorable FA Cup tussle against Torquay United in which Charles's men took the Third Division side to a first-round replay. The first match, at Edgar Street, ended 0–0. At Plainmoor, Ken Sandercock gave Hereford a shock lead after four minutes but Torquay went on to win 4–2. Charles 'came within a hair's breadth' of heading his side level when it was 3–2.

The season was overshadowed by the tragic deaths of two Hereford players. On 20 January 1969, Evans and Purcell were killed in a car crash in heavy fog on the notoriously dangerous Heads of the Valleys Road near Ebbw Vale. The pair, who both lived in Swansea, were en route to Edgar Street where the team coach was waiting to take the team to Nuneaton for a Monday night Camkin Cup match. Three vehicles were involved in the crash – Evans and Purcell's Riley Elf, an estate car and a van. When the two players failed to turn up the coach left without them and the players and club officials did not learn about the crash until after the match. Hereford secretary Reg Tidball telephoned Bill Humphries who broke the news to Charles and his players in the dressing-room. 'John sat in the bath and cried like a baby,' recalls Peter Timms. 'Like John, they were Swansea lads. It broke his heart.'

Days earlier Evans and Purcell shone in the 4–1 Herefordshire Senior Cup final win over Newport County in which Charles scored all four of Hereford's goals. According to Ted Woodriffe, he gave 'a vintage performance at centre-forward'. Afterwards the ever-modest Charles said he felt embarrassed. 'I never like a match to look like a one-man show,' he said. 'All the lads played well and I would have liked the goals to have been shared out.' At 38, with thinning and greying hair, Charles was still a formidable force, albeit at non-league level. He was in good shape, no pot belly or 'love handles' yet. 'He was built like a weightlifter with big shoulders and a narrow waist,' says Dudley Tyler, who Charles signed in 1969. Alan Scarrott, though, noticed his legs. 'They were fairly marked. You could see he had been kicked throughout his career. There were no scars, they were just worn.'

The side limped on for the rest of the season, minus Evans and Purcell, finishing 14th and 20 points behind champions Cambridge United. That summer the club had a new chairman, Frank Miles, the man who helped Harold Rumsey bring Charles to the club three years earlier. Hereford born and bred, Miles owned West Country Carpets which had nine stores in the West Country, South Wales and Hereford. His ambition was to take the club into the Football League and to achieve his dream he promised a shake-up at Edgar Street. 'The general discipline of the club will be tightened 100 per cent and training and match practice will also be organised. This club is going to be run on business lines.'

Miles admits Charles would not have been his choice as manager. 'He had a wonderful name in football and wonderful experience,' he says. 'But it's the old story, a good engine driver doesn't necessarily make a good stationmaster. Sadly, that was the case with John.'

Charles's management style was certainly eccentric, as his former players testify. He had never heard of team sheets and would pick his starting 11 off the top of his head, usually in the dressing-room minutes before the game was due to start. 'Kick-off would be five or ten minutes away and we wouldn't know what the team was,' says Peter Isaac. 'I'll never forget one game against Cheltenham. We were changed and about to go onto the pitch. John was geeing us up and the lads who weren't playing came into the dressing-room to show their faces. John English, who was a striker, said, "All the best lads!" John looked at him and said, "You're supposed to be bloody playing!" He had obviously forgotten about him. Organisation wasn't one of his strong points.'

Fred Potter, a goalkeeper Charles signed from Burton Albion and the man who replaced Isaac in the Hereford goal, recalls a match at Kettering. 'It was 2.45 p.m. and John still hadn't come into the dressing-room to tell us the team. The referee came in and said, "Look, you're supposed to give me a team sheet 45 minutes before kick-off." I was getting changed and the referee said to me, "Why are you changing and no one else?" I told him I was the only goalkeeper here so I must be playing! John's training sessions were fantastic but his man-management and organisation were, excuse the expression, crap.'

Ricky George, who joined Hereford in March 1971 and who went on to score the winner in the club's famous 2–1 win over Newcastle United in the FA Cup in 1972, adds, 'I remember sitting in the dressing-room before a game. We were all wearing our suits. John came in and said, "Come on boys, get changed. We kick-off in 20 minutes." One of us said, "What's the team John?" And John got a packet of cigarettes out, leaned against the wall and started picking the side. "Fred in goal . . ."'

Ronnie Radford, like George, joined Hereford in 1971 and he encountered Charles's unique approach to football management in his first game. It was before a pre-season friendly against Shrewsbury Town at Gay Meadow. On this occasion, a team sheet was brought into the dressing-room by Peter Isaac, by then the club's trainer. Radford's name was on it but the Yorkshireman did not know where Charles wanted him to play. 'I had got changed and was waiting for John. He always came into the dressing-room very late. We were about ten minutes away from kick-off and he still hadn't turned up. Anyway, we were about to go out when John came in. I asked him, "Excuse me, John, but where do you want me to play?" He looked at me and said, "You're a midfield player, aren't you?" I said, "Yes." And he replied, "Well, play midfield." And that was it! It could have been central midfield, left side or right side. So I played in central midfield because that's where I chose to play.' Ken Mallender, a left-back Charles signed from Norwich City, recalls another incident before the same match. 'We were about to walk out onto the pitch when John realised that there were 13 players in the line. He took two of them out. "You and you, sit with me," he said.'

The rare team talks were hardly stirring. Peter Timms recalls a pre-match talk before an FA Cup tie against Rugby Town in 1969. 'He started with the goalkeeper, then the right-back, then he came to me, saying, "I'll come back to you later." Then he carried on with the rest of the players, but he never did come back to me. That was my team talk.' George remembers one pep talk for a midweek match. 'I can't remember who we were playing but the next game was against Dover, who were top of the table. Suddenly John went all serious. "Now, we've got to win tonight. Well, we haven't got to. But if we do it will be a good game Saturday." All the players just fell about laughing and then John started to laugh. We were still laughing when we went out onto the pitch but we won 3–0. I have to say John took the mystery out of management for me. He used to twiddle his fingers at the two centre-halves during matches. That meant he wanted them to dovetail. One had to take the front forward and the other the forward behind him. That was the closest he got to tactics.'

After matches, there were no post-mortems, no analysis. Charles would show his face in the opposition's dressing-room and say, 'Well played, lads' – he did this whatever the result – before jumping into the bath, dressing and driving home to Cardiff. The ritual presented a major headache for Isaac if the next match was in midweek and away from home. 'We had to pick up certain players at certain points for away games. For instance, we picked up Ronnie Radford at Cheltenham and Dudley Tyler at Swindon. But because John always disappeared straight after a match I had to ring him up at home and ask him who was playing in the next game so we knew who we had to pick up. Then I'd have to call those players and tell them,' says Isaac. 'All that could have been avoided if John had made a list of players he wanted after the Saturday game. Sometimes he didn't even know we had a game midweek!'

Lack of organisation was one weakness, so too was his genial disposition. Charles was not ruthless enough for the world of football management. On the pitch he never wanted to hurt an opponent physically and off it he never wanted to hurt his players' feelings. Reflecting on his time as Hereford's player-manager years later he confessed that he 'didn't particularly like having to tell players they were left out of the team'. Not long after signing for the club, Ricky George discovered Charles's habit of avoiding confrontation.

Hereford were playing Yeovil Town at Edgar Street and George was struggling with an ankle injury. During the week Charles told the little Londoner he would be involved. 'John was always standing in the doorway at the ground waiting for the players to arrive. When I turned up he always had a big grin on his face,' explains George. 'This night he said to me, "Hey you, Douglas

Fairbanks. Come into my office." He always called me Douglas Fairbanks, I never knew why. So I followed him into his office. I didn't know he even had one. They had just built it for him in the close season. The chair still had cellophane over it and his desk was bare. It had obviously never been used.

'He said to me, "Sit down, boy." Then he said, "Great, isn't it?" I asked him what was great. "My office." Then he told me, "I'm gonna leave you out tonight, boy." I asked him why. "Because of your ankle." I said I was fit. "I think you're feeling your ankle." I promised him I was fit and that I really wanted to play. "Oh all right, you play." I started laughing, then he started laughing. I realised years later that he was trying to drop me. He was looking for the kindest way of doing that and so he brought up my ankle.'

Alan Scarrott recalls a dressing-room bust-up between him and Charles during a game at Bath. 'I had a poor first half and John gave me a blast, which wasn't like him. In the heat of the moment I turned on him. This was quite normal inside a dressing-room. But when I had a go back he didn't say anything. He couldn't be hard, it just wasn't in him.'

Before the start of the 1969–70 season Charles brought 24-year-old Dudley Tyler – whom he called 'a late developer' – to Edgar Street. Tyler was to prove his best signing. After Hereford recorded another FA Cup giant-killing in 1974 by beating West Ham United, the East End club were impressed enough with the winger to pay £25,000 to take him to Upton Park. Charles, says Ken Mallender, deserved the credit for the Tyler sale, even though the deal was done when Colin Addison, Charles's successor, was in charge at Hereford. 'Dudley had great feet and control but he would put his head down and run all over the place. It was John who moulded and directed him. He stopped him running around like a headless chicken.'

Another notable arrival that summer was the former West Ham centre-half Ken Brown from Torquay. Charles sounded out Brown about a move to the Southern League club after Hereford's FA Cup defeat against the Devon side at Plainmoor the previous season. 'He said if I fancied leaving Torquay he'd love to have me at Hereford,' says Brown. 'I had another year left on my contract with Torquay and I didn't particularly want to drop into non-league football.'

Then came a change of manager at Plainmoor with Alan Brown replacing Frank O'Farrell. 'My face didn't fit so I decided to go to Hereford. Players would join Hereford simply because John was there. I wouldn't have heard about Hereford if it hadn't been for John Charles.' Brown, who was living in London, would catch a train to Newport where he was collected by Charles who gave him a lift to Edgar Street. While he drove, Charles told Brown stories about his time playing in Italy. 'I had a year with Hereford and I have to say it was one of the best years of my entire playing career,' he adds.

At one stage in the 1969–70 campaign, Hereford were serious contenders for the league title. At the end of November, after a 1–0 win at Brentwood, the side went top of the Southern League Premier Division for the first time under Charles. They looked like champions elect when they hammered Hillingdon Borough 7–0 at Edgar Street. Charles scored four goals in that victory. 'We have been building up for this,' the player-manager told the *Hereford Times* after the match. 'It had to come. We've been playing some great football recently without proper reward for our efforts.' The home supporters were unaware Charles had argued with his chairman before the match. Charles often turned up late for training which infuriated Frank Miles. 'He wasn't setting a good example by arriving late for training and sometimes Peter Isaac ended up having to take over,' says the former chairman. Miles believes the sports shop he had opened in Cardiff was to blame for his tardiness. 'Training would start at 7 p.m. and he would turn up at 7.30 p.m. or 7.45 p.m. This happened quite frequently.' Miles would have preferred Charles to relocate to Hereford. 'I would have been happier had he moved. I don't know if I ever asked him about that but I think I would have been wasting my breath.'

Despite words from the chairman, Charles's punctuality failed to improve. Jim Finney, the former World Cup referee who replaced Reg Tidball as club secretary in 1971, briefly worked with Charles shortly before his sudden departure from Edgar Street early in the 1971–72 season. 'He was so laid back it wasn't true,' says Finney. 'For a midweek match we would expect him to be at the ground at about 4 p.m. to make sure everything was in order. On one occasion, an evening match was postponed at about 6.30 p.m. and

John wasn't even at the ground. He arrived at 7.15 p.m. and someone told him, "Sorry, John, the match is off." And John said, "Why the bloody hell didn't you ring me this afternoon. I wouldn't have bothered coming!"'

At the end of the 1970–71 season Charles took his players to Brest, in northern France, for an end-of-season friendly. The bulk of the team assembled at Hereford where a coach was waiting to take them to Southampton where they would board a ferry to Cherbourg. 'We nearly missed the boat because John was late getting to Hereford,' recalls Ricky George. 'Apparently he got up late. He was very casual. The manager arriving late is not the sort of thing players expect to see. I heard stories that when he was playing in Italy he would arrive to play for Wales and all he had on him was a toothbrush in his top pocket.' George recalls a trip to Germany during his days playing for Charles. A reception was held for the team in a Dusseldorf hotel. 'Did you have a comfortable journey?' Charles was asked. 'Yes,' he replied. 'We flew *Luftwaffe.*' He meant, of course, Lufthansa, the country's national airline, and not Nazi Germany's air force.

Despite the early promise, Hereford's championship challenge faded in the second half of the 1969–70 season. Defeats at Dover and Yeovil were a huge setback but it was over the Easter period that the dream died. The side took two points from their three Easter fixtures. They lost a Good Friday clash at Worcester 1–0 before taking a 4–0 beating against eventual champions Cambridge United at the Abbey Ground. A 1–0 win over Worcester prevented the holiday period becoming a total disaster. Charles's side eventually finished tenth. They also came close to making it to the third round of the FA Cup. After disposing of Rugby Town they faced Chelmsford Town in the first round. Chelmsford had beaten them 5–3 in a Southern League match earlier in the season. In the week of the game Charles called his players in on Monday and Wednesday for extra training 'to avoid the mistakes of the previous game'. It paid off with Mick Lewis scoring the only goal of the tie. That meant a second-round draw against Newport County of the Fourth Division. Even though they were without an away FA Cup win for 13 years, confidence was high in the Hereford camp. A bullish Charles said he felt his side had a 'better blend of youth and experience than County' and that they could 'play as well as any Fourth Division club'.

The part-timers were just three minutes away from forcing a replay at Edgar Street when Alan Wood headed a controversial winner to give the Welsh club a 2–1 win. Ken Brown claimed Wood held him down as he jumped for the ball. Referee John Sier waved away the Hereford protests. 'Diabolical,' snapped Charles when asked about Sier's decision to let the goal stand. Hereford's modest finish to the season did not stop Charles being linked with several managerial posts in the Football League, namely at Plymouth Argyle, Hull City and Bournemouth. His former Leeds teammate, Peter Harrison, urged him to apply for the vacancy at Bournemouth. 'I said to him, "Why don't you go for it? With the name you've got, you'd surely get the job." I told him I'd come with him and help him with the coaching. "Oh, all right," he said. But he never wrote to Bournemouth. I saw him a couple of weeks later and asked him about the job. He said he didn't bother applying.' It was not the first time one of Harrison's plans involving his former housemate failed to come to fruition. 'When we were at Leeds John and I talked about opening up a fish and chip business,' he recalls. 'We were both up for it but we never got round to doing anything. Who knows, we could have been bigger than Harry Ramsden!'

In May 1970, as a result of the speculation surrounding Charles, Miles offered him a 12-month contract. Charles accepted. 'With so much talk of league clubs being interested in John I was not certain one way or the other what decision he would make,' the businessman told the *Hereford Times*. 'But both myself and my fellow directors are extremely pleased that he will be with us at Edgar Street next season.' In the contract Miles insisted on a clause that said Charles would spend more time in Hereford concentrating on the management rather than playing side. 'I have no doubts that John Charles, with all his experience in football, is the man for the job and I have every confidence in him,' continued Miles.

Hereford began the 1970–71 season in brilliant fashion. They won ten of their first thirteen matches and were sitting on top of the table. They also drew a Football League club – in this case Fourth Division Northampton Town – at home in the first round of the FA

Cup. In the boardroom, meanwhile, Miles plotted the club's election to the Football League. In an era of re-election, the bottom two clubs in the Fourth Division needed to win the votes of the other Football League clubs and 'associate members' if they wished to avoid being replaced by a Southern League Premier Division rival. Miles and his directors, armed with china bulls – a gift from the club – visited the country's Football League clubs to argue Hereford's case.

Charles helped his club's cause by beating Northampton who reached the fifth round the previous season. The Cobblers, managed by Charles's former Wales teammate Dave Bowen, were 2–0 up at Edgar Street with 33 minutes remaining. Hereford centre-half Alan Jones, another Swansea lad recruited by Charles, reduced the arrears. With three minutes left on the clock, Brian Owen sent the 10,401 crowd into ecstasy when he netted the equaliser. At the County Ground, Hereford recorded one of their most famous results. They attacked Bowen's side from the kick-off and Billy Meadows put the visitors ahead in the third minute. Eleven minutes later, Owen, the hero of the first match, nodded Hereford 2–0 in front. Northampton's Frank Rankmore pulled one back in the 58th minute. Charles, who began the match as a forward, came back to help his defenders. The Cobblers piled on the pressure in the last half-hour but the part-timers held on and Northampton's 14-match unbeaten run at home came to an end. It was one of Hereford's greatest victories, up there with the 2–0 Welsh Cup win at Cardiff City in 1958 and the 1–0 FA Cup win over Millwall in 1965. 'The best game I ever saw John play for Hereford was the replay with Northampton,' explains Fred Potter. 'He was a Goliath at their place. I knew that anything that came over John that day was my ball because nobody was jumping higher than him.'

In the next round, Hereford landed a plum draw – Third Division Brighton at Edgar Street. Hereford's ground was packed to its 12,769 capacity and fans saw Charles head his side in front in the 61st minute. Ricky George delivered a corner and Charles's classic header dropped under the crossbar. Brighton came back. Nobby Lawton, who had skippered Preston North End in the 1964 FA Cup final, levelled four minutes later before Kit Napier, another former Preston player, scored the winner in the 73rd minute. Brighton goalkeeper Bryan Powney denied Charles a 77th-minute equaliser when he brilliantly saved his power-header. Afterwards Pat Saward, Brighton's manager, paid the losers the finest of compliments. 'If Hereford do not gain admission to the league next season there is no justice in the game.'

Hereford possessed no realistic chance of reaching Wembley in the FA Cup, but they did in its non-league equivalent, the FA Challenge Trophy. They beat Bury Town, Gloucester City, Banbury United and Macclesfield Town to reach the semi-finals. Hillingdon Borough, a side they had beaten twice in the Southern League that season, awaited them at Leicester's Filbert Street on 3 April 1971. 'We have beaten them twice and can do it again,' proclaimed Charles. Hereford had beaten them 6–0 at home and 5–0 away and were overwhelming favourites to make it to the final. 'The wives were choosing their Wembley outfits,' recalls Miles.

Wembley fever gripped the cider-making heartland. Two trains were hired to take supporters to Leicester and 4,000 made the trip to Filbert Street. Before the match, the chairman and his player-manager clashed again, this time over Charles's decision to play himself. 'There were ten minutes to go before the match started and John hadn't put his team sheet in,' says Miles. 'He hadn't played for about two months and he put himself in the team.' Hereford were unrecognisable from the side that thrashed Hillingdon earlier in the season and the Londoners tore up the form book to win 2–0. Charles, who began the match in defence but finished it in attack, was heartbroken. 'It was my greatest ambition to finish my playing career at Wembley,' he said afterwards. 'But what I feel most of all is that we let our own supporters down.'

Both goals came from defensive errors, the first from a sloppy Brian Potts back pass and the second after a Mike McLaughlin miskick. 'Had we won that trophy it would have helped our cause to get into the Football League that year,' explains Miles. Charles's decision to play when he was not 100 per cent match-fit may have been a factor in the defeat, but some of his former players believe he should never have selected new signing Potts at right-back ahead of Roger Griffiths. 'The semi-final defeat against Hillingdon was the biggest disappointment of my career,' says Fred Potter. 'John had got this lad Potts who had hardly played for us. He shouldn't have played him against Hillingdon but he did and he made the mistake that led to their first goal.'

Ricky George missed an open goal in the first half when Hillingdon were leading 1–0. Had he scored, it may have changed the outcome of the game. 'I was devastated and I apologised to John,' says George. 'He just grinned at me and said, "What are you being sorry about? I've seen Sivori miss easier ones than that." I'm sure Sivori hadn't missed an easier chance but it made me feel so much better. I think the way he supported his players was his best quality. I remember walking off the pitch at half-time in one game at Edgar Street and one of the directors had a go at me because I missed a couple of chances. "You're bloody useless, George!" John heard him, ran up into the directors' box, got hold of him and said, "Don't you ever talk to my players like that!"'

There was more disappointment in the Southern League. Distracted by their cup campaigns, Hereford lost the Premier Division leadership. At the end of March they slipped to eighth spot but were only four points behind leaders Cambridge United with seven games in hand. They were unable to make their spare games count and a mediocre finish to the season, which included defeats against Bedford, Poole and Margate, consigned Hereford to fourth place. A season so full of promise ended with a bare trophy cabinet. 'His lack of man-management, just having those final few details, stopped John winning something at Hereford,' says Potter. Adds Roger Griffiths, 'We were always there or thereabouts with John. We were a good football side. He wanted us to play good football.' According to Ken Mallender, Charles 'knew what he wanted from his players but had trouble getting it across to them'.

Miles ploughed on with his election campaign. A ten-minute documentary arguing Hereford's case for Football League graduation was made. Accompanied by Charles and the Lord Mayor of Hereford, Bill Griffin, Miles travelled to London, to the Café Royal in Regent Street, to present his club's case to the Football League. In a year of near misses Hereford lost out to Barrow who finished last in Division Four.

Charles earned himself another 12-month contract at Edgar Street. He was figuring less and less on the playing side but his tally of 15 goals during the 1970–71 campaign brought his total to 137 since joining the club from Cardiff in 1966. George recalls, 'When Billy Meadows and I arrived for pre-season training John said to us, "I'm full-time now. Anything you want, or any problems you've got, come to me and not the chairman." So Billy asked him for a ten-pound-a-week rise. John said, "You'd better see the chairman about that."'

The players were aware relations between Miles and his manager were strained. It was no secret the chairman wanted a say in team affairs, much to Charles's annoyance. Alan Scarrott remembers a match at Chelmsford. 'We were out on the pitch and John called me into the centre-circle. He got me close to him and then whispered, "The chairman doesn't want you to play today but I do." I did play in the end but we all knew Frank was trying to have a say.'

Charles was bothered by his chairman's keen interest in team selection. Sometimes he called his old friend, Joe Wade, a former Arsenal player who settled in Hereford after finishing his playing career at Edgar Street. The pair had known each other since Charles's Leeds days and at lunchtime they would meet up at The Crown and Anchor pub, Wade's local. Wade, who owned a sports shop in Hereford and Leominster, had already helped Charles open his own shop in Cardiff by linking him up with companies such as Dunlop and Slazenger. 'John was troubled and he asked for my advice,' says Wade. 'I think he had lost confidence in the club. He was very successful at Hereford and all the players loved him. I told him to stick it out.' Wade experienced Miles's style for himself. Following Charles's departure he took over the Hereford side on a caretaker basis until Colin Addison's appointment in October 1971. 'We were playing at Worcester and Frank came into the dressing-room. Alan Jones was beefing about something, I can't remember what exactly. Frank had a habit of coming in and taking over the complaints of players to the detriment of the manager. I told him to get out. He didn't give orders when I was in the dressing-room.' Miles admits he 'probably did interfere' with team affairs. 'Apart from being the chairman I was also managing the club. I was doing more than I had to. When John wasn't there I had to get involved.'

The 1971–72 season was barely a month old when the *Hereford*

Times announced the end of the Charles era at Edgar Street. It said business pressures had forced Charles to resign, that it was an 'amicable' parting and that there was 'a certain amount of nostalgic regret' on both sides. The news was greeted with disbelief since the side had lost only one of their first eight matches. Charles issued a statement. 'Since I took over part-time four years ago the club has made tremendous strides and the job has altered as a result. I now believe Hereford are entitled to a manager who is able to live on the spot and give his full attention to the running of the club with the aim of gaining league status.'

Charles said that after signing the last contract he hoped to spend three days a week at Hereford but his 'business commitments in Cardiff' prevented that. 'It was also suggested that I should move to Hereford but I must think of the education of my children,' he continued. 'They had an unsettled life during their infancy when I was playing in Italy and now they are doing well with their studies I do not want to uproot them and move them to a new location.'

When Miles was asked to comment, he replied, 'We are parting company on the very best of terms. With John's business interests in Cardiff it has often been a big strain for him to travel 70 miles to Hereford and back to keep an eye on club affairs and I fully understand his position.'

Jim Finney was assigned the task of clearing out his vacant office. When he opened the bottom right-hand drawer of Charles's desk he discovered mounds of unanswered correspondence. 'There were hundreds of letters he hadn't replied to,' comments Finney. 'There were invitations to speak at dinners, invitations to take part in quiz nights, invitations for him to be guest of honour at certain events.' Finney also came upon a 'great pile' of autograph books. 'Kids had sent them to the club for him to sign and he had obviously just thrown them in his drawer.' To ensure the young fans were not left disappointed, Finney signed the books on Charles's behalf and returned them. 'Everyone was upset when John left,' says Ricky George, 'although some would have said it was bound to happen.' Ronnie Radford said the players 'missed Charles terribly'. He adds, 'He was so much a part of us. We missed him as a man, a footballer and a friend. At the same time, I think everyone realised John wasn't going to take us any further.'

Miles hired 31-year-old Colin Addison to replace Charles. An inside-forward who had played for York City, Nottingham Forest and Arsenal, Addison joined Hereford from Sheffield United on a player-manager basis. To Miles's delight, he led Hereford into the Football League that season. The magnificent FA Cup replay win over Newcastle played a huge part in their ascension. Yet 11 of the 12 players who featured in one of the competition's great upsets were signed by Charles. Addison was the only non-Charles player. 'John left Colin the basis of a good team and Colin had the management skills to take us forward,' explains Fred Potter. Ken Mallender agrees. 'Colin was of a different generation. He had been on coaching courses at Lilleshall. He was a lot more organised than John.'

CHAPTER THIRTEEN – DIAL 'M' FOR MERTHYR

After being shown the door by Hereford, Charles devoted more time to his sports shop but it was not long before another club tried to lure him back into the managerial game. Maldwyn Davies, a flamboyant bingo hall owner and managing director of Merthyr Tydfil Football Club – at the time floundering in the Southern League Premier Division – saw the 40 year old as the ideal person to revive The Martyrs' flagging fortunes.

Merthyr were hailed as the best non-league side in British football during the late 1940s and early 1950s when they won the Southern League championship four times in five years. When Davies approached Charles in January 1972, the South Wales Valley club's position was critical, on and off the field. The team had won only four games all season and relegation seemed a certainty. The club was losing around £600 a month and constantly faced the threat of going bust. Gates at Penydarren Park were at an all-time low – one home match, just before Charles was hired, attracted a pitiful crowd of 196, the second lowest in the club's history. Merthyr owed its existence to Davies' generosity. A successful local businessman, he paid the club's wage bill out of his own pocket for a year. He even bought the team a 17-seater Ford Transit minibus to be used for away matches, which trimmed £1,000 off travelling expenses each season.

From January 1970 until Charles's appointment a year later, Davies was also Merthyr's team manager, which might explain the team's wretched results. He had never played football. Davies was simply a lifelong supporter of Merthyr who watched the team from the Penydarren Park stand. He insisted, however, that he had 'sufficient knowledge of the game to run and pick the side'.

His view of how Merthyr should play was romantic but naive and flawed. Like every supporter, he adored Merthyr's great side of 1949–54, the side of Bill Hullett, Bill Jarman, Frank Squires, Jenkin Powell and Stan Davies. Davies aimed to copy their style so he fielded a side of five forwards, three half-backs and two centre-backs. But this was now the 1970s. Football had moved on and the 'WM' system that flourished during the 1950s was doomed to failure. Dilwyn John, the goalkeeper who had joined The Martyrs after spells with Cardiff City and Swansea Town, recalls, 'Maldwyn was a football addict but he knew nothing about football. His team talk would be, "You're on a ten-pound win bonus today lads." And that would be it. Another time he said, "Today we're going to play with a sweeper, four at the back and five forwards." One of our players asked him, "Who's going to play in midfield?" He looked at us and said, "Oh, the forwards can come back."'

Merthyr was a club in crisis in January 1972. It was wallowing at the bottom of the Premier Division and losing a pot full of money every week. There were also discipline problems in the dressing-room. During the Christmas period, Davies fined ten of his players two pounds each for failing to turn up for training. Striker Colin Crotty walked out when the club refused to pay his wages after he skipped a Welsh Cup match against Ammanford to attend his brother's wedding – he later changed his mind and returned. Davies threatened to withdraw his financial backing if results did not improve. None of this seemed to bother Charles who readily accepted Davies' offer. The former Leeds, Juventus and Wales superstar was announced as player-manager on 18 January, the day after Charles watched Merthyr's 1–1 draw with Folkestone at Penydarren Park.

'John Charles is the man we wanted and we are delighted that he has accepted our offer,' said Davies who boldly predicted Charles would bring the Southern League title to Penydarren Park within two years. He admitted the side Charles inherited was not good enough to stay in the Premier Division but his new manager was optimistic. 'I see it as a challenge but I think we can get somewhere if I get the players I want and who I am now trying for,' he said. 'I won't say we can get out of trouble but we can at least get near to doing that. I feel there is a good nucleus around which I can build.'

Luring a world-famous name such as Charles to the football outpost of Merthyr Tydfil proved a hassle-free affair. Ken Tucker, the club's secretary at the time, explains, 'Maldwyn knew John was available. He also knew he was living down the road in Cardiff so he decided to get him. He asked him if he would like to come up to Merthyr for a chat. John said yes and the same afternoon he became Merthyr manager.' The talks took place at Davies' home, which backed onto Penydarren Park. 'In a way, John joining Merthyr was a bit of a formality,' continues Tucker. 'He was eager to get back into football, Merthyr was one of the prominent non-league clubs in Welsh football and he wanted to stay in South Wales.'

Charles shook hands with Davies after agreeing to a forty-pounds-a-week salary. 'It was a modest figure for someone of John's stature but for the club it was a very high wage,' adds Tucker. 'There wasn't a great deal of money at Merthyr. Maldwyn was funding the club single-handedly.'

Davies had been forced to bring in a new manager. A couple of weeks before Charles was appointed, the board held a two-and-a-half-hour crisis meeting which resulted in the resignation of one director, Bernard Lewis. He said he was no longer prepared to provide financial assistance 'because without a tracksuit manager the club is going nowhere'. Davies in charge of the first-team affairs saved the club money but it harmed results and poor results were to blame for the woeful crowds. It made sense to push the boat out financially and hire a manager to revitalise the team. With Charles at the helm it was hoped Penydarren Park would once again host crowds of 12,000.

After agreeing terms with Davies, Charles, wearing a white Italian suit and white shoes, was given a tour of Penydarren Park where he was introduced to the players and backroom staff. 'I shit myself when Maldwyn told me John was going to be the new manager,' says Frank Hagerty, then trainer at Merthyr. 'A man of his stature coming to Merthyr! I thought, "What's he going to do to us!" I was worried about my job. I didn't know what was going to happen because a new manager always wants to bring with him his own people.' Hagerty's job was safe. Charles had no plans to bring in his own backroom team. In any case, there was no money for him to make changes.

Charles was promised a free rein in team selection. He would also supervise training every Monday and Thursday, starting at 7 p.m. and finishing at 9 p.m. Former Merthyr winger Mal Gilligan recalls his first training session. 'I couldn't believe it. He had us doing circuit after circuit. He just crucified us. Even the best trainers at the club were nearly throwing up. Just when you thought you had done enough he'd say, "Do it again." Most of us had been at work all day – I was a carpenter/joiner – and we were shattered before we arrived for training. John's idea seemed to be, "If I can't get them to play football then I'll get them fit" but if you're not fit by January you're never going to be fit.' Adds Gilligan, 'John wanted to show the forwards how to head the ball so he had me on the wing crossing. I had to put in cross after cross after cross. Talk about concentration! On a pitch as bad as Penydarren Park's, it was difficult to cross accurately. I knew John wasn't going to go far as a manager. I think the Southern League was his level.' Gilligan was soon put out of his misery. At the end of the season he was one of four players released by Charles. Tucker, on the other hand, was impressed with Charles's first session. 'He was showing the players how to head at goal. He had one player taking corners and John was shouting, "Right-hand corner" and "Left-hand corner" and he was heading the ball exactly where he said he would. It really was a masterclass in heading the ball.'

Charles's first game in charge was a home match against Barnet, then in third place in the Premier Division. He was greeted by a 768 crowd. It was a far cry from the club's heyday 20 years earlier but it was a vast improvement on recent attendances. The fans were hoping Charles would play against the London side but he monitored his team's display from the dugout. Barnet spoiled his big day, leaving South Wales with a 2–1 win, but Charles was reasonably pleased with the way his players performed. 'I am more satisfied with them than I was last week,' he said after the game. 'They are showing a bit of a system. They are now beginning to look like more of a team.' Asked if he could keep them in the Premier

Division, he replied, 'There are plenty of games to go yet.' The *Merthyr Express*, the town's weekly newspaper, was less upbeat. After the Barnet defeat, the paper felt that Merthyr's hopes of avoiding the drop 'seem as slim as The New Seekers teaching the world to sing in perfect harmony'.

Charles knew he needed to sign fresh faces and fast. To free up the cash needed to bring in new blood he told four players they could leave on a free transfer – Gilligan, full-back Brian Davies, winger Harry Robinson and forward Mike Hayes. However, no one wanted to join Merthyr. 'Players don't want to come to us unless we offer good money and we have not got a lot of money to offer,' moaned Charles.

The dire results continued. There was still a mathematical chance of survival but the club appeared resigned to life in the Southern League's Division One (North) after a 3–0 home defeat against Chelmsford. Afterwards Davies, who became the club's chairman in February 1972 following a boardroom shuffle, spoke of a three-year plan at the club. Charles declared he was concentrating on building a new team for the following season. He could not wait to get started. After a 4–0 defeat at Cambridge in March he said he was 'disgusted' by his team's performance and accused some of his players of a lack of effort. The same month Charles encountered a problem which was familiar to Davies. Eight players – Dennis Morgan, Les Harris, Brian Davies, Clive Lloyd, Terry Collins, John Bird, Harry Robinson and Brian Williams – said they were unavailable for a Monday night match at Chelmsford. A livid Davies said only Collins and Bird had 'acceptable excuses' and threatened to sack some of the other six. In the end, all eight were fined.

Charles waited until April for his victory as Merthyr manager, a 2–1 win against Romford at Penydarren Park. 'HOO-RAY!' was the headline in the *Merthyr Express*. The season failed to end on a winning note. A 6–0 hammering at Telford followed, then a 4–0 thumping at Gloucester. By the time Guildford rolled into town, Charles's men were a dispirited bunch longing for the summer break. The supporters, like Charles and his chairman, accused them of not trying. The team also knew the directors had met in Penydarren Park's version of the 'Night of the Long Knives' and decided each one of Merthyr's 16 players was free to leave the club if they refused to accept the reduced terms for 1972–73.

For the Guildford game, Charles chose his starting line-up 18 minutes before kick-off – echoes of Hereford – and the disgruntled players put on the first shirt they picked up in the dressing-room. Dilwyn John, the goalkeeper, played on the left flank. Dennis Morgan, a full-back, played in goal. Charles decided to play. He wore the number 9 jersey but played in midfield. Guildford won 2–0.

The last home game of the season, against Margate, ended in a 3–1 defeat and only 216 people turned out on a cold, windy afternoon to watch the doomed Martyrs. A dismal campaign closed with a 2–0 loss at Dover. Merthyr were relegated well before their trip to Kent.

Charles worked on building a new team. Only four players decided to stay on lower wages which allowed him to recruit new faces. His new signings included centre-half Doug Rosser from Swansea, midfielder Alan Smith from Newport County, striker Paul Caviel and inside-forward Alwyn Owen. The latter two had starred in the Merthyr League for Troedyrhiw Boys Club. Charles invited two of his former Hereford players, Ricky George and Billy Meadows, to join him at Penydarren Park. The pair wanted thirty-five pounds a week and a £1,000 signing-on fee. There was no way cash-starved Merthyr, who were also in the process of building a £25,000 clubhouse, the Jubilee Club, could meet their demands.

After a busy time wheeling and dealing in the transfer market, Charles went to Diano Marina for a ten-day holiday before returning to Merthyr to start pre-season training on 17 July 1972. Hopes were high after a 3–1 win over Fourth Division Newport County in a friendly but it was a disappointing start, The Martyrs losing 2–1 at Rugby Town. To shore up his defence Charles signed Mel Nurse, a former Wales international, from Welsh League club Pembroke. Nurse had won 12 Welsh caps and, like Charles, he was a Swansea man. During his two years in the Valleys town, Charles publicly lost his temper once, in a home match against Bromsgrove. Nurse was playing at centre-half and John was at centre-forward. 'One of their players came across my blind side, slid in and bang! We were both on the ground,' remembers Nurse. 'I heard a crack.

This player had broken my leg. I looked across the grass and I could see him lying on the ground. I looked again and all of a sudden he had gone! Big John had seen what had happened, ran back, picked him up by the neck and was dangling him four feet off the ground.'

After the match Charles went looking for the Bromsgrove player and had to be restrained by half a dozen people. According to Ken Tucker, Charles was 'foaming at the mouth'. Ieuan Evans, a member of Merthyr's backroom staff, adds, 'It was a deliberate foul on Mel and John saw red. We told him the player had gone. He had. Straight after the game he jumped into a car and disappeared. I think he had a gypsy's warning that John was after him. That was the only time I ever saw John ruffled.'

Nurse's debut was Merthyr's first home game of the season, against Tamworth. Charles was without his two Newport-based players, Smith and striker David Williams. They were unable to reach Penydarren Park in time because the road from Newport was blocked by an overturned lorry. Caviel took Williams' place alongside Charles in the Merthyr attack and scored the only goal of the game to send the 1,360 crowd home happy.

Charles again donned his boots for a Southern League Cup tie against Redditch and 'showed that he's still got plenty of zip' by setting up both goals in his side's 2–1 win. 'If I wasn't standing outside the dressing-room at half-time with a cigarette ready for him John was upset,' says Frank Hagerty. 'He'd have a smoke at half-time and the cigarette was still in his hand as he made his way back to the pitch. He'd walk around the touchline with it and just before running onto the pitch he would throw the cigarette on the floor and stub it out with his boot.'

A decent start to the season – a 1–0 FA Cup replay defeat against Barry Town saw The Martyrs concede their first goal in seven matches – did not prevent the manager adding to his squad. He persuaded Carl Slee to return to the game after the former Swansea defender quit football to become a newsagent. Midfielder George Young came from Newport County and striker Dave Smith from Cheltenham. In the dressing-room Charles retained his penchant for playing practical jokes. 'He would tie a knot in your laces, tie a knot in your socks or tie the sleeves of your shirt together,' reveals Hagerty. The players saw another side to the Gentle Giant on the way back from a match at Tonbridge. While the team stopped at a service station Clive Lloyd, Merthyr's inside-forward, hid a bag of Brussels sprouts under the kit bags at the front of the bus. 'John was sitting in the front and I could see him sniffing,' recalls Colin Pritchard, the team's bus driver. 'After a little while John said, "There's an awful smell in this bus." Clive said it must be the boots or the kit. John started going through the bags and found the sprouts. When he found out they belonged to Clive, he blew his top. He thought Clive had nicked them but he hadn't. Clive had got talking to this fruit and vegetable seller at the service station who gave him the sprouts. But John gave Clive a hell of a rollicking. He told me to stop the bus and he made Clive throw the sprouts away at the side of the road.'

The next home match after the FA Cup loss at Barry was against Atherstone in the Southern League Cup. The attendance of 513 provoked an angry response from Phil Howells in the *Merthyr Express*. Charles had every right to feel depressed because his team was taking shape. They were unbeaten at home and had conceded just two goals in nine matches. 'Merthyr,' wrote an angry Howells, 'have the unenviable tag of possessing some of the most disloyal fans in the whole Southern League. John Charles is a respected name throughout the world. Wherever he goes, he adds crowds on the gates and autograph hunters are never far away but Merthyr couldn't care less.'

The Atherstone gate was 288 down on the previous home match and 847 down on the first home game of the season. Explains Ken Tucker, who was the club's secretary for 18 years, 'Merthyr is a strange place when it comes to football. The crowds never rose dramatically when John was the manager there. At Merthyr you had to be top. Being third, fourth or fifth wasn't good enough. If you were doing well they'd support you but if the side was an ordinary one then the gates would hover in the hundreds. The people only came out for the big games.'

Charles no doubt agreed with the adage that the town was ruled by 'the three Bs' – betting, bingo and booze. The people of Merthyr no longer cared about football, despite having the likes of Charles as a figurehead. Howells launched a far more savage attack on the town's apathy towards its football club the following year when

Charles guided The Martyrs into the second round of the FA Cup. The first-round replay tie against Macclesfield drew 1,500 to Penydarren Park but the next Southern League home fixture saw the gate drop by a third. 'If an award was to be made for the worst sporting town in the world it would surely go to Merthyr,' said Howells. 'Their so-called sports fans will jump on the bandwagon of success. They will come along to see the big match once every year or so, but after that it's back to the afternoon pint and a huddle around the television *Grandstand* programme just to show how great their interest in sport is.'

Merthyr were among the promotion contenders in the first half of 1972–73. They boasted a mean defence, marshalled by Nurse. Charles, whose knees and burst of speed had gone, was still a force in the air. He was capable of scoring that match-winning goal. Charles headed the winners against both Wellingborough and Redditch. 'He may have been 41 or 42 but people still couldn't get near him when he jumped for the ball,' says Dilwyn John. 'Some of the goals he was scoring, even at that age, were tremendous.' Beginning to feel the aches and pains of a long, bruising career in the game, Charles wore bandages underneath his socks when he played for the Southern League side as support for his ankles. 'You never knew John was going to play until the last minute. He tended to pick his games at Merthyr,' remembers Ieuan Evans. 'He wasn't the John Charles of old but he would still do enough for us to open our mouths in awe.' Evans recalls one match, at Milton Keynes. A couple of players were unable to make the trip including goalkeeper Dilwyn John so Charles told left-back David Jones – known as 'Dai Bananas' because he worked for a wholesale fruit merchant – that he would be taking John's place. He handed him the goalkeeper's jersey.

'Put that on,' said Charles.

'John, I've never played in goal before!' replied Jones.

'Put it on!'

'I've never been in goal before!' repeated the player.

'Don't worry,' reassured Charles. 'You save the ones on the floor, I'll get the ones in the air. No heroics from you today. Don't come off your line.'

Charles played in defence and, as he promised, looked after his makeshift goalkeeper. To everyone's amazement Merthyr left

Milton Keynes with a 1–0 win. For the same game Colin Pritchard helped Charles with a few matchday chores.

'Who's that, John? Is he your coach?' asked one home supporter after overhearing Charles issue Pritchard with a set of orders.

'No,' replied a grinning Charles. 'He's my coach driver!'

Merthyr held Third Division Bournemouth 3–3 in a friendly played on Halloween to mark the opening of the Jubilee Club. Brian Clark, Bournemouth's forward who once played for Cardiff City, was impressed enough to tip the Welsh side for promotion back to the Premier Division. There was also talk that Charles was in the running for the vacancy at another Division Three club, Swansea City, where Roy Bentley was asked to resign after a run of poor results. Charles was reported to be among the 30 who applied for the job, which eventually went to former Manchester United goalkeeper Harry Gregg.

At Penydarren Park the promotion charge continued. Stevenage were beaten 3–0, then came a 2–0 win at King's Lynn. After a 1–1 draw with Cheltenham Charles persuaded another Welsh international, midfielder and former Cardiff teammate Barrie Hole, to join The Martyrs. Hole made his debut in a 4–1 home win over Gloucester. Maldwyn Davies was hoping for gates of 1,500 but only 545 came to see this match. It was one of only a handful of games Hole played for The Martyrs. Tired of football, he wanted to concentrate on his newsagent business in his native Swansea, which was an hour's drive from Merthyr. 'John came into my shop and asked me to come up to Merthyr with him,' says Hole. 'I said yes but I was only there for about four or five weeks. I didn't want to play football any more. I didn't have the hunger to play – and I used to dread driving up there from Swansea.'

A series of away defeats during the spring wrecked the team's chance of promotion and Merthyr finished in sixth place. 'John was at Merthyr during a very difficult time,' says Tucker. 'The club's finances were limited. It wasn't just wages but the floodlights, laundry, rent, plus there were taxes to be paid. He signed players he knew, like Mel Nurse, but they were at the end of their careers. I think John had difficulty getting young players to the club, players who could do the running.'

Charles's men reached the quarter-finals of the Welsh Cup in

1973 where they faced his old club, Hereford, at Edgar Street. Before the game he received a standing ovation from the Hereford supporters and then, as a sweeper behind the back four, he played one of his best games for Merthyr. They held the home side to a 0–0 draw. The 8,462 attendance meant Merthyr's share of the gate receipts amounted to a welcome £1,500. No wonder Davies, fed up with the poor crowds at Penydarren Park, agreed to switch the replay to Hereford rather than play it at apathetic Merthyr. The team's chances of reaching the last four were drastically reduced but Davies was guaranteed another four-figure cheque. In fact, the money received from both these matches was more than the club would take from all 21 Southern League home matches that season. 'The Merthyr fans have not played fair with us and we owe them nothing,' said the chairman. 'Home gates have been abysmal despite the fact we are unbeaten at Penydarren Park. Why should we supply the cream when they won't support the bread and butter matches?' Charles and his players were unable to produce an encore in the return game and lost 3–0. Davies was not too unhappy. He knew a cheque for £2,000 was on its way to Penydarren Park. As the town's newspaper said, 'MERTHYR CRASH BUT TAKE CASH!'

Charles managed to lure another big-name player, winger Barrie Jones, to Penydarren Park in the summer of 1973. Capped 15 times by Wales, blond Jones hated his time in Merthyr and is reluctant to talk about his stint with the non-league club. 'The travel arrangements were a joke, the board was a joke, the whole club was a joke,' says Jones. 'The whole experience was enough to put someone off football and it was a shame to see a great player like John Charles managing a club like Merthyr. I only went there because of John. Looking back, I wish I had never gone. I wish I'd stayed at Worcester.' He adds, 'We used to go to away games in this minibus and it was an embarrassment getting on and off it. It was like an ice-cream van and some of the away trips were four or five hours on the road. The travel arrangements were an absolute joke. For instance, we had a game at Burton and Doug Rosser and I arrived at Penydarren Park at 8.30 a.m. to pick up the minibus but when we got to the ground we found the bus had already gone! It had left 15 minutes earlier. We ended up having to drive after it.'

Derrick Bryant, who scored more than 200 goals for Minehead, was another recruit. Nick Deacy, an apprentice steel engineer at the Guest, Keen and Nettlefolds steelworks in Cardiff and who played for Cardiff Corries, proved to be Charles's big discovery. Tipped off by a former Cardiff City player called Bobby Brown, Charles watched Deacy in action. He made the short trip from his Cardiff home to the playing fields in the city's Llanishen area where the Corries played. Charles liked what he saw and decided to visit Deacy at his home in Cardiff's Heath suburb to invite him to join the Southern League outfit. 'There was a knock on the door and my dad went to answer it,' says the former striker. 'He came back into the room and said, "It's John Charles for you." Dad was a big football fan and he couldn't believe what was happening.' Deacy signed amateur forms with Merthyr, joined Hereford in September 1974 and went on to play for PSV Eindhoven in Holland. He appeared 12 times for Wales. 'I look back at my career and I owe it all to John. If he hadn't taken me to Merthyr I might never have left the steelworks.'

Charles arranged three attractive pre-season friendlies, against Bristol City, Derby County, who had won the First Division championship a year earlier, and Wolves. Merthyr beat Bristol 2–1 with goals from Deacy and Caviel before losing 3–1 to a Derby side that rested all its star players except Welsh international midfielder Alan Durban. They also lost 2–1 to Wolves, a game rearranged to a new date after the start of the season. More than 7,000 people saw the three matches, bringing much needed cash to the club.

Not so popular was the new garish kit Charles introduced at the club. Gone were the black and white stripes, replaced by a lilac kit with yellow down the sides and around the collar. 'John thought we should have a new image but it was the worst kit I've ever seen. It was awful,' says Ken Tucker. Charles had been influenced by the bold colours worn by some of the Italian sides. Fiorentina played in purple, Palermo in pink and black while Bologna, Genoa and Catania wore red and blue. 'The supporters didn't like the new kit,' adds Tucker. 'A lot of them followed the team of the 1940s and 1950s and were very traditional in their outlook. It wasn't one of John's better ideas.' It was not long before the new strip was dropped and Merthyr reverted back to black and white.

The 1973–74 campaign, Charles's last with the club, opened with a 4–0 victory against Dunstable at a sun-soaked Penydarren Park. In three games out of four, Merthyr found a last-minute winner. 'There were two games on the trot when John headed a last-minute winner at the far post,' says Ieuan Evans. 'I remember him running back to the centre-circle laughing.' Terry Collins, one of the club's directors, adds, 'There was many a time when we were losing, we'd win a corner and John would score from it. It was a bit like *Roy of the Rovers*.'

After a strong start to the season there was the inevitable talk of promotion but the FA Cup proved a fatal distraction. For only the third time in the club's history The Martyrs made it to the second round. A fixture backlog, caused by the cup run, meant the team occasionally played two games in two days, on the Saturday and the Sunday. This punishing schedule affected results and at one stage Charles's men went seven games without a win. Merthyr's promotion hopes evaporated.

The cup adventure began with a 3–0 win at Barry Town. They drew 0–0 at Glastonbury before beating the West Country side 3–1 in a replay, Charles netting Merthyr's second. Next came a victory over Mangotsfield and Charles's header, which sealed a 2–0 win, was the talk of the town for days. Barrie Jones delivered a corner-kick and his header was so powerful that John Ferris, Mangotsfield's goalkeeper, made no attempt to save it. Deacy, who played many times alongside the greying Charles in Merthyr's attack that season, says, 'John couldn't run, his legs had gone. Derrick Bryant and I used to do all the running for him, but he could still head the ball. His timing in the air was impeccable. John was in his forties when I was there but he played most of the games that season.'

Macclesfield stood in the way of a place in the first round proper. At the Moss Rose Ground Charles played as a sweeper behind the back four. The plan was to force a 0–0 draw and take the Cheshire club back to the Valleys. It worked although the visitors had a lucky escape when Macclesfield missed a penalty in the 58th minute. The result was remarkable considering Merthyr arrived in the silk-weaving town with the bare minimum of 11 players. One absentee was Deacy who was scoring freely for his new club. Charles arranged to give him a lift to Cardiff Central Station. The pair were to catch the train to Merthyr and from there, travel to Macclesfield in the team bus. Charles, though, never turned up at Deacy's home. 'John said he forgot he had to pick him up. I couldn't believe it,' says Terry Collins. 'It was a vital cup game and Nick was one of our star players.'

Deacy believes Charles deliberately 'forgot' to collect him. He wanted to play in the match which meant either Deacy or Bryant would have to make way for him. Charles loathed telling players they were dropped from the team so 'forgetting' to pick up Deacy avoided an awkward situation. 'We were catching the train at 9 a.m. and he said he would pick me up at 8 a.m.,' recollects Deacy. 'It had gone 8 a.m. so I rang his home. His wife said, "He's on his way." Then it got to 8.45 a.m. and I rang his house again. His wife said the same thing. "He's on his way." But it turned out he had gone straight to the station.' Merthyr beat Macclesfield 2–1 in the replay. 'I scored the winner in the last minute so what had happened before the first game was all forgotten,' adds Deacy.

For beating Macclesfield, Charles and his men were rewarded with a trip to the Dorset coast. They were drawn away to Weymouth, who were also managed by a Welshman, the former West Bromwich Albion and Wales full-back, Graham Williams. Weymouth also had forward Mike Trebilcock playing for them. Trebilcock's name was synonymous with the competition. He scored Everton's first two goals in their dramatic 3–2 win over Sheffield Wednesday in the 1966 FA Cup final.

On the morning of the game Charles was shocked to discover his chairman sleeping in the back of his car, a Mercedes parked outside Weymouth's ground. The night before Merthyr's biggest game in years, Maldwyn Davies had downed a few whiskies too many. 'Maldwyn looked a mess and he hadn't shaved,' remembers Terry Collins. 'John got hold of him and said, "You can't go to the game like this!"'

Charles escorted his chairman into the town centre. In Hodges, a menswear chain, he bought Davies a sports jacket, trousers and shirt to wear to the match. Freshened up and sporting his new apparel, Davies no longer looked like a man who had knocked back 'a skinful' the previous night. 'John knew Maldwyn would have to meet the Weymouth directors. He was manager of Merthyr and that was something he took pride in,' adds Collins.

Charles became close friends with Davies during his stint at Merthyr. Davies frequently holidayed in Italy with his player-manager. They had much in common. Both smoked and drank (Charles was known as 'John Tonic' in the Jubilee Club because when he wanted a gin and tonic he would buy the tonic water while Davies bought the gin) and they shared a passion for football. But Davies' thirst for alcohol occasionally irritated Charles. 'We were signing a player – I can't remember who it was – and John was showing him around Penydarren Park,' remembers Collins. 'He took him into the Jubilee Club and there was Maldwyn in a drunken stupor. John noticed what state Maldwyn was in. He told the player, "You can't meet the chairman because he's not here tonight." He was too ashamed to introduce him to Maldwyn.' In August 1973, Davies was banned from driving for two years and fined seventy-five pounds for driving with excess alcohol in his blood.

Weymouth was arguably Charles's finest hour and a half with The Martyrs although the lack of 'good luck' messages from the mining town galled him. There was a telegram of congratulations from Macclesfield after Merthyr beat Weymouth but nothing from Merthyr. Perhaps Phil Howells was right – the people of Merthyr were as interested in sport as they were in learning Hindustani.

Once again Charles played at sweeper and he helped his defence to shut out Trebilcock and the other Weymouth forwards. Bryant scored the only goal of the afternoon to send Merthyr into the second round. 'There were no sticks of rock on sale and the amusement arcade on the seafront had its shutter up but it was Merthyr's happiest day at the seaside,' said the *Merthyr Express*.

The Martyrs were 90 minutes away from a potentially money-spinning third-round tie. Hendon of the Isthmian League were their second-round opponents. They were a strong amateur side – they had just knocked Southern League Premier Division side Barnet out of the competition – but Merthyr had home advantage. For a short while the media glare fell on Merthyr's football team. The club was featured in the HTV television programme *Sports Arena* while Charles, now 42, found himself in demand with Fleet Street's football journalists. The London press had largely ignored him since his return from Italy ten years earlier.

In the week leading up to the match Charles insisted on an extra training session, on the Wednesday, which took place at the town's Afon Taf High School. The third round eluded Merthyr, who were brushed aside 3–0 by Hendon. The team was unrecognisable from the one which had triumphed in Dorset. Hendon took the lead after three minutes. They finished off Charles and his jaded Martyrs after the break with two goals in as many minutes. Charles played himself in attack but he was well contained by Hendon's Cardiff-born defender Alan Phillips.

The tie was over after 57 minutes when Phillips, abandoning his position at the back, headed home Hendon's third goal, which triggered a mass exodus from Penydarren Park. The lack of cup fever in the town before and during this game baffled the *Western Mail*. Merthyr-born Mario Basini, the newspaper's diarist, was among the 3,000 crowd. 'There was no fervour at Merthyr on their big day. No flags out to greet the visiting team, no band playing, no masses of black and white scarved supporters. None of the *hwyl* that belongs to the Welsh valleys . . . The supporters were more like men going to a compulsory union meeting than to cheer their side on to paths of glory . . . They hadn't seen a crowd like this at the Park for years, they said. But you could be forgiven for thinking it was Hendon's home ground. That was the difference between the sets of supporters.'

The third-round draw, which took place one hour and 40 minutes after the final whistle, made the defeat all the more sour. Hendon earned a mouth-watering tie against First Division Newcastle United at St James's Park. For Merthyr, that tie would have been worth £10,000. 'That defeat against Hendon still hurts today,' admits Deacy, who blames the defeat on Charles's pre-match preparations. Before the game the team gathered at the Castle Hotel where they lunched on steak, toast and tea. 'The club knew it was going to get a good gate so John decided to splash out on a pre-match meal. The kick-off was at 3 p.m. and at 2 p.m. we were eating steak and chips! We got to the ground at 2.45 p.m. and we played on full stomachs. We got stuffed. Hendon were a good team but we didn't help ourselves that day.'

The slap-up meal in the Castle Hotel may well have cost Merthyr a place in the third round but it made a welcome change from the usual pre-match routine. Finances were so tight that the club scrapped the one-pound meal allowance given to players for away matches.

On one occasion, after a game in London, the team was treated to a free meal when the club minibus stopped at a Swindon fish and chip shop. The Italian owner, a Juventus fan who displayed a photo of Charles in a Juventus strip on the wall, recognised Merthyr's manager and told the players, 'The meals are on the house.'

Usually, players had to be satisfied with a cup of tea and a piece of toast at a motorway service station. 'They gave us ten shillings [50 pence] for something to eat after away games,' says Barrie Jones. 'What could you buy with ten shillings? You were lucky if you could get a cup of tea. There were some good players at Merthyr and we could have won the Southern League but the club was run so badly.'

After the cup defeat Merthyr found themselves 13 points behind league leaders Burton Albion but they had four games in hand. Erratic results, however, consigned them to another year in Division One. There were memorable wins. Redditch were hammered 8–1, a match that saw Deacy score four goals, and they also dished out a 6–1 beating to Whitney with Deacy hitting a hat-trick. Merthyr's free-scoring forward was soon attracting the attention of Football League clubs. His name was linked with Bristol City, Manchester City and Bournemouth. Deacy was convinced he would be bought by a Football League club but was still at Merthyr come the end of the season. When he discovered Charles had refused to sell him, he stormed into his office at Penydarren Park and threatened to quit. Charles rang Davies at his bingo hall to inform him of Deacy's displeasure and took the player to see him. Deacy was offered professional forms and promised a signing-on fee. 'Maldwyn took five hundred pounds out of his till and started counting them out in front of me,' recalls Deacy.

At the end of the 1973–74 season Charles headed for his holiday apartment in Diano Marina. His new contract remained unsigned and Swansea manager Harry Gregg, a close friend, had offered him the youth-team coach position at the Vetch, a job he eventually accepted. Before making his final decision Charles went to see Mel Nurse at his Seahaven Hotel on Swansea's seafront for advice. 'He said, "Mel, I've been invited to join Harry Gregg at the Vetch. What do you think?" I said to him, "Swansea is a Football League club. Merthyr is a Southern League club. If I was you, I'd join Swansea,'" explains Nurse.

In the summer of 1974 Charles returned to the club where, three decades earlier, his glittering career began.

He left Merthyr without fulfilling his promise. After a 1–1 draw against Weymouth in April 1972, Charles vowed he would take them back into the Premier Division. There was no bad feeling from his former club. 'John had gone as far as he could with us,' admits Ken Tucker. 'Swansea had always been the love of his life and he always wanted to be involved with The Swans. He used Merthyr to progress to a Football League club and we were delighted about that. We were always pleased when someone progressed from the club. There was no animosity towards John when he left. There was no acrimony. In fact, he still used to come back to see Maldwyn.'

Charles spent two years at the Vetch, developing the club's youth programme. 'I thought with the name John had we would attract good young players to the club,' explains Gregg. 'There was no better name than his to bring to a Welsh club.' Charles brought through youngsters such as Robbie James, Alan Curtis, Nigel Stevenson and his own nephew, Jeremy Charles. All four helped The Swans rise from the old Division Four to Division One. 'John was great with the kids,' continues Gregg. 'I remember his first week with me. We were having a kickabout behind the ground and John went to head the ball. As he did so one of the apprentices accidentally kicked him in the face and knocked out his two front teeth. They were implants, John had lost his original teeth years earlier. John was in real pain because he was kneeling down and his head was between his knees. But he got up and just said, "It's OK, it's OK". He could have gone after the lad but he didn't.'

His duties with the youth-team players were not enough to fill an entire day so Charles found himself doing the chores he once did as a groundstaff boy in the 1940s. 'I went to the Vetch one day and I saw John helping the groundsman to paint the stand,' recalls Nurse. He was supposed to be Harry Gregg's assistant. I said to him, "You didn't come here to paint the stand. Tell them they can jump into the river!" But that was John, he was so placid.' Gordon Daniels, then the club's secretary, adds, 'In a way, it was sad to see someone of his stature having to do those sort of jobs but he was filling in time. He was looking after the youth team but that wasn't a full-time job. But John didn't mind doing those things because he loved being in a football environment.'

In January 1975, after a dreary run of results that sent The Swans plummeting to the depths of the Fourth Division, Gregg resigned. Charles tried to stop the former goalkeeper from quitting. 'Don't do it, Harry. Don't do it,' he told Gregg before he went in to see the directors. Charles was heavily tipped to replace Gregg but within hours the board unveiled Harry Griffiths as caretaker manager. Gregg had recommended Charles for the job. 'I told the directors they should make John manager. It was his hometown club, he could bring players to the Vetch and he would draw in the crowds. They may not have gone for him because he was my recommendation.'

In the summer of 1976 Charles left Swansea. Griffiths had revived the team's fortunes and, after leading the side that finished 22nd in the table in 1974–75 to 11th place a year later, he was rewarded by being given the manager's job on a permanent basis. Although he never made his feelings public, Charles was bitterly disappointed not to have been named as Gregg's successor. He decided on a fresh start, a life away from football. He chose the retired footballer's favourite, the pub trade. The Gentle Giant never fulfilled his ambition of managing a Football League club.

CHAPTER FOURTEEN – FALLEN IDOL

On 23 December 2001, Charles celebrated his 70th birthday with his second wife, Glenda. It was a low-key affair. The couple watched a comedy film in their modest, semi-detached home in Birkenshaw, a village between Leeds and Bradford. During his time in Italy he earned an estimated £100,000, a whopping amount in the late 1950s and early 1960s. He should have become Britain's first millionaire footballer yet Charles has lived frugally on a state pension since turning 65. The fortune he amassed while playing for Juventus and, to a lesser extent, Roma, was eaten away by a series of disastrous business ventures and a costly divorce. When Charles earned his lire in Turin there were no agents or financial advisers looking after his future. 'I was a sucker for anyone who said he could double my money,' Charles once said with typical honesty. 'I may have been a good footballer but I'm a lousy businessman.'

His Turin restaurant, King's, was his first business failure. Charles sank £15,000 of his own money into the doomed project. The restaurant closed in 1963 and the player forked out a further £20,000 to clear his debts. 'John did a lot of things behind my back. I should have taken charge more,' says his first wife, Peggy. 'He lost a lot with the restaurant. I should have demanded to know what was going on with it.' The restaurant's financial loss meant they could not buy their home in Cardiff. They only had enough for a deposit. 'We had no more than £10,000 in the bank when we came back from Italy,' reveals Peggy.

The sports shop in Cardiff, which he opened with the former Wales international rugby player, Alan Priday, shortly after he signed for Hereford, was also a disaster. Charles and Priday became friends when, as two prominent sportsmen in the city, they found themselves being invited to the same social functions and charity events. The pair became closer when their wives gave birth at the same hospital, Northlands, at the same time. It was there Peggy gave birth to their fourth son, David.

After visiting hours they would leave together for a drink at their local pub, The Butchers Arms. 'One night we went for a drink and John said, "How would you like to go into business with me?"' recalls Priday. 'I asked him what he had in mind and he started mentioning various projects.' It was Priday who came up with the idea of a sports shop and John Charles Sports Ltd opened in December 1966. It was situated on the suburb's main road, just a few minutes drive from Charles's home, and sold sports equipment. Priday says he had no intention of staying in the business for more than two years. 'The plan was to build this business so John had something to go to when he finished playing football. I was working for an engineering firm and that was where my main income came from. John was going to be in the shop most of the time. I would be involved on weekends.'

Priday soon discovered his partner was not cut out to be a businessman. 'One Saturday morning I was in the shop doing some stocktaking. John went to the newsagents, bought his *Daily Mirror* then called into the paint and decorating shop because the girls who worked there would always make us a cup of coffee. He came back into the shop and sat in his big, black chair and started reading the paper.' In came four men who played for a local football team, Caerau Athletic. 'They wanted socks, jerseys, bibs, corner flags, two balls and the captain wanted a pair of boots,' continues Priday. 'They looked at me and then John. I told him we had some people from Caerau Athletic. He looked up, said, "Morning, lads" and carried on reading the paper! I couldn't believe it. I told John to get the jerseys and the boots and I got the rest of the stuff. I told him not to charge the captain for the boots. "I'm not doing that!" John said. I explained to him that if he let him have the boots the whole team would come to the shop for their gear. After a lot of persuasion he gave him the boots and later on we had an order worth £230 from the team which was a lot of money in those days. But John just couldn't see the sales side of things. He didn't have any business acumen. He would also let people he knew have things without paying. You'd find, say, a cricket bat put aside for Harry Griffiths. John would say, "Oh, I'm letting him have it." I'd tell him Harry had to pay for it. Seven or eight months later and we'd still be waiting for the money. He couldn't see it was business. He was very generous and a lot of people took advantage of him.'

After two and a half years, as agreed, Priday withdrew his capital. Charles was now on his own, although the business was reasonably established and starting to make a profit. But he was trying to kick-start a career in football management and was rarely seen in the shop, which was usually staffed by Priday's elderly father, Les. The business soon nosedived. Peter Harrison, whose wife worked in the shop for around 12 months, recalls, 'People who had brought footballs into the shop to be pumped up and laced were coming in and asking if they were ready. They would be in a box with dozens of other balls that hadn't been done.'

Saturday mornings were potentially the busiest time for the sports shop, yet this was the day Charles's absence was guaranteed because it was matchday. Charles would be away on football duty, first with Hereford and then Merthyr. Then there were the out-of-season football tours abroad with his guest team. Mauritius, South Africa and Rhodesia (now Zimbabwe) were among the distant destinations for Charles and his friends and they would be away for weeks on end. 'If John had some business acumen the shop could have been a little gold mine because there were a lot of schools and football teams in the area and they all would have needed kit and equipment,' says Priday.

Above the shop Charles opened a sauna and introduced a chiropodist but it failed to spark any upturn. In 1973 he cut his losses and sold up. He was £9,000 worse off. 'It was such a shame what happened to John Charles Sports Ltd because I remember going to a trade fair in London with John when we were opening the shop and all the manufacturers wanted to open accounts with us,' says Priday. 'They could see the potential in someone like John Charles owning a sports shop.'

Like many of his contemporaries, Charles drifted into the pub game to make a living. After finishing with Swansea City in 1976 he looked around South Wales for a pub to run but found nothing suitable. He decided to pay his old friend and former Elland Road teammate, Harold Williams, a visit in Leeds. Williams, who became a landlord after retiring from the game, was successfully running The Railway Inn and Charles knew he would have connections in the West Yorkshire brewery industry. 'I came back from a game of golf one day and found John and Peggy in my pub,' says Williams. 'I asked them what they were doing in Leeds. John says, "Nothing." Then Peggy said they were looking for a pub. I asked John if that really was the reason why they had come up and he said yes.' Williams called one of his contacts at Whitbread and told him John Charles and his wife wanted a pub. 'The guy at the brewery asked me if John would be any good with a pub,' continues Williams. 'I said I thought he'd probably be bloody useless, but put John in a pub in Leeds and he'd fill it.'

In October 1976 the Charleses were given The New Inn in Churwell, a mile or so from Elland Road. Williams was spot-on with his prediction. People flocked from all over the country to patronise the pub, just to meet 'King John'. 'In the beginning you couldn't get through the door. I'm not kidding – it was heaving,' he explains. 'They were coming from all over Yorkshire, all over the north of England.' One evening Jim Finney popped in to say hello to his former Edgar Street colleague at the same time as a coach party arrived. Finney was flabbergasted when he discovered it was from Nottingham and had driven up especially to see the landlord. The pub was on the way to Elland Road and was a magnet for Leeds supporters en route to the game. 'The brewery were delighted to offer Dad a pub,' says Peter Charles. 'He had a far better chance of making it in Leeds than he did in South Wales because he was far more popular with the Leeds people.'

Charles, it seemed, was tailor-made for the licensing trade. After trying – and not really succeeding – in football management, and after failing with a restaurant and a sports shop, he appeared to have found his niche. Their second son, Melvyn, who had studied at catering college in Cardiff, worked at The New Inn with his parents, and Peter, who was also attending catering college, helped out during the holidays. 'The pub was a winner,' says Peggy. 'We were doing very well in the beginning. It was really busy.' With his father constantly being invited to functions across the north of England, combined with his commitments with the Leeds United Ex-Players Association which played charity matches most Sundays, Melvyn soon found himself doing most of the donkey work along with his mother. 'We were running the pub on a daily basis. Dad was just a figurehead,' he explains.

Among the staff was Charles's former Leeds colleague, Keith Ripley. 'The pub was a licence to print money,' he recalls. 'It was a damn good pub. It had a little restaurant and the meals were superb. Everything was there for it to be a success. I thought John could have been a good landlord. He was a very sociable person who could get on with people. Every day the pub was packed out, from wall to wall.'

After a year or two, life at The New Inn began to turn sour. The gruelling pub schedule was starting to chisel away at the marriage. The couple started to argue and fight.

'We just grew apart,' admits Peggy. 'Being with someone 24 hours a day was terrible. We had never spent that much time together when John had his football, then all of a sudden we were in each other's company constantly. It was a living hell.' The rows intensified and in 1978 Peggy walked out of the pub, closing the door on their 25-year marriage. 'I didn't leave him for anyone else. I left because it was impossible, absolutely impossible, to run a business with John.'

His laid-back approach to running the pub infuriated his wife and sons. Strangers were allowed behind the bar and sometimes he failed to open up on time. 'In the evenings we opened at 7 p.m. but to John it didn't matter if we opened at 8 p.m.,' says Peggy. The pressure on the couple increased when their 11-year-old son, David, was diagnosed with tubular sclerosis, a rare neurological disease. He needed an operation to remove a brain tumour and lost the feeling on his right side.

Charles said the marriage ended because they 'had just got fed up with each other and didn't see eye to eye any more'. Peggy went to work in another pub, which was run by friends, before taking an accountancy job. She has never remarried. 'I wasn't surprised when Mum and Dad split up,' says Peter Charles. 'It was inevitable. They had started arguing and it became pretty bad towards the end. Dad was hardly in the pub because he was always being invited to functions and in the end it came to a head. Pub life can break couples up.'

Charles then met the woman who eventually became his second wife, Glenda Vero. She helped him to run The New Inn before the pair decided on a fresh start. They took over the tenancy of the Gomersal Park Hotel, in Gomersal, just outside Leeds, in 1984. Out of all his business ventures, this proved to be the most traumatic. It cost the Gentle Giant £10,000 and he nearly ended up in prison. Charles and his partner left the Gomersal in March 1987 but 11 months later the one-time football superstar found himself hauled in front of Huddersfield magistrates for non-payment of rates. Charles owed Kirklees Council £943. He proved a hard man to pin down. The council served him with ten notices. Twice bailiffs were sent to the hotel and there were also two warrants issued for his arrest.

Charles told his pursuers he would pay £100 before making the rest up from the proceeds of a testimonial match Leeds were arranging for him. The match was never organised and Charles flew to Canada to take up a technical director's post with Hamilton Steelers in the Canadian National Soccer League. Charles abruptly locked the doors of the Gomersal in March 1987 to join the Canadian club which had offered him a three-month contract. No one knew he and Glenda had gone to live on the other side of the Atlantic, in Stoney Creek, near Toronto, and their 'mystery disappearance' made the front page of the *Yorkshire Post* in July 1987 when Dewsbury Licensing Magistrates discussed the fate of the Gomersal's special hours certificate. The magistrates heard Charles had left the hotel four months previously and had not been seen since.

His low-key departure from Leeds to Canada was in complete contrast to the hullabaloo that surrounded his move from Leeds to Turin 30 years earlier. The certificate, awarded to the hotel 'for music, dancing and substantial refreshment', was revoked.

After four months in Canada he returned to Leeds but made no attempt to pay off the rates arrears. 'We have had a long struggle to try and collect these rates,' Martin Collison, the council's senior recovery officer, told the court. Charles said he was on the dole, receiving £70 a week in unemployment benefit and could not afford £943. He told the magistrates he could raise £100 'in a few hours' and could wipe out the rest of the debt with the money he would receive from a testimonial match Leeds were staging for him and Bobby Collins the following month. (When Charles went to Turin to ask Juventus's Welsh striker Ian Rush if he would play in his testimonial match he dished out some advice to the former Liverpool player – 'Don't squander your cash. Profit from my unhappy experiences.')

Charles said he was hoping to receive £10,000 from the testimonial against Everton but the court was having none of it. It said the 56 year old had shown 'culpable neglect' in not paying the rates and Charles was told he would be sent to jail for 60 days unless the amount was paid. He was led away by a jailer and taken to Huddersfield Police Station. From there he telephoned Glenda at the home they rented in Birkenshaw and told her what had happened. Not expecting a prison sentence, she burst into tears. 'When he left home this morning we thought that once he explained the situation, the magistrates would give him a further chance to pay,' she said on that bleak afternoon in March 1988.

After Charles had spent five and a half hours in a cell waiting for the prison bus that would take him to his 'home' for the next 60 days, Glenda arrived at the police station. She had £943 with her and refused to say where the money had come from. Leslie Silver, then Leeds United chairman, was later unmasked as the Good Samaritan. He could not bear to see Charles, the club's greatest ever player, thrown into prison. 'John was the finest player we ever had at Leeds United,' said Silver two days after bailing out the Gentle Giant. 'In the past we have tried to help him in every way we can. We have even offered him jobs at the club.' Juventus also extended a helping hand. Charles could have worked for Società Assicuraziva Italiana, the insurance company owned by the Agnelli family where many ex-Juventus players ended up. He was also offered a job with Fiat but Charles turned the Agnellis down, opting to stay in Britain.

Thanks to Silver's generosity Charles was a free man. Looking sheepish, he quickly ran down the steps of the police station, gave a thumbs-up sign and said, 'It's good to be out.' He then got into his nine-year-old Vauxhall Carlton that he had parked outside the magistrates' court and which Glenda had since picked up. His partner was critical of the way the former footballer had been treated. 'I think the magistrates have been harsh. They don't have to treat him like this. John does a lot of work for charity. The money would have been paid next month from the benefit match. It's just a relief to see John again.'

From Huddersfield Police Station he was taken straight to Morley Snooker Club where he was due to play his friend and ex-world snooker champion, Joe Johnson, in a charity snooker match. He arrived an hour late. Before he showed up the compère told the spectators, who included the Lord Mayor of Leeds, Doreen Wood, that Charles was late because 'he's had a slight upset this afternoon'. Charles did not want to dwell on the day's events. Raising his fingers to the top of his head, he told reporters, 'I've had it up to here. We managed to pay the money. It's all over now. I'm very relieved.'

The newspapers had a field day with the story. They wrote about 'the fallen soccer idol', 'the skint sportsman' and 'the tragic downfall'. By the late 1980s Charles was penniless. Melvyn, who went on to run his own pub, The Gascoigne Arms in Garforth, would find out just how desperate he was for money during this period. Melvyn had been given the Wales jersey his father wore on his international debut in 1950 by someone who had done cleaning work at Manselton School in Swansea. For years the framed jersey hung in Charles's old school but now it was unwanted. So the red shirt was transported to Garforth to hang proudly in Melvyn's pub. 'A few weeks after putting the shirt on display Dad came into my pub,' recalls Charles's son. 'I showed him the shirt. He looked at it, had a drink and then left.' The following morning the cleaner alerted Melvyn to the shirt's disappearance. Someone had taken it off the wall and walked away with it. 'I presumed it had been stolen,' explains Melvyn. A couple of months later Melvyn attended a dinner at the Yorkshire Sporting Club in Bradford. Part of the evening involved an auction of sport-related memorabilia. 'All of a sudden this bloke came into the room carrying the shirt that had been hanging in my pub! I then found out it was Dad who had taken it. He got £1,200 for it. When I asked him why he took the shirt he said it was because it was his, which I suppose was fair enough.'

Charles received £20,000 for the testimonial he shared with

Bobby Collins and this helped him back on his feet. Apart from the money he lost with his businesses he was also involved in a costly divorce. His marriage to Peggy was legally terminated in 1982. 'It hit me hard financially,' said Charles years later. 'It was half and half, and she wanted half.' The judge ordered him to pay Peggy £10,000. Charles could only afford £2,500 so the rest was to be paid in instalments. Some of his testimonial money – £2,500 – went to his first wife. 'If people say I took his money, it isn't true,' she says. 'After the first payment it took him a long time to pay me the rest. I had to wait eight or nine years.'

Rather than dividing Charles and Glenda, the rates crisis brought them closer together. Six weeks after the trauma at Huddersfield Magistrates Court the couple married in a simple ceremony at Leeds Registry Office. They may have fallen on hard times but there was a touch of the extravagance Charles was once so accustomed to as they arrived in a white Rolls Royce. Peggy sensed her ex-husband was about to tie the knot when he paid her an unexpected visit at her home in Garforth. He asked for the decree absolute that proved they were divorced. 'I asked him what he wanted it for. He said it was for insurance purposes! Of course I knew what he really wanted it for.'

He had one last stab at a business, opening a shop that sold baby clothes and toys in Cleckheaton, in between Bradford and Leeds. It was the brainchild of his new wife, but like his other ventures it ended in closure. The shop was unable to compete with the bigger stores such as Mothercare, although the fact the clothes reeked of nicotine because Charles was always smoking inside the shop can hardly have helped custom. Selling expensive children's attire imported from Italy on a West Yorkshire council estate was bound to end in tears. In a candid interview with the *Western Mail* in January 1995, Charles described the Cleckheaton shop as 'the biggest blunder' he made. 'It wasn't the right thing for me and in the end it just slipped away. It was a shame because Glenda put a lot of effort into it.'

During the 1990s Charles slipped quietly away into early retirement. He continued his involvement with the Leeds United Ex-Players Association, raising money for their favourite cause, kidney machines. A state pension became the only source of revenue for a man who, when he was in Italy, was earning ten times as much as his British contemporaries and, if he was playing today, could command a weekly wage of between £130,000 and £150,000. His shirts, caps and medals, which would fetch considerable sums in today's football memorabilia market – and which would have provided him with a nice nest egg – have long gone. Over the years he has given them away, mainly to be sold in aid of charitable causes. He also sold off his Diano Marina apartment during the late 1970s.

Considering his achievements on the pitch and his standing in the world game, the awards and tributes have come surprisingly late in his life. In 1999 he was awarded an honorary degree by the University of Wales, Swansea. The following year he donned a cap and gown for a second time to receive an honorary doctorate from Leeds Metropolitan University.

In 2000 he was voted Leeds United's Player of the Millennium. In 2001 he became the first foreign footballer to be inducted into Italian football's Hall of Fame, ahead of names such as Diego Maradona and Michel Platini. A few months later, at an event to mark the 125th anniversary of the Football Association of Wales at Newport's Celtic Manor Resort, Charles was named as the greatest Welsh footballer of all time, ahead of Ian Rush and Ivor Allchurch. 'I don't care what has been said about me over the years or what I have won,' a moved Charles told the audience, 'this is the greatest and proudest moment of my life.' He said it meant more to him than the honour he had just received in Italy. 'This is something that comes from my countrymen and I could not be prouder.'

The following June, after years of campaigning by his supporters, Charles's contribution to 'the beautiful game' – he was never booked or sent off – was finally recognised by Buckingham Palace when he was awarded the CBE in the Queen's Birthday Honours List. 'What does that stand for?' asked Charles when his wife, who opened the letter from Buckingham Palace that dropped on the doormat of their Birkenshaw semi, told him he was going to receive the CBE. He said he was 'a bit shocked' by the award. 'It came right out of the blue. I certainly wasn't expecting it. I thought everyone had forgotten about me.' The letter relaying the news came in a normal, white envelope. 'I read the letter about five times before I could take it all in,' said a thrilled Glenda who said she 'never gave up hope' of her husband being honoured. 'John was ignored for so long, possibly because he's Welsh,' she explained. 'If you look at the Honours Lists, you don't see too many non-English people on them.' He was presented with the CBE by the Prince of Wales in October 2001. 'I told Prince Charles I had met his mum before, when she visited Turin, so it was nice to be seeing her son this time,' he said after the short ceremony at Buckingham Palace. For his supporters, the CBE is not enough. A campaign for Charles to be knighted is ongoing.

In March 2002, aged 70, he was awarded the Freedom of Swansea, following in the steps of Prince Charles and former President of the United States Jimmy Carter. By now it was public knowledge he was not enjoying the best of health. He was fighting cancer and suffering from Alzheimer's disease. Charles was diagnosed as having bladder cancer in 1997 but Glenda, who underwent a bowel cancer operation in 1991, kept the news private. Only family and close friends knew. 'It isn't something you want to go public with,' she said in September 1999, after admitting her husband was receiving radiotherapy and chemotherapy for the cancer.

Doctors discovered a tumour on Charles's bladder in 1997. It was removed but cancerous cells returned after three months so he underwent a course of chemotherapy and radiotherapy. The disease returned in April 2001 and he needed more chemotherapy. The cancer has been controlled, although Charles visits the hospital for regular check-ups, sometimes staying overnight for tests. He remained unfazed by the illness. 'I have some good days, some not so good. What can you do? You have to keep going. I get painful twinges occasionally but I still enjoy life.'

In December 2001, while giving an interview for a television tribute to celebrate his 70th birthday, Glenda admitted her husband had Alzheimer's disease, an incurable condition that attacks the central nervous system. This explained Charles's fading memory and inability to recognise old friends and teammates. Former Cardiff City and Wales colleagues Colin Baker and Alan Harrington, who were among his neighbours when he was living in Rhiwbina, were invited to his Freedom of Swansea function. When they introduced themselves to 'Charlo', he did not recognise either of them. 'It was very upsetting because we were very friendly with him,' says Harrington. Nearly every Sunday the Charleses and the Harringtons would go for a drive near the sea, either to Rest Bay or Southerndown. Charles also spent a lot of time in the Harrington household when Peggy and the children were on holiday in Diano Marina and he was living on his own. His family would spend the entire summer holiday in Italy but Charles was unable to accompany them because pre-season training started in July. 'He'd come round every night with his spaniel, Candy, for a cup of tea,' says Harrington. 'Then he'd come back at eight in the morning for breakfast. Sometimes he'd call by to ask my wife, Gloria, if she would do his washing for him!'

The Gentle Giant makes the occasional trip to Turin, where he is still revered, to watch his beloved Juventus. He was invited to the Stadio Delle Alpi at the end of the 2000–01 season, for a match against Atalanta. Juventus moved from the Comunale to the futuristic Delle Alpi, built for the 1990 World Cup in Italy, as soon as the tournament had ended. The Comunale, the venue of so many of Charles's triumphs, is now used for training. As he walked around the running track that circles the pitch, the *tifosi* chanted, '*Gio-va-nni! Gio-va-nni!*' (Giovanni is the Italian for John). Charles wiped away tears. The late Kenneth Wolstenholme accompanied Charles and Glenda on this trip. 'Little children who had never seen him play were asking for his autograph,' he said. 'Where we were staying there was a wedding reception. We strolled out onto the balcony to see what was going on. Suddenly we heard a voice shout "John Charles!" The wedding guests wanted him to come down and the photographer started taking pictures of John with the guests. I don't know what the bride and bridegroom thought.'

Now Charles's only pastime is watching football. Accompanied by his best friend, Harold Williams, he rarely misses a match at Elland Road. There he watches footballers earning five-figure weekly salaries. But Charles does not begrudge them their money. He believes today's footballers are entitled to their huge wages. As a massive earner himself during the 1950s, his view is not surprising. 'They deserve it. It is they who entice the crowd through the turnstiles, they are the people the crowd are paying to see. Good luck to them. I think it's wonderful they are getting all that money.'

Charles has always maintained he has no regrets. He once said if he could turn back the clock, he would not change a thing. 'I've had a great life out of football and gone to places where people will never go, without having to pay a penny,' he said in 1995. 'I've done things which I wouldn't have done if I was a coal miner or a road sweeper.'